TRI

Triad contains three contemporary works of fiction.
Brief biographical notes on the authors are given
on pages 6 (Ronit Lentin), 58 (James Liddy) and
120 (Tomás Ó Murchadha).

TRIAD
Modern Irish Fiction

Tea with Mrs Klein
Ronit Lentin

Young Men go Walking
James Liddy

Ivy Lodge
Tomas O Murchadha

WOLFHOUND PRESS

© 1986 Ronit Lentin, James Liddy, Tomás Ó Murchadha.

All rights reserved. No part of this book may be reproduced or utilised in any form or by any means electronic or mechanical, including photocopying, filming, recording, video or by any information storage and retrieval system without prior permission in writing from the publisher.

Triad is a fiction collection. All characters, incidents and names have no connection with any persons living or dead. Any apparent resemblance is purely coincidental.

First published 1986 by
WOLFHOUND PRESS
68 Mountjoy Square, Dublin 1.

British Library Cataloguing in Publication Data

Triad: modern Irish fiction.
    I. Lentin, Ronit. Tea with Mrs Klein
   II. Liddy, James. Youg men go walking
  III. O Murchadha, Tomas. Ivy Lodge
823'. 01'8 [FS]   PR1309.S5

ISBN 0-86327-056 5
ISBN 0-86327-057 3 pbk

This book is published with the assistance of
The Arts Council (An Comhairle Ealaíon),
Dublin, Ireland.

Cover design: Jan de Fouw
Typesetting: Redsetter Ltd., Dublin.
Printed by Billings and Sons Ltd.

TEA WITH MRS KLEIN
Ronit Lentin

RONIT LENTIN, born in Israel, came to Ireland in 1969. She has since worked in television and written extensively in Hebrew and in English. *Stone of Claims* and *Like a Blind Man* are two previous novellas published in Tel Aviv. Her radio plays were broadcast by Israel Radio and RTE. She is married to Louis Lentin and has two children.

1

Who can it be, she asks herself, irritated. There is always someone at the door. Must be the tinkers again. Always coming at the most awkward hours. Always wanting something. Have you anything, missis, a little help? Bloodshot eyes. Filthy. As if I have anything to give away. If only they knew how little I have for myself. I am sure they have more than I have.

Anyway, what sort of time is this to be calling? She glances at her watch. Normal people would be eating their lunch now, she is glad to find out she hasn't been raging for nothing.

She peers through the glass. It's impossible to see clearly since she changed the transparent glass a month or so ago, substituting for it an opaque rectangle. She hates people peering into her life. The black-clad figure doesn't look familiar behind glass. Black trousers, black jacket, pink face. She opens the door before his arm is lifted to ring the bell a second time. A priest. A priest in a dog collar, the words go through her mind.

The caller, in an over-friendly voice, says, 'Good morning, Ma'am.'

'Good morning.'

'I am visiting all the new houses on the estate,' he says. 'My name is Father Daly.'

Giving himself the title, she muses.

'I am collecting names and details of all the people in the parish. May I come in?' All this, presupposing that he would be welcome.

She glances down quickly, smoothing her jumper and her old skirt with an angular, arthritic hand. 'I am not Catholic,' she says. 'But if you want to, you can certainly come in,' and before she can invite him into her living-room, he is already there, standing in the middle of the floor, an uncertain smile on his face. 'Sit down, please,' she says cautiously, pointing to a green velvet easy-chair. Fancy coming in here, as if he owns the place. Priests, so sure of themselves. She sits opposite him, on the edge of her chair, her hand primly positioned on her knees, her bust round and heavy, saying nothing, waiting for him.

'You are new here,' he starts, taking out a small blue notebook.

'I have actually been living here for the past eight months,' she says, her eyes sad and empty. 'But, as I have already told you, I am not a Catholic.' She gives him no more. Let him ask the embarrassing questions. After all, this is his job.

'May I know what religion . . . I mean, what are you?' He is a trifle embarrassed.

'I am Jewish, Father,' she says, his Christian title coming natural enough.

'Is that a fact? I thought you weren't Irish.'

'But I *am* Irish, Father. I was born in Limerick. I've lived in Ireland all my life. Apart, that is, from a few years across the water. Following the children, you understand. After my husband passed away.'

'Yes, I know how it is. It's difficult to remain put, alone, where tragedy strikes.'

'How right you are. Apart from the fact that one has to help the children. With their children.' She is beginning to warm to this stranger. So few people nowadays have time for an old woman living alone.

'How many children have you?'

'Five, thank God. And eight grandchildren.'

'Go away! Five? Really?' says the priest automatically.

She doesn't answer. Still waiting. If he came here wanting something, let him come out with it. After all, he must have come for something. She examines him with a hostility typical to her. He has thick lips, and very white teeth. Could be dentures. His spectacles cast a dark shadow on his pale eyes. But without knowing why and in spite of her natural hostility she likes him a little.

'So you are Jewish,' he says, looking her straight in the eye.

'Yes. Why? Does it astonish you?' So you are Jewish. If he does not like Jews, let him get it right out. Must be anti-Semitic. The thought scares her.

'You don't look Jewish,' he says. 'There are some other Jewish families in this estate. Did you know that?'

She does not. She asks for their names. She mentions that she knows the relatives of one of these families. Everybody related to everybody. Like one big family one sees only at funerals and weddings. Too big.

'I would like', he says, 'to have a complete list of all the people in the parish. Even those who do not belong to the parish.' He chuckles, enjoying his own sense of humour. 'Do you mind if I ask your name? For my list?'

'Klein, Gertrude Klein.'

'A German name,' he says. 'Did your family come from Germany?'

'No. From Lithuania. Most Jews in Dublin came from Lithuania. From a small village, Achmian in Lithuania. We all come from there.

They say we are all related in some way.'

'How come that you have a German name then?' He is curious now.

His interest tempts Gertrude to talk. 'Originally my husband's family came from Austria, or it could have been Germany. Many years ago. Or so they say. One of them married into a Lithuanian family. Jews in Europe have always crossed borders without actually moving. Because countries kept being conquered and changing rulers. This is how one finds a Klein in Lithuania. My father's family name was Lipshuetz. Another German name. When he passed away my brothers decided that Lipshuetz was bad for business. So they chose to change it to Laurence. My husband's family on the other hand, those who are alive, still call themselves Klein. Mind you, Klein is an easier name than Lipshuetz, don't you think?' What am I telling him all this for? He must think I am completely mad, it can't possibly interest him. This goy. 'But you must be bored to death, Father. Can I offer you a cup of tea?' Without waiting for his reply, Mrs Klein goes to the kitchen.

Father Daly looks around. He knows these houses. He too lives in one of them, one of the few hundred little boxes which shot up overnight at the foot of the green hills. He lives and works in the estate in accordance with the diocesan policy of planting priests in the heart of their parishes.

The room is not very different from many other rooms he sees every day. No holy virgins here, no holy-water fountains, no crucifixes of course. But there are two easy chairs, one brown leatherette armchair and a dark wooden chair, a few coffee tables with glass ashtrays and framed photographs of smiling children, and on the television set a flower pot with the price tag of the local supermarket still on. Yet there is nothing in this room to indicate Mrs Klein's personality. He takes it all in quickly, professionally, accustomed to making instant judgements of house dwellers according to the contents of their living-rooms.

Mrs Klein calls to him cheerfully from the kitchen, 'Do you take milk, Father?'

'Yes, please.' He is already on his way into the kitchen. 'Can I help?'

'No thank you, Father.' For some reason the stranger's presence in her kitchen does not embarrass her. She feels safe. She carries into the living-room the tea things and some shop biscuits on a plastic tray. 'I don't have any homemade cakes today, unfortunately. In fact I haven't been baking that much recently.'

'Not to worry. It's good of you to make tea for me. I am sure you have just finished lunch,' he says, smiling calmly.

'I never eat a lot on my own. I get tired', she says, 'cooking for myself all the time. After all those years. Imagine peeling potatoes for seven people every night, Father. Roast potatoes every night, apart from

Tuesday, that is. Tuesday was our night out. We used to go to the pictures and then we went to eat in the Savoy Restaurant. You are probably too young to remember the Savoy. For five shillings you could eat a really good meal there.'

'It isn't a matter of age. I am not that young Mrs Klein. I didn't grow up in Dublin, but even I heard of the Savoy,' he says softly, trying not to underplay the importance of the good old days when she used to dress up and go out, wearing her string of pearls every Tueday to eat half a roast chicken with Brussels sprouts or a well-done steak with baked potatoes.

'You are a country boy so? Hard to believe.'

'Yes. I too was born in County Limerick. Not too far from the city. We must have been born quite close to each other, you and I.'

Born near Limerick. Maybe his father was one of the lunatics who attacked us. Aloud she says, 'Really? It's a small world. Someone rings the doorbell, you open the door and find the local parish priest, who, it turns out, was born not too far from you. How fascinating.' Gertrude Klein gets excited thinking of how she would tell all this to her daughter Doris.

'You can say that again,' he says and sips his tea. 'Do you like it here, Mrs Klein?'

'To tell you the truth, Father, I love my house. It suits me fine. If only it was closer to town I would be really happy, the buses here are so slow, it takes almost an hour to get there.'

'You go to town a lot?'

'I like going in to see the shops, to see what's new, to keep in touch. Apart from that, there isn't even a small shop here in which to buy bread, or eggs. It's not easy for a woman my age, you know, dragging to the shopping centre.'

'But surely you know that at the other end of the estate there is a small shop? She doesn't have much, but she does keep bread and eggs. It's not too far, only five-minutes walk.' Father Daly has always complimented himself on his practicality. In fact, he prefers giving his parishioners practical advice than spiritual guidance.

'I never knew that,' says the Jewish woman opposite him, suddenly looking frail and lost. 'I never meet anybody, you understand. My neighbours never talk. I say hello and they barely nod, barely turn their heads. It's impossible to make friends here. I have been living here now for eight months and yet I only know the woman on my left. Where did you say this shop was?'

He explains how to get to the shop. Then he finishes his tea and decides it is time to visit the next house. He has to finish his little survey before meeting with the bishop, a meeting at which a decision would be made regarding the building of the new church. It all depends on the number of people in the parish. For the time being he says mass in the gym hall of the local school, and twice every Sunday in the small chapel of a convent down the road.

She offers another cup of tea, something to eat, talks about the estate, about the shops in town, about the neighbours, repeating herself, lonely, longing, holding on to his company. He responds to her longing and stays another hour, his hands stuck deep in his trouser pockets, trying desperately not to hold this strangely brittle woman and hug her, as he would his own mother.

At three-thirty he knows he really must go. He gets up and makes his farewells.

Why am I holding on to him for such a long time? He will think I have nothing better to do. 'I am busy too,' she mutters, 'I have a lot to do today. I only hope I haven't delayed you too much.'

'Not at all. On the contrary. It's a pleasure to stop running and relax for a while with a cup of tea.'

She looks at him, examining his round face at length and says lightly, trying hard not to sound too deliberate, 'Perhaps, if you have some time, you could come here again. I'll always have a cup of tea for you. And sympathy. Tea and sympathy, as they say.' She chuckles, embarrassed.

Father Daly chuckles too. He shakes her hand, and says very warmly that he'd love to come and see her again — one of these days. 'In the meantime,' he adds casually, 'God bless you.'

She looks on and sees him ring the bell of her neighbour's house. Once. Twice. No reply. He goes to the next house and Mrs Klein goes in, thinking that soon he will be talking to somebody else. In somebody else's world.

The priest continues to preoccupy her thoughts throughout the day. At four-thirty Doris comes with the children. Gertrude talks to her enthusiastically and in great detail about Father Daly's visit. Her daughter listens, indifferent, and doesn't ask questions. Gertrude plays with the children, makes tea for them and is full of life. Why am I feeling so great, because this goy was sitting here today for an hour and a half, drinking my tea? But somehow she cannot wait for his next visit.

As on every evening, she eats early. She prepares the food, eats quickly and without pleasure, washes up fast, wishing to get rid of a burden.

After the meal, she goes upstairs and undresses hurriedly. She takes off her old jumper and her stained skirt, undoes girdles and corsets. Now she feels relief. She doesn't look at her body in the long mirror standing in the corner of the room. She hasn't looked at herself for years now. She pulls her floral nightie over her head. Over this she puts on an old woollen dressing-gown. She doesn't remove her make-up but stares at her face as she sits at her dressing-table. Not bad, Gertrude, not bad, for your age. She scrutinises her profile in the three-way mirror and applies another coat of lipstick to her bloodless lips. You look tired, my lady, you look tired. The pale blue watery eyes encircled by red blood snakes. You look tired.

This happens every evening as she prepares for the highlight of her day, a few hours in front of the television set. A last look in the mirror and, stepping lightly, she goes down to the living-room, fixes the cushion on the green chair, her chair, has a quick look in the daily paper, makes up her mind, and turns the knob.

*   *   *

Gertrude Klein returned to Dublin a year before, after some years in England.

When her husband died she sold the family home because it was then too large for her. Her oldest daughter, Joan, and husband, a Chester lawyer, asked her to come and live with them. At first Gertrude didn't want to. She actually tried to live for a while in a flat in Dublin, not far from the old family home.

She busied herself buying new furniture to suit the little flat. She sold the old heavy pieces which had filled the living-room and the dining-room, reserved only for Friday nights and holy days. The furniture in their old home had been chosen by her husband and she was actually glad to get rid of it and buy things she liked, although she didn't admit this to a living soul. She even had to sell the old beds because they were too large to squeeze into the little flat. Doors nowadays are too small, the owner of the removal firm told her.

After the first few weeks, the flat furnished and appointed, the old furniture sold and the new curtains hung, Gertrude had nothing more to do. With the house gone, the meaning of her life went too. It was never the same, after her husband's death. She stopped cooking regularly, used to sit idle for hours. She never made friends with anyone and was alone most of the time.

Joan and her husband decided 'something had to be done with mother'. They managed to persuade her that her place was with them, in Chester. By then she was rather glad to be persuaded.

Gertrude's constant illusion that she always did exactly what she wanted, and thought right and proper, became stronger with the passing years. As a young bride she was too busy to notice that the children arrived almost every year, without her being able to protest or do anything about it. Joan was born ten months after Gertrude and Daniel's wedding. Alex was born thirteen months later. Rose and Doris followed within a year and four days of each other, Rose being Alex's junior by less than two years.

At thirty-one, Gertrude found herself with four small children. She never asked herself whether she had really wanted them. She decided that was enough and went, bravely, to see her obstetrician, some six months after Doris was born, asking him to 'do something' so that she wouldn't have more children. Instead of solving her problems once and for all, the doctor explained the safe-days method. He never did find out, perhaps because of their reserved exchange of formalities, the extent of Gertrude's ignorance. She had been certain she only had to ask the doctor and he would seal her womb for ever.

For the next four years she adhered religiously to the safe-days method, not letting her husband near her during her fertile period. When her sisters asked if she had completed her family, she always replied yes, almost fanatically.

It took her almost four months to discover she was pregnant again. Since her cycle had never been regular it was impossible to know, she would say later. For two or three months she protested when asked teasingly by her sisters if she was pregnant again. Too often she had complained to them of nausea and pains in her legs. On the fourth month everyone knew. Gertrude was fuming. I could have done something about it, she thought during this fifth pregnancy, if I only knew. She had a hard time until Henry was born and she never quite forgave him for it.

Though for years Gertrude pretended to be mistress of her fate, she was actually lacking in confidence. At first she was too busy to notice that things were happening to her, but when Henry was born she started to feel that someone up above was against her, that something was making it hard for her. This resentment was to last and made her constantly suspicious of the whole world.

After Henry's birth Gertrude decided to take herself in hand. This time she was lucky, an infection necessitated a hysterectomy. Later, she would say to the younger women of the family that no woman should wait until she had a hysterectomy, that one had to take care and not get trapped. Long years with small children had affected her badly, Gertrude Klein didn't want to be caught unawares again.

Daniel Klein was a businessman. He was a smallish, cheerful man who used to take a pint of stout every evening after work in the pub across the road from his shop. While at home he listened to the radio most of the time, but since he did not have any particular interests he and Gertrude had all the time in the world to spend in bitter arguments.

The children remembered only the eternal feuds. They never saw their father's cheerfulness, reserved for his drinking companions, and his endless enthusiasm about new business ideas.

He had a stationery business and at different times tried making money in various ways. Amongst other things he had a small printing workshop for wedding and bar-mitzvah invitations and new-year cards; a personal stationery service, quite a novelty in those days; an agency for ballpoint pens when they came into vogue; and a typewriter-repair service. There were good days and many bad times.

Beyond her family, Gertrude had only one interest: her singing. After she married she gave up appearing on the stage, although she went on singing in the Jewish choir. She always said she gave it up because of Daniel, who denied he had ever forbidden her to sing. Thus the motif which would crop up again and again, spoiling things, appeared already at the beginning: the sacrifices she made for her husband and children.

*   *   *

Father Daly's second visit isn't planned. Mrs Klein returns from town one day and walks home from the bus stop. Father Daly stops his car, calling out her name. The fact that he remembers her name and bothers to give her a lift causes her pleasure. Perhaps he isn't like the others. She offers him a cup of tea and he accepts. They enter her house calmly, without tension, as if accustomed to doing so. Even during those first minutes a bond is formed between them. An intimacy.

She puts on the kettle and begins to take off her coat and change her shoes. 'I always change my shoes the minute I come in,' she says apologetically. 'I learnt this from my poor husband. As soon as he walked in the door, he went upstairs and put on his slippers. "Gertrude," he used to say, "I am just changing my shoes." Me too, especially in the last few years. My feet swell and I find it impossible to remain in my shoes the whole day.'

'I also spend a lot of time walking about and the moment I come in I change my shoes and put on a heavy jumper. Even in summer. Makes one feel at home.' Father Daly enters the living-room, sits on a green chair opposite a photograph of a plump child and holds his head in his cupped hands.

Gertrude comes silently from the kitchen. What, is he sleeping here, bubbles her anger. He doesn't hear her come.

'Tired?' she says softly.

Father Daly lifts his head. 'A little. Last night I sat up with a family who lost their daughter. Eighteen years of age. Poor child. A road accident.'

'Terrible. There is nothing worse than the loss of a child. I haven't experienced it, thanks be to God. But my poor mother lost two of her children. They were babies at the time. I can still hear her scream. She cried night after night. In the mornings her eyes were red and she was tired and nervous. We also cried, couldn't bear to see her grief. When father came back on Thursday nights or Friday mornings to find us all tired, depressed and emaciated, he used say that we mustn't mourn on the Sabbath.' Why am I telling this goy all this, he will think we were utterly primitive.

'What did your father work at?'

'Used to sell things. In the villages. An old-fashioned travelling-salesman.'

'Really?' Not so tired any more, he is curious now. 'What did he sell?'

'Anything.' Gertrude Klein moves into the kitchen to make the tea. She continues talking in a loud voice, clear and still young. 'The Jews, you understand, when they came here they thought they were coming to America. The boat owners diddled them, charged them fares to America, put them down here and told them this was America. They had to make some sort of a living, as most of them had no money left to go and look elsewhere. This was how many of them started selling things in the Irish villages. They got on great with the customers, since most of them came from small villages in Lithuania themselves. They didn't know much English, naturally, so when they found out this country was called Ireland it made them laugh. In Yiddish ire is eggs. Since then we call the Irish, you, that is, Beitzimers, beitzim being the Hebrew for eggs.' She chuckles, entering the room with a tray laden with cups, biscuits, spoons, teapot, milk jug, sugar bowl. Seeing her guest's attentive face, she adds, 'You probably don't find it quite so funny. One has to know Yiddish in order to understand this.' She starts pouring the tea.

'I always thought your language was Hebrew. We studied a bit of Hebrew in the seminary.'

'You don't say,' says Mrs Klein between biscuits. 'No. We only pray in Hebrew. My father wouldn't allow us study Hebrew as a language. No. Yiddish is the real language of the Jews. Everybody knows Yiddish. I know a little Hebrew, a few blessings, that's all. I can't read it. They didn't teach the girls, you know. The Jews don't teach their daughters too much. Providing you knew a few blessings, something about dietary laws and caught a husband as soon as possible, you didn't have to study. Today of course things are quite different. Another biscuit?'

He eats another biscuit. Mrs Klein's strange world is spreading before him like a web and so he encourages her to tell him more about her father.

'He was, as they say, a vikle. Weekly, that is. Used to call for his money once a week. He went through the villages, you know, offering the women all kinds of things. He'd leave the stuff with them and make them sign a piece of paper. Then he returned every week to collect his dues. When he went back he brought with him all sorts of other things, silk scarves, dress materials, cooking pots, you name it, even holy pictures. This was before most villages had shops. His life was not easy, he spent most of his time on the road. I loved going with him when he went on short spins, one-day spins. My mother didn't let me go for longer, because father used to sleep rough. Not too clean, his sleeping places, back rooms of public houses, even barns which farmers let him have for a halfpenny a night. It was a hard life and we were always short of money. We used to share our clothes, pass shoes from one child to the other. That's why everyone in our family has foot problems. Even then shoes weren't exactly cheap.'

'No. I know the score. We too didn't have it easy. My father was a postman and we never had enough money. Sometimes we received presents from ladies who lived in real houses with front gardens, not like us with our small cottage. Our kitchen was our living-room and eight children slept in two bedrooms. Like sardines.'

'So you know how it is. Cold in the winter, not enough coal to light the fire. The boys sent to play football outside to keep warm and the girls sent out to get milk from the neighbouring farm. I had to go every day. Once a week one of the others came with me, for eggs. Two and a half dozen cracked eggs. Cheaper, you know.' She finds another thing in common with the priest and it unnerves her. He must think we were poor ignorant people like his own family, the family of a country postman. 'In spite of it all,' she says, 'my father was a real scholar. When he came home, he washed his hands and sat down to his studies. Our house was small but our front room, the living-room, was some sort of a synagogue. There used always be men there, studying the Old Testament or the Talmud. Or praying. I can still hear the murmur from that room.' Now she continues oblivious of Father Daly's presence, remembering, talking to herself. 'The rest of his time, particularly Sundays, he spent with my brothers, teaching them the Law, reading the Bible and the prayers. Is it any wonder he had so little time for us, the girls? He did love us, I am sure of that, but he rarely thought of us. I managed somehow to take an interest in music. Singing in fact. But only because of my sister Sheila, who studied the piano at school. The nuns in our school were very musical.'

'The nuns?'

'Yes. We went to the local convent school. I am sure my father was simply sure of our resistance to all temptation . . . . Where was I? Yes. The nuns taught us to play and sing and they decided that Sheila and I were particularly talented. First Sheila. She started playing the piano.

She used to go to the convent to practise every day after school. Until my aunt heard where she was going. She found a second-hand piano and bought it for Sheila, so she wouldn't have to go into the convent in the afternoons. Father shuddered when he saw the piano. I remember, it was a Thursday evening, he had just returned from the country. "Do you want", my aunt screamed at him, "your daughter to spend her entire day in a convent? The mornings aren't enough?" He looked at her and didn't say a thing. He only asked that the piano be positioned upstairs so that when the men came to study with him they wouldn't see it. He also forbade Sheila to play while there were people in the house. It was tough for her. A few years later my turn came. The nuns decided I had a good voice and that Sheila would be able to accompany me on the piano. I had it easier, I could at least practise anywhere, even in the bath.'

'And your father?' says the priest. 'What did your father say?'

'When I started singing, he was quite old. When I was thirteen, he was over sixty. Somehow, he became more and more preoccupied with his books and his religion and didn't pay the same attention to the family. He may have simply been fed up battling with us all. Or perhaps he realised that I would get married anyhow and this would put an end to my career. Which was exactly what happened. He was a wise man, my father.'

'And what happened to your singing when you did get married?'

'My late husband simply wouldn't hear of it. He wouldn't let me continue appearing with my sister. We used to appear in charity concerts, you know. Mainly within the community. Mind you, we appeared once even in the Theatre Royal, in a big concert. It was wonderful.' Gertrude's face lights up as she remembers. 'They were all there. Jimmy O'Dea and Noel Purcell, everyone. It was truly wonderful. Sheila and I gave some Strauss operetta songs. We were, you may laugh, the classical part of the programme, everybody sang such light stuff. But my late husband would simply not hear of me continuing. You know how it is, I was a good Jewish wife, doing what my husband wanted. Everything for the husband and children, as they say.' She pauses for a while, looking at the priest. 'You know, sometimes I feel the good old days never existed. They seem so unreal, so far away.' She sighs, pinning her gaze to the wall in front of her.

The visitor says nothing. The air is thick to the touch. He is like a fly caught in a web of honey. His world seems suddenly irrelevant, unreal. The chapel and the school, the parishioners and the bishop, all sink suddenly and he focuses on Mrs Klein's honey.

'You know, Father,' says her voice, sweet and shy, 'I have five children, bless them and spare them, and here I am, sitting and talking to a priest. Incredible. My poor father would have turned in his grave.

If he only knew.'

He smiles apologetically. He cannot understand what brought that on.

'I have nothing against you personally, Father, I want you to know that,' she hastens to add, sensing his perplexity. 'But you do realise that priests and nuns weren't exactly the most popular in our house. My mother told us that her grandmother used to spit three times over her left shoulder against the evil eye every time she saw a nun in the street. Hard to believe, isn't it? We, of course, did nothing of the sort.'

'If you'd started spitting you'd never have stopped,' says the priest. 'there were so many priests and nuns in Limerick in your time.' He chuckles.

Mrs Klein joins him, saying, 'You took the words out of my mouth, Father. That is exactly what I was going to say.'

He understands me, she thinks after he leaves. And it annoys her. All those things I told him about my father, about my music, about the hard times. He knew exactly what I meant. Not like Alex, not even like Joan, or Doris. Always arguing, as if they had been there. Correcting me when I tell them things. He can listen. But I should not tell him too much. Priests, when they know too much, they might just use it against you.

In spite of it all, she knows she will go on talking to him, as long as he continues coming. Throughout the day she is humming to herself, her voice high and ringing, though cracked somewhat.

*   *   *

Gertrude Klein started developing young. When she was twelve her mother wound a piece of cloth around her bust, tying her young breasts, flattening them out. Gertrude did not know there was another way. She was brought up not to ask questions. But the warmth which filled her limbs during those first years of womanhood couldn't be bound by a piece of cloth. She used to quench the warmth with a groping hand between her legs, moist fingers climbing and pushing, extinguishing the burning fire. Her sister, Pearl, who slept in the same bed, used to wake up from time to time when Gertrude lay awake fumbling and restless for hours on end, and wonder why her little sister wasn't asleep. She couldn't sleep, it was too hot, too cold, were the only answers Gertrude could conjure up, well used from a tender age to hiding her feelings.

Pearl and Sheila had fiancés and Gertrude loved to listen to them talk about their young men, exchanging stories in their shy reserved way. They were good girls, Sheila and Pearl, but Gertrude didn't

believe their reticent tone somehow. Had she had a fiancé she would
have kissed and kissed him, her lips smeared with cherry lipstick, her
eyes veiled, longlashed, like in the pictures she sneaked in to see
whenever she had a penny or two.

Pearl was too conservative, too religious for Gertrude's liking.
Always praying and preaching.'Gertrude knew that Pearl would make,
like their mother, a good wife, a fastidious mother, strictly kosher,
adhering to all the purity laws. Her young man on the other hand was
a very jolly fellow who always sneaked a few coppers to Gertrude.
These she hid so that her mother wouldn't find them and make her give
them back. She felt sorry for Pearl's Joey. Pearl would nag him to death,
like her mother nagged her father. But Joey seemed happy and her
father was too preoccupied with his studies to pay any attention to his
bickering bitter wife.

Mother was a tall woman, with long auburn hair tied in a linen
kerchief. Gertrude loved to see her comb it out in the mornings. Her
face was handsome but sombre, her hands long and arthritic. She
taught her daughters, who weren't sent to secondary school, to cook,
clean, polish silver and brass, sew and knit, embroider and bake. 'This
is the school of life,' she would say. There was as lot of talk about clean-
liness and scrubbing so when Gertrude's young brother said, many
years later, that the house was actually filthy, mother blew her top. If
she said the house was clean, clean it was and that was that.

Gertrude wasn't very close to her mother and invested all her young
love in her sister, Sheila. Her little body trembled when she listened to
Sheila playing the piano, wishing that she too, could play like that one
day.

Sheila was the one to discover the cloth binding on her bust.
Gertrude actually managed to hide it from her sisters for a long time,
changing her clothes in the bathroom, which was on the first floor, far
from the bedrooms and from her sisters' scrutiny. One evening Sheila
found her weeping, rubbing her sore breasts. She burst out at mother,
who was just then passing from bed to bed, stroking a child here, cover-
ing another there. Mother promised to buy Gertrude a brassière.

The following day was one of the most important in Gertrude's life.
A day she would always go back to in her memories as the day she
became, officially, a woman. Asking questions about her body and its
sensations was forbidden, so she didn't attempt to ask her mother why
she suddenly had blood on her knickers. Again it was Sheila who disco-
vered it and took the frightened Gertrude in hand, sat her down and
explained to her what was happening. This was the first and last lesson
in sex education she ever got. For the rest of her life she would remain
a frightened child of twelve, with a half-extinguished flame burning
away inside her. Like her mother before her, she would go on treating

her emotions and the emotions of others light-heartedly, without ever admitting the real fire she had known and hidden, many years before Daniel and a whole lifetime before Father Daly.

* * *

'The reason I am alone', says Gertrude Klein to Father Daly, who surprises her one winter morning, 'is because my children are scattered all over the world. A typical Jewish family, you might say. Come to think of it, a typical Irish family too, isn't it? Always looking for luck elsewhere. I would have given a lot to have them closer to me, but I am not so sure it would have made such a big difference. Take my Alex for instance. Does he come occasionally to find out how I am? No. If it wasn't for his wife, Barbara, I wouldn't see him at all. He simply doesn't think of his old mother. I could die here, you know, with him only ten minutes away. Yes, I know he loves me, but he doesn't show it. I know my Alex, you can be sure of that.'

'So often', the priest puts on his confessional voice, 'people simply don't know how to say I love you. Especially within their own families. Perhaps', he suggests, 'he is simply not sure that you love him. Perhaps it is a simple case of lack of confidence.'

What does he ram this penny psychology down my throat for? She catches herself silently grumbling about Father Daly, and doing so, her face twists, her eyes shut tightly, as if in pain. 'Lack of confidence?' says the voice behind the pain. 'My Alex? No, Father, not my Alex. He has too much confidence. I don't think that he cares tuppence if I love him or not, as a matter of fact.' Admitting it too easily. Take care, Gertrude, he may think you are really miserable. 'Mind you, he is very busy, is my Alex. Always thinking of his work. He is in marketing, an expert in some new marketing methods. Doris is different. She comes here at least once a week without fail. We talk on the telephone every other day so that we both know exactly what's happening. Alex has to be asked over and over again what's new, is he well, you know. His wife is the one who tells me about him. But it is not too easy with her. She is not from here, you understand. She is from Montreal. From a large Jewish community and she never stops complaining about Dublin, about Ireland, about the community. Not that I don't agree with her in much of what she has to say. It's hard to blame her. She is a highly educated girl, PhD in literature, and here she is, at home with the children, cooking and cleaning. But all this makes it difficult to talk to her sometimes, she sees everything in such black-and-white terms.'

'It's difficult to be in a strange place, move countries without anger or resentment against the people around one, although the locals of course are not to blame for the alienation,' says the priest.

'Difficult? Difficult you said?' She speaks fast now, without thinking. 'She has it difficult? And what about me? After all the years, always moving from one place to the other, from one house to another, first Limerick, then Dublin, then England, then Dublin again. Always moving, without taking roots. What does she know, Barbara, about new places? This is her first move, the first time she's left home. And after all, what's so bad here? There are Jews here, no? There are no pogroms here. No one burns shops and beats up Jews here, like in Limerick in 1904. True? And there is social life here, there's theatre, concerts, not like the years I had small children and there was nothing to do, nowhere to go. What did we have in Limerick in my day after all? Only mad priests and . . .' she stops. Alarmed. In her rage she forgot who she is talking to. This time I've really done it. She has exaggerated not in her words, for which she apologises to Father Daly, but in exposing to this stranger, part, small as it may be, of the tensions which are her family life. She doesn't usually admit to chinks in the façade. Inadvertently she has spoken of loneliness, of fear. The fear of staying alone, of dying in an empty house. A fear she has outgrown but that she still adheres to, pulling it out like a joker from deck of cards whenever she is in need of a moral victory. Herself versus the others — the constant battle for no-man's land, for a peace of mind which she never had.

The cleric says again and again that he understands.

Slowly and deliberately she replies, 'You know, Father, sometimes when I am talking to you I forget myself. Because with you I feel safe. Honestly.' These words are an enormous effort for her.

He doesn't say anything. He sits and gazes, amazed, at this woman. He knows there is something there, underneath the apologetic chuckling cover. Something deep and sticky, which he cannot understand. Here is a totally different world than the one he meets daily in the chapel, over cups of tea in the other semis, in the confessionals. But what he sees as different is only external, only personal circumstances, historical background. It's only this natural curiosity, the reason he has become a priest sitting on the other side of the confessional listening to sticky whispers of invented and real sins, which brings him back to Gertrude Klein, again and again.

*   *   *

One of the things Gertrude always regretted was not being given the opportunity to study. After primary school the girls stayed home because their father didn't approve of secular education for girls. Even the boys he agreed to send to school only after family pressure. 'What do they want with Irish and mathematics, for what do they need the history of the British Empire? What they do need is to study the Torah and some bookkeeping and get a lot of experience.'

But the Jewish community in Limerick was small, everybody was related to everybody and people put pressure on Lipshuetz to leave the boys with the Christian Brothers, where they studied history and geography, English literature and mathematics, Irish and French and a host of other things old Lipshuetz never heard of. At sixteen, he put them into the business so that he could stop working and concentrate on his own studies.

Gershon, whom the sisters called Gerry, had a natural flair for business. He took over his father's rounds, and then got a chance to become a partner in a jeweller's shop. The first few years were difficult. He bought cheap and sold at a small profit. He knew the villagers from his rounds, knew who had jewels and offered the women a couple of pounds in cash, which they usually fell for since they rarely had any money in the house.

Soon, with most of the gold gone from the country houses in the counties of Limerick and Clare, you could find the best selection in Gerry Laurence's shop.

In the first years, when Gershon went on his rounds, to return to the city only for two or three days a week, Gertrude, his junior by some twelve years, used to help in the shop. She loved to stand behind the counter selling jewellery. She preferred this to running the house, which she had to do since her mother's death. She acquired a posh accent, learnt a few professional-sounding words and advised hysterical girls about their engagement rings. 'Every hand has only one suitable ring,' Gershon used to say and Gertrude, so influenced, had believed since then that there was only one way to do things.

Moishe, called Maurice, also had a good head for business. He acquired, unwittingly, a good scrap-iron business from one Rosenberg, whose grand-daughter befriended him. Since none of Rosenberg's sons wanted to deal in scrap, considering it a dirty business, Moishe, smelling money, got into the firm as the old man's assistant. Rosenberg liked him and, when he died, left him his fortune.

Moishe and Gershon were the last Jews to remain in Limerick after 1904. Both took non-Jewish wives, so now it is difficult to speak of a Jewish community in that city.

*   *   *

'I was a child, almost a baby, during the Limerick pogrom,' Gertrude Klein tells Father Daly, who now visits her fairly regularly. 'Four years of age. Now you know how old I am. Alright, I admit it. I shall soon be seventy-five. Born with the century, nineteen hundred.' Gertrude pauses for a minute.

Father Daly obliges. 'Seventy-five? I wouldn't have believed it, Mrs Klein. I simply cannot believe it. I thought you were sixty-five at the very most. The very most.'

'Seventy-five, Father. In five months and three days to be exact.' She is counting the days to this very important date, in fear more than in expectation, like she did before her fiftieth, her sixtieth and her seventieth birthdays. Always scared something might happen. 'But why am I counting days and months for you, Father? I started to tell you of the pogrom in Limerick. I was four years old. This is what they told me afterwards. I can't remember too much, I was only a baby. But I can remember the fear. And what the grown-ups used to say at home about Father Creagh's sermons.'

'I never knew there had been a pogrom in Ireland. In fact, I always thought it marvellous that there is no anti-semitism in Ireland,' he says.

There is no anti-semitism in Ireland my elbow. Who is he trying to kid? Both of us know the Irish are not exactly in love with the Jews. Come to think of it, nobody else is in love with the Jews either. She recalls having said this again and again to her children in the past. 'I am not saying that there is anti-semitism now, Father,' she says cautiously. 'But there's no doubt about Limerick in 1904. There definitely was a pogrom in Limerick, it's a well-known fact. Perhaps there is no anti-semitism now only because there aren't enough Jews in Ireland.'

'About three thousand,' says the priest out of the blue. 'I went to the library and did some reading.'

'Anyway,' she says, covering a small smile of satisfaction, 'it all began in January 1904. With the Graf wedding. My sisters never stopped talking about this wedding. Blue velvet, and a motorcar just to go from one end of the street to the other rather than walk. After the wedding, to which all the Jewish community went, naturally, the sermons started. Rich people's weddings, you know how they can be. Graf was a money-lender, one of only two money-lenders, mind. This is important because it was a crucial part of Father Creagh's sermons. He was, you'll excuse me, Father, a madman. The Hitler of Limerick. I know he was a priest, but I am sure that what he was saying was against the Christian spirit.'

'What did he say?' Father Daly gets her back to the facts.

'Something about the Jews being vipers in the breast of the Irish population. He was speaking at a Redemptorist meeting, after the Graf wedding. I remember that my father told me he had read in the paper that we, the Jews of Limerick, would you believe it, crucified Jesus. In person. How could we have done it? We weren't even there when he was crucified, were we? Isn't it funny?'

Father Daly doesn't respond. He too had been educated to believe the Jews crucified Christ. Seeing he does not say anything, she glances at him uncertainly. He looks her straight in the eye, smiling, trying to soften.

'He talked plenty about all our sins. The Jews' sins, that is. Nonsense about how we kidnap children, Christian children, and murder them for their blood, for our Passover. But all this was nothing compared with what he said about us, the Jews of Limerick. He said we came to Limerick apparently the most miserable tribe imaginable, these were his exact words, and that later our rags were exchanged for silks. That we have wormed our way into every form of business, trading under Irish names. How does a Jew manage to make money, he asked. He told the people that we, as pedlars from door to door, pretend to offer articles at very cheap prices, but in reality charge several times the value of the same item in the shops. He said we force ourselves upon the people, that we impose the weekly payment system — remember, I told you about the vikle system, Father — so that people would pay for an article again and again. The Jew, he said, has a sweet tongue when he wishes . . . .'

Gertrude Klein uses Father Creagh's words almost exactly, playing the part as she heard it being played so often during her childhood. She glances briefly at the cleric, awaiting a reaction. When none is forthcoming, she goes on.

'He said the mayor's court seemed like a special court for the benefit of the Jews — this was how much he exaggerated. I am amazed', she says in a small voice, fluttering her paled eyelids, 'that people actually sat there listening to all this. Must have been his power of persuasion. There are such people, you know. He also said that by bringing in merchandise from England we crippled local trade and industry. We come to Ireland, he said, to fasten ourselves like leeches and to draw blood when we have been forced away from other countries. He said all that,' she goes on, suffocating a small sigh, 'all that and more. People in our community never stopped talking about it for a long time.

Father Daly moves uncomfortably in his seat, but she continues, unruffled. 'After his speech, would you believe it, only three people left the hall. The others, we were told, all sat there and clapped and clapped for about five minutes. It was awful, you must agree, Father, because as a result of his hysterical sermon they attacked us, pelting us with mud, breaking our windows and throwing stones. And there was a boycott, six months long. All business stopped. No one had money, even those he called money-lenders and blood-suckers.' Gertrude sighs, wringing her hands. 'God, I remember the fear, even though I was only little, we couldn't get out of the house for a good few months, couldn't buy things. Father never did any business, never stopped praying. After a couple of weeks some help arrived. From London. Food parcels and some clothes for the children. I can still smell those awful parcels, mouldy. Some people were beaten up and shops were destroyed. Poor Mr Martinson, he was beaten up by several men and ran for help into our house, covered in blood. I was only a child, but this was something I shall never forget. And Mr Racusen — he was beaten up when he went out to sell milk. He had no one to sell milk to and had to get rid of his cows. Every Monday the people from the confraternity meeting came down our street, walking together, like a wall. Frightening. Our blinds always down, the curtains drawn. Always dark, night and day. And outside the Jewish shops — the police guarding.' She pauses, sighs again.

'Many Jews left Limerick after the . . . after that?' asks Father Daly, again preferring to anchor in facts.

'Most of them. To tell the truth, I never quite understood why father stayed on. He even returned to his rounds after the pogrom and Gershon joined him, before making a go of that jewellery shop of his. Gershon was in Limerick until his death a few years ago, you know, but he was not really Jewish.'

'What do you mean, not really Jewish?'

'He married a Catholic girl. His children are Catholic and he, like so many Jews, only happened to have been born a Jew. A mistake you might say. My other brother, Moishe, Maurice, is also married to a gentile. But they at least have no children. Religion passes on through the mother with Jews.'

All this time they are sitting, tense, on the edge of their chairs as if waiting for something. When she offers him a cup of tea his face lights up, relieved.

Father Daly's world is simple and his moral philosophy totally clear. Like Mrs Klein's. But this time their standpoints are opposed and he can't help agreeing with some of Father Creagh's words. Although he has always claimed he abhors violence, he knows of the poverty in Limerick at the beginning of the century and realises the injustice. Those penniless Jews coming to Ireland and becoming rich by exploiting the villagers' wives may have been, as Father Creagh said, bloodsuckers and money-lenders. But he says nothing because, most of all, he hates upsetting people, particularly in their own homes.

But Gertrude Klein cannot stop. Making the tea, she goes on, her voice shrill and high, from the kitchen. 'They spoke of our riches,' she shouts, 'but believe you me, we were far from rich. Father may have sold them something they didn't want from time to time. He may have persuaded them, but he never cheated them. And he worked hard. God, he worked hard. He used to come home, I remember, in the last years of his life, he used to come home torn, torn.' Her voice turns to a shriek. 'Each week he aged, each week another white hair, another wrinkle.' At this point she reaches the room, carrying the tray. She almost bangs it on the little table and when she lifts her hands to pour the tea, they shake so violently that she has to stop and straighten up, an attempt to calm herself. 'You should have seen him,' she says, regaining her breath. 'Grey with tiredness. Always on his little cart, with the old donkey. Rain, wind, snow, anything. He was on his way. He wouldn't talk about his work much. Said it wasn't very interesting, that it was more interesting to talk about his studies. But one thing I do remember. How he complained of being cheated. Naive. That's what my father was. Naive. They signed the piece of paper alright, and said they would pay, but would they pay? Not at all. Week after week, they wouldn't pay. And I can assure you father didn't cheat them. So naive, he was so naive.' Gertrude Klein weeps and in her excitement she is shaking, as if falling, looking for support in a chair, a wall, anything. When she finds it in the priest's solid arm, she leans against him unashamedly, a grateful smile on her white lips.

'Sit down, sit down, Mrs Klein. Sit down. You must rest a while. You are over-excited.' Father Daly sits her down on the armchair. 'I'll pour the tea. Sit down, Mrs Klein.'

She looks at him, her face bloodless, her eyes very blue and woven with red snaky veins. She stares at him, looking for something in his face, finding only silence and blandness.

He looks at her, smiles with his mouth only and says, 'It's alright. It's alright.'

But at the same times his eyes tell her something else. Something hostile, strange, about those Jews. She takes in only the eyes, not the words. She sits up and with very white hands, a large diamond twinkling on a thin finger, pours out the tea, cooled in the meantime, into the china cups. Sugar, milk, stir. Cautious sips, hard swallowing sounds and silence.

And in the silence, exposure threatens her once again. Although she knows instinctively that she is safe with him, he takes on Father Creagh's shape in her mind's eye — his eyes so near her face, so hostile — Father Creagh standing on a pulpit, talking. 'Blood-suckers . . . vipers in our midst . . . money-lenders . . . enemies of the people . . . enemies of the people . . . enemies of the people . . . .' The voice burns in her head, she is dizzy and weak, nauseated. 'The Jew has a sweet tongue . . . money-lenders . . .' says Father Daly's round voice and she tries to push him away, her hands weak. Push him away, push his pink face away, his almost-orange face, his sweaty forehead, his steamed-up spectacles. Push him away.

*   *   *

2

Gertrude Klein wakes up in her bed and finds her daughter Doris beside her. She is cold and the room too white, too bright against her sore eyes. She blinks, taking in Doris's figure, the large body, the elongated head, the dark eyes. 'What are you doing here, Doris? Something has happened to the children? What happened? Why did you come, it isn't Tuesday, is it?'

Doris says something garbled, but Gertrude has to know. She is in bed and there is light outside. She never sleeps in the afternoon, so what is she doing in bed in the middle of the day?

'How will I manage to sleep at night, Doris? Why am I in bed in the middle of the day?' She is fully awake now, completely lucid. She knows she has done something strange, that something had happened, but doesn't remember fainting after she told the priest about Limerick. All is detached, disconnected, sudden.

'You were tired, Mother,' Doris says vaguely, 'that's all. So you went to sleep and I came in and found you in bed.'

'What nonsense. What do you mean, you came in and found me in bed? You don't even have a key. Who let you in?' Suddenly the whole thing falls into place, Father Creagh, the pogrom, Father Daly. 'Did he let you in? What happened to me?'

'You fainted, mother. It was lucky my number was with Mrs O'Grady. He went to see if she knew of anyone he could contact on your behalf. He had a good fright. He even called a doctor. And then me.

'And what did the doctor say?'

'He said you were over-excited. The excitement weakened you. People often faint when they get over-excited. That's all.'

'Which doctor could this priest have called? Not Dr Rose surely?'

'How could he know of Dr Rose?' says Doris impatiently. 'And he wanted someone to come immediately. He got a fright, I told you already. Doctor McNamara, from the estate, he came. He came immediately and gave you a check-up. He wouldn't even take money, Daly told him to put it on his bill.'

Gertrude says nothing. So I have fainted again. One day I could faint in the bath and drown or in the kitchen and break my neck. Not such a bad idea, to go like that. Better than cancer. Better to faint all of a sudden and be done with it.

Doris smooths her mother's blankets, pats pillows and says it's time to eat something.

I have nothing in the fridge, Gertrude panics. What will Doris think.

She never buys food for more than two days and today would have been her shopping day. She simply has to get out of the house at least once every two days, otherwise the house depresses her in its emptiness, shutting her in. She enjoys going into the small supermarket, buying half a pound of marge and half a dozen eggs and then into the fish shop, for a fillet of plaice for supper, discussing prices, the freshness of the fillet. Sometimes she goes into the Jewish delicatessen and buys a little potato salad or chopped herring to brighten her meals. She doesn't starve herself, far from it, she eats plenty of sliced white bread, drinks many cups of tea and stuffs her face with shop biscuits, but rarely sits down to a proper meal by herself.

Now, however, she knows that Doris won't find anything in the fridge. 'You know, Doris,' she says in her most cheerful voioce, 'I am not at all hungry.'

'You have got to eat something,' Doris says dryly. 'What is there?'

A heavy silence.

'I haven't been to the shop today, Doris, you understand, dear. I didn't have time. Father Daly came early this morning. He sometimes comes at the most incredible hours. The first time he came here it was just after lunch, ten-past-two, would you believe it? For him there's no problem, naturally. He probably has a housekeeper, and no worries. He eats, wipes his mouth, probably with a starched napkin, perhaps even belches or makes other horrible noises, and gets up and goes.'

'Mo-ther!' Doris says, the word clearly divided into two impatient syllables. 'What about something to eat? I am going downstairs to make something for you. Stay in bed like a good girl, yes?'

'You drive me crazy, all of you,' says Gertrude. 'Barbara also talks to me about not eating every time she comes here. Babbles on about vitamins and vegetables. You don't think that I starve myself, do you?'

'No. Of course not, mother. But sometimes I think you could look after yourself a little better, that's all.' The voice is colourless, tired, disinterested.

She's going to root in my cupboard, Gertrude thinks, irritated. What do they care what I have in my presses? When they come I always have a good meal for them, don't I? So what do they want with my cupboards?

Gertrude bakes now only when the old guilt bothers her. She used to boast of her cakes, of her numerous homemade delicacies which filled the house with their aroma. The fact that the children retained different memories, memories of over-cooked meals, of mother guarding her cakes religiously for 'when daddy comes home from work', is a minor detail now. If anyone dares to confront her with the other point of view she is so hurt that it simply isn't worth their while.

Doris finds half a bottle of milk and a packet of cooking margarine in the fridge. There isn't even an egg. In the cupboard she finds two tins — tomato soup and baked beans — some flour, sugar and about ten rolls of toilet paper. On the table a jam jar with a quarter-pound of rice, another one of tea. Doris cooks the rice, serving it to her mother with half a tin of baked beans.

'Doris, you are a genius. You managed to make a meal from next to nothing.' Gertrude tries to sound cheerful. As a matter of fact she is furious. Now she has no more baked beans, which, with an egg, could have made an excellent supper.

Doris stabs her sixth cigarette in the cut-glass ashtray. It would be better to sell off all this Waterford glass, she thinks, and fill the house with food. But what nonsense. The problem is not money. Gertrude simply doesn't believe in filling the house with food. She absolutely loves shopping. Something to do. Saves her from going mad. Apart from that, she says that food doesn't keep. She still lives in the pre-preserved-food era. One cannot freeze meat, she claims, or fish, it's simply not the same. Sometimes she does buy frozen peas, but eats them on the same day so they won't go bad. She buys tinned food, stating categorically that she doesn't have the energy to cook fresh food.

Gertrude eats the rice, wipes her pursed mouth carefully and tells Doris to put the rest in the fridge. 'I never throw anything away,' she says, half-jokingly.

Doris smiles to herself and goes downstairs to wash up.

When she comes back up, her mother is asleep. One of her hands hangs outside the bed and her mouth gapes wide open, black. She seems old suddenly, helpless, no more the composed woman whose equilibrium is never interrupted. Usually Gertrude takes care to remain cool in every situation, her manners perfect, not letting anyone see what goes on in her head. It's the fainting, Doris thinks, she is tired.

Father Daly comes on the following day. Doris opens the door and to his chirpy question, 'And how is our invalid today?' answers vaguely, her face wrinkled with worries, 'Thanks, she is not too bad, considering.'

He realises instantly that something is bothering her, a cigarette in her nicotine-stained hand, her mouth quivering. Therefore he says in his mourners-comforting voice, 'I know it is scaring to see your mother so weak suddenly. It's a shock. Perhaps you'd like to tell me what happened, what it is that's bothering you?'

She steps back, protecting herself from this invasion, from this confident stranger. Father Daly chooses to interpret this retreat as an invitation to come into the house and before she knows where she is, the door shuts behind him and he becomes, once again, part of Gertrude Klein's life and for the first time, Doris's life too.

'Something happened,' he says again, his vouce reassuring. 'Would you care to tell me about it? Your mother and I, I don't know if she told you, became quite good friends recently. I like her very much and would like to help her. And you.'

She tries to keep her cool, at least outwardly. 'Nothing particular happened, Mr Daly.' She deliberately refrains from using the religious title, which sounds so natural when her mother uses it.

'I'm glad to hear it,' he says, his voice unbelieving, slightly cynical. 'May I go up and visit her?'

'You see, Mr Daly,' she starts nervously, speaking fast, 'she almost didn't wake up at all since yesterday. She ate something and then slept the whole time, her mouth open, making strange noises in her sleep . . . like, like an old woman. An old and sick woman.'

'Have you called a doctor?'

'No,' she looks vaguely guilty but adds, 'it's not a matter for a doctor, I am sure of it. Something is happening to her, she is changing. What happened between you two before she fainted?'

A quick glance saying, so this is what's bothering you, you are afraid of my effect on the old woman. Then he looks directly at her, his eyes round, his pink face open. 'Nothing in particular. We just sit and talk, drinking tea. Yesterday, for example, your mother told me about Limerick, about what happened to the Jews there, about the pogrom. And about Father Creagh. She got rather excited and passed out.'

'She told you about Limerick?' Doris finds it hard to believe.

The priest doesn't answer. Waiting for more.

She peers at him, her eyes yellow and her face grey, like someone suffering from insomnia, examining his silence and making nothing of it. 'She, I mean mother, something is bothering her. Perhaps the Limerick memories scared her suddenly. She is always so, so calm, her behaviour so correct. And suddenly this. As if she is scared of something. Something rather vague. Do you think it's Limerick?' She is really asking what he thinks of her mother's condition, what is happening to her, admitting to having missed something.

He is used to it. His parishioners often ask him questions, trying to understand, through him, what is motivating them. They often ask him to make a decision for them and more often to agree to a decision they have already taken but feel rather guilty about. He has to be their spiritual guide too, reminding them of their duty to Jesus, the cross they have to bear. But he mustn't think of Doris in these terms, even though he can't help thinking she should remember her duty to love. 'I don't know your mother long enough to arrive at any conclusions,' he says finally in a slow deliberate tone. 'But it seems to me she got excited not only because of Limerick. I think, and correct me if I'm wrong, that she is a disappointed woman, disappointed by her isolation and her distance from her children.' He enunciates every word carefully and ends like a slow piece of music, waiting for the applause.

No applause comes. Doris's reaction is almost violent. 'I think you are mistaken, Mr Daly. My sister-in-law, Barbara, also talks a lot about mother's loneliness and isolation. But I happen to think that mother is perfectly happy, that this is how she wants to live. She could have come to live with us, you know, we asked her to. But she prefers a house of her own, a place to which she can come back, where she can be alone, eat small meals and sit for hours in front of the television, not talk too much, not make any effort.' Her voice is almost metallic, her face sombre. 'You may not know, but she had a hard life. She had a large house, five children and a husband whom she had to care for. Now she prefers to rest. I have come to this conclusion a long time ago. I am glad, however,' says the voice, cool now, formal, 'that you don't think that she got over-excited because of Limerick. And now . . .' but she says no more.

Father Daly is astonished to hear her blame herself. For a minute there he thought she was worried, but now realises the finality of it. Doris does not want the responsibility for her mother's life but realises its emptiness.

'I would like to see her, just to say hello,' he says, gropingly. 'May I?'

'She is asleep now,' she says, hostile, 'perhaps tomorrow morning.'

'Doris,' comes Gertrude's high voice from upstairs, 'who are you talking to?'

He avoids looking at Doris, who replies, her voice shrill and loud, sounding exactly like Gertrude's, 'Mr Daly came to see how you are . . . . He would like to see you,' she adds reluctantly.

'Please tell him to come upstairs,' says the mother, and Doris, resentment in her eyes, points towards the stairs. 'There you are, Mr Daly, mother is in the front room. I understand you know these houses.'

'Thank you, Missis,' he says, country-style, but Doris doesn't let him get away with it. 'Ross,' she says sharply, 'Mrs Ross.'

She lets him go up alone, enter her mother's room alone. She stays at the bottom of the stairs, lighting a cigarette. After a couple of minutes she follows him.

The first thing she sees when entering the room is her mother's pale smiling face, sunk deep in the soft pillows. But the eyes are calm again.

'You are not serious, Father,' the voice is saying, excited, 'I simply fainted, all of a sudden? It's strange, you know. It happened a few times in the past few months. I have found myself on the floor in front of the television, or by my bed. The doctor gave me some pills, but they mustn't be doing the job.'

'Doctor McNamara says you'd better have a check-up. He gave me a letter for St Vincent's. It won't cost you much, he also gave me a form for the Eastern Health Board. They will cover the expenses.'

'Why didn't you tell me you have been fainting?' says Doris, sharply breaking the calm.

'But Doris, I didn't want to worry you,' Gertrude says apologetically. 'Apart from that, I did tell you Dr Rose has given me pills for low blood pressure, didn't I?'

'Why didn't you tell me you have been fainting, Mother?' Doris repeats, insistent. 'You should have told us. You cannot stay in the house by yourself, it can be dangerous.'

'It's not at all dangerous. At the most I could break my neck and it would be final, a quick death, no suffering. Not like poor Harry, suffering so many years from cancer. Harry,' she explains to Father Daly, 'was my nephew. Poor thing. Got cancer and was in hospital almost four years, dying slowly. His wife had such a hard time with the kids, you cannot imagine. Since then I'm always scared of cancer. An awful thing. Anything is better than cancer — '

'What rubbish!' Doris's sharp voice cuts short her mother's careful sentences. 'We shall talk about it later.' She looks at the priest, his round face emotionless, and bossily sits herself on Gertrude's bed.

'I suggest, Mrs Klein, if you don't mind, that you have that check-up anyway. It can't do any harm. Then you can decide what to do. They can send the results directly to your own doctor if you wish, or you can go back to Dr McNamara to get a second opinion.'

'Thanks. Nice of you to have organised all this. The check-up is a grand idea.' She glances at Doris, 'What do you think, Doris?'

'This is ridiculous!' Doris explodes, astonishing both her mother and Father Daly. 'You're letting a priest, a Catholic, organise your life. But you wouldn't listen to a word I say. I think you've overdone this friendship, frankly. What would grandfather have said? A talmudist's daughter making friends with a gentile, and a priest at that.'

The silence lasts only a couple of tense seconds.

'Doris, are you out of your mind? I do think you'd better apologise to Father Daly. Why this narrowmindedness? Who says one has to make friends only with Jews? And how many friends do you have? Jewish friends I mean. And how often do I see you, or Alex? OK, I see you twice a week, but Alex only twice a year, when Barbara drags him over. You should be thankful I am not alone all the time, you know.' She is panting heavily now, her words shooting out like bullets.

'You are complaining?' Doris is almost screaming now. 'How many times did you come of your own accord to see the children in the last couple of years? Yes, you come when I come for you, I know. But do you ever think of coming over yourself? For Alex I cannot speak, but you'd better think of what you're saying.'

'Doris,' Gertrude is breathing heavily now, her face scarlet. 'What are you saying? What are you saying?' Her voice which shrieked seconds ago, dies out now and she is lying down again, motionless, her mouth pursed, panting.

Father Daly takes her wrist in his experienced hand but soon lets the thin, arthritic arm fall again. 'She is alright,' he says. 'She only got excited. I'll call Dr McNamara, she may need another injection.'

Doris starts sobbing. 'Mother, I am sorry. It's my fault. I'm sorry, I didn't mean . . . .'

Father Daly lays a steady hand on her shaking shoulder and says, 'You shouldn't blame yourself. But you should also remember it for the next time. People often say things they don't really mean, when they get upset. You should remember.'

Doris cuts her sobbing with a sudden jerk, straightens her back and looks at him hatefully. 'It's all because of you, you dirty little priest. Because of you she has suddenly changed. Everything was alright, nothing has happened for years, since father died, in fact. Everyone lived happily ever after and things were just fine. But since you arrived on the scene, everything is collapsing.'

He does not answer. He looks her straight in the eye, then goes down the stairs to telephone Dr McNamara.

Within two weeks Gertrude is on her feet again, strong and chirpy. The check-up shows low blood pressure and the doctor says only that she has to avoid over-excitement and physical effort.

During these two weeks Doris spends every day with her. The two talk very little. Doris shops, cleans, cooks, serves meals and medicines. Barbara comes three times a week to relieve Doris, who is looking exhausted and unhappy. As usual, Barbara never stops chatting, about the kids, about Alex, about the world. Alex fixes up the television by Gertrude's bed so she is able to spend her evenings watching the box. She refuses point blank to move to Doris's.

Father Daly comes from time to time to see how she is, but never stays long because of Doris's hostility. Then one day about a month after the faint he finds her on her feet and on her own, for a change.

She starts evoking to him, or rather to herself, the Gertrude of the years gone by. 'You have no idea, Father,' she says when they are sitting in front of the fire, a cup of tea in their hands, 'to what extent Doris reminds me of myself, years ago I mean. Always doing what has to be done, working so hard, never stopping for a minute. Poor thing, she comes here early in the morning, cleans my house, washes up the dishes from the night before, makes my breakfast, helps me wash, makes something for lunch and runs back home, cleans her own house, cooks for the kids. When they return from school at three-thirty she feeds them, sticks them in the car and hurries back here. Then she cleans up my lunch things, makes my supper and washes my kitchen.

Yes, every day she washes the kitchen floor, like it's going out of style. The number of times I told her it isn't necessary, but she doesn't listen. Then she makes us a cup of tea and prepares my supper. If it's a hot meal she stays on until I finish, and if it's cold she might go off a little earlier. What diligence, Father, there's no end to it. I can only think about myself, how I slaved all my life, working away for everyone else. And do you suppose someone helped me? My husband never as much as washed a cup or a saucer. Not to mention boiling an egg or making a cup of tea. The girls always had excuses, homework, ballet, piano lessons. I had help alright, but I was always busy, help or no help. What a life. And to think of the music I sacrificed in order to be my husband and my children's personal slave. He was always busy, always working, meeting his cronies, you know. But,' she adds dutifully, realising it has to be said, 'we had a wonderful life, Father, a wonderful life.'

'And the children,' she says some time later, 'do you know what happens with children, Father? When one is young, one wants them to remain babies for ever. We used to always say that they'll have plenty of time to face the cruel world. So one does everything for them. Covering up the flaws, as it were, so they wouldn't see them. And then they grow up and everything is different, altogether different. Our beautiful life together, a houseful of children, a happy marriage and what is left of it all? Three or four letters from across the ocean, a phonecall from across the channel every couple of weeks, and heartbreak tales.' She looks at the cleric, examining his reactions carefully.

He doesn't say a thing. He feels there is another side to the story, a side Gertrude is not prepared to expose or is unconscious of. He merely listens. She and her family have become part of his life and he feels responsible for this fragile woman sitting in front of him, holding tight to her cup of tea.

'Take Rose for example. Married a non-Jew. Nice guy. Very ambitions. A doctor. In order to advance in his profession he wanted to move to the States. In New York he started climbing slowly up the social ladder. Golf at the right clubs, drinks with the right people, you know the score. Rose was left alone in a small flat with a screaming baby, without friends or relatives. so it didn't work. Naturally. And to think what a marvellous pianist she had been. We sent her to London to study piano, in the Royal College of Music, if you please. We sent her to London and she goes and falls in love with this goy, if you pardon the expression. Today she is up to her eyes in analysis and other American nonsense. She lives alone in a smallish flat in New York, Jeremy pays her expenses and looks after rich patients in California. So what did I guard her from the cruel world for, can you tell me? We didn't tell them anything. Sparing them like. Now I think we would have done better to tell them. During the war we did not tell them anything. They have, of course, heard of the Blitz, but we didn't tell them about the concentration camps and all that. We were never short of food and they were as happy as Larry. What did we do it for, can you tell me?'

Gertrude pauses for a while, almost in tears. 'And Doris. Do you think Doris is a happy woman? She found this David, God knows where. A good boy, but God what a weakling. Literally licks her boots, you know. it would have sickened me, I can tell you. And she is growing older by the minute, one can see she has no challenges in life, if you follow me. Her life begins and ends with the kids. Her education, her career, everything — all gone by the board.'

Father Daly moves uncomfortably on his seat, crosses his legs and looks at Gertrude.

'But Henry tops them all. Today I get a letter from him. From London. He has made up his mind to marry his girlfriend. She isn't Jewish, naturally. Why bother and find a Jewish girl? He doesn't ask me, he tells me. There won't be a ceremony, they are getting married in a registry office. I am not invited. I suppose I should feel grateful he let me know at all. A sudden letter. After not hearing from him for six months. Maybe he knows her only a couple of weeks? Who knows what sort of girl she is? He is working in the bank, the Bank of Ireland. Hasn't done too badly since he got started with them. He is my baby, you understand. On the one hand I am very glad he decided to get married at long last but on the other, he is so unstable. How can he know she is the right girl for him? I suppose I am being a Jewish mama. I suppose it's ridiculous to worry about one's baby, who is forty years of age, isn't it, Father?'

He almost says something, to tide her over, but she doesn't give him a chance.

'I hope you'll be able to meet them all. They promised to come for my seventy-fifth birthday, in three months time, in April. You shall see them, so nice, so polite, just like me, Father, always hiding their problems, you know. It is very important to me to look right, to wear the right clothes, to say only the right things, and as little as possible. Don't you think it's ridiculous? That it's high time to start speaking my mind?'

And later she says, 'I'm afraid of the meeting with the children. Of course it will be great to see all the grandchildren, to be together once again. I haven't seen Rose for six years and Henry I last saw two years ago. But what will it do to us? When I see Alex, I can hardly talk to him. I am afraid they'll all be like that, strangers.'

And, before he leaves, almost as an afterthought, she says, 'When my poor husband was alive, we had a good life, but it wasn't easy to live with him. Not easy at all. He always wanted me to do what he said and

I think that my children would also like me to be all sorts of different things. But how can I be different than what I am? My husband would not let me go on singing, he insisted on arranging the furniture his own way, that I dress just so. I did everything he wanted. Not always without argument, I admit. Everything for peace and quiet, you know. To give up one's whole life for the sake of peace and quiet is a mistake, Father. I know now. Since I've met you I've been thinking a lot about this. I can talk to you. You can listen, you know. Considering the fact that I have five children, bless them and spare them, it's crazy that here I am, pouring my heart out to a priest.'

She has already said this in the past, but it never stops to bother her, partly because Doris never stops giving out to her about this strange friendship, as she calls it. 'It is impossible', Doris had said 'that he comes here simply out of friendship. He wants something from you. Perhaps a promise you'll become a Catholic before you die. Collecting souls for his album.' 'What nonsense,' Gertrude had laughed angrily in reply, but in heart of hearts she too has doubts.

*   *   *

Gertrude's wonderful life with her husband wasn't all that wonderful. Daniel had his own life and the house was nothing for him but an eating place, a place to wash, sleep and kill time between other occupations. He had very little patience with her chatter, her incessant complaints, her martyrdom.

She couldn't explain the rage she was subject to on very trivial matters. She wasn't violent and her attacks were sort of weepy, imploring. She could get quite het up when a pudding she planned for two meals got eaten in one. She would hide the fruit cake in illogical places, so that a peckish child wasn't able to take a slice. A roast chicken the family was going to finish, cold, the following day, would find its way to a hiding place in the wardrobe.

When the children grew, they found her out and she would break into long sermons about greed and waste when she found half the chicken gone during the night, or the fruit cake reduced to crumbs. Daniel would cut her short and since he wouldn't play along with her, Gertrude would sink deeper into the game, waving her hands and sobbing.

Doris could still remember the crying and shouting from her parents' room, her fear as a young child, when father shrieked at mother and when mother sobbed and sobbed. Mother was always weepy, she was a victim. When the children grew, they got used to the pattern.

Gertrude met Daniel after having completely despaired of getting married. She was living with her parents after she left school and the Limerick of those days didn't offer young women many opportunities.

Pearl, who had moved to Dublin, was always introducing Gertrude to potential husbands. She dabbled in match-making in her spare time, thus supplementing her husband's income. He never managed to get his own business and was still repairing watches in a small jeweller's shop. Pearl, a heavy woman by now, lines, kerchief and rolling hips, was rather devout and wanted Gertrude to marry an orthodox man.

Gertrude hated those introductions, as they were called. She was small, her bust heavy and her hips round. But she had a nice face, healthy looking chestnut hair and a slender waist. Her eyes had always been watery, but her nose was straight and her mouth heart-shaped. She had acquired, working in her brother's shop, a posh accent and generally she made as they say a good impression. She hated the meetings Pearl arranged for her in Dublin since the potential husbands were usually bearded and dressed in traditional garb and wide-brimmed hats. She hated them also because of her painful shyness.

The meetings usually ended with the potential husbands leaving without expressing any interest in the scared little mouse they had just met. Gertrude too was not enthusiastic. She had her own dreams.

The man to whom she would give the treasure burning within her would be a man of the world. He would be dressed according to the latest fashion, would have very good manners, would be very romantic. She was deeply affected by the romances she had read and by the moving pictures. She was full of sticky sensuality, flickering her eyelids in front of the mirror. She used to pet herself and touch her secret places, which caused her such pleasure when she lay alone in the bed in which she turned from a young girl to a woman. Like her future tantrums which she wouldn't be able to control, she had wells of desire she wasn't able to understand in those years after the first brassière.

None of the young men she met at Pearl's managed to get close enough to extinguish her flame. She used to leave these meetings anguished and angry at herself for having been tempted once again. She left, cool and disappointed, yet with her flame rekindled because of renewed hopes for something else. Her hope aroused excitement, re-dipping her in circles of desire, the exit from which she had to make on her own during the cold nights under the flannel nightie and the four woollen blankets. An incomplete exit, leaving parts of her behind within the circle, like dead bodies in no-man's land.

Funnily enough, she met Daniel too at Pearl's. He wasn't one of the potential husbands, as he wasn't orthodox enough for Pearl and had the reputation of a libertine. It was known in the Jewish community that he bet on horses, that he did not refuse a drink and as for his livelihood, it had been neither regular nor secure.

Gertrude was about twenty-five at the time. There was something young, eager, childish in her body and face, which turned from fresh to bitter later on. She managed to dress well, classically, but fashionably enough. Her budget wasn't too big: money she had managed to scrape together and the odd handout from her brothers. From time to time she would get hand-me-downs from Sheila and her friends, who regarded 'marrying Gertrude off' a priority.

Daniel had come to Pearl's house to consult Joey about a watch he was planning to buy. He was about thirty-three at the time, cheerful, dressed in a well-cut suit. He joked with Pearl and her younger sister, charming the two of them. Daniel had a contagious, aggressive charm, which would turn with the years into a yiddishy sense of humour, an argumentative, dominant nature, but was during the first few weeks almost intoxicating to Gertrude.

She was hypnotised. From the first moment she knew that here was the man of her dreams. When he told her of New York and London, even of Paris, she almost melted away. She didn't notice that he wasn't listening to her, that he was only barely there, that all he wanted was a new audience. Daniel, on the other hand, was excited by the impression he made on this young woman whose eyes expressed willingness to do anything he would ask. The actor found a stage, the audience bought a ticket. The lights went out and the first act had begun.

During the next few months they saw each other fairly often. Usually in Dublin. Gertrude now spent most of her days at Pearl's and Daniel used to come and fetch her to the moving pictures or to the races. He continued betting, usually for small sums, sometimes winning, more often losing. They went to dances in the Metropole and would walk, holding hands, in O'Connell Street, looking in shop windows, or ride together on the tram along the river.

Pearl wasn't too excited about the idea of them getting married. Gertrude's father didn't know to what extent the relationship was serious. Sheila, with whom Gertrude talked about Daniel when at home in Limerick, was a little more sympathetic. But on the whole everybody was delighted, since Gertrude was no longer young and they were afraid she would remain an old maid, a burden to her family.

Daniel loved Gertrude's shyness, her eagerness to agree to anything he said. She didn't add much to a conversation, but was always pleasant, her manners perfect. He was drawn to the heat radiating from her, not a warm heat but a hard heat, demanding a reaction, alluding to gratifications. During their stolen minutes between the public hours, when his hand slid in apparent innocence along her bust, touching the secret places, she would shiver, moving him and scaring him at the same time.

Finally he asked her permission to go to her father in Limerick and formally ask for her hand. She said yes, so he arrived at her father's with a bottle of kiddush wine and a box of chocolates. He explained how he intended to keep her, explained about a shop he was about to open, made an excellent impression and managed to charm the old man.

Gertrude still has a well-retouched photograph of herself, a bride dressed in yards and yards of Limerick lace, and of Daniel, a groom dressed in a morning suit and a top hat. The ceremony itself has faded from her memory.

The promise remained only half-fulfilled. Daniel wasn't able to quench Gertrude's thirst. Gertrude expected something far in excess of what she got. But both presumed this was how it had to be and both were satisfied with short gropings in a dark room under the woollen blankets. Gertrude could not refrain from thinking that there was not a great difference between this and her own groping hands under the flannel nightie.

*   *   *

'Remember I told you about my party?' Gertrude asks Father Daly.

Father Daly, who comes often to visit her these days, doesn't answer. He knows she doesn't expect one. But this time she doesn't continue. She looks him straight in the face, her eyes very watery, very blue.

'Yes,' he says, embarrassed at being caught. 'Of course I remember. All the children are coming?'

'This is exactly what I wanted to tell you. They are making such a fuss over this birthday, you cannot imagine. Rose is coming from New York, Jeremy is paying her expenses. I haven't seen her daughter since she was a baby. Joan and Mike are coming from Chester, with their three children. Doris and Alex are in Dublin, of course. But Henry, nobody knows what's with Henry. If he's coming, and if he's bringing her.'

'Have they got married yet?'

'I don't know. Isn't it ridiculous? I have children and I don't even know if they're married. I dare say this only to you. If I told this to anyone else, they would have looked at me as if I fell from the moon. I got a letter, I told you, saying they're getting married in a registry office. I wrote immediately, I always write immediately. I don't like to be the one not to write. I wrote and wished them all the very best, said I hoped they would be happy and asked for a photograph of the wedding. So that I could see how she looks. I also invited them to come and visit, saying I would very much like to meet her. Madelaine, that's what she's called. Madelaine.' She looks at him, awaiting a reaction, knowing from experience that he reacts only seldom.

He decides to say nothing. So she goes on. 'I got no reply. He simply ignored my letter. And letters from Joan, Alex and Doris. Everybody wrote. Joan even telephoned. He was very nice on the telephone, and said he would ring her back, but said very little. Perhaps something happened. Maybe she left him, this Madelaine. Maybe he is sick, or something. The whole thing sounds somewhat fishy, I think.'

'Sometimes,' the priest says very cautiously, 'men around forty, when they finally decide to leave home and have a family of their own, are afraid that people will poke their noses into their business.'

'Finally leave home?' she is actually shooting forward with the rage his words arouse in her. 'Finally leave home? You make me laugh. Excuse me, but my Henry has not been at all tied to the family or to me for at least twenty years. But after all he is still my baby and I am worried about him.'

'But what can you do, short of going over to see him?'

'Everybody says to me, just go to him if you are so worried. They forget I am almost seventy-five. No one offers to go over for me, you know. They say it doesn't matter if I cannot stay with him, I can always stay in a hotel. And on the other hand, the fear I may not find him, that something happened to him . . . .' She stops. She knows her fears are totally unbased. Why should she go to Henry, she thinks, when it's his duty to keep in touch with his mother? Why should I be making this effort? Because Gertrude Klein never commits herself, she prefers, as usual, to stay put, advising, asking and not asking, not really wishing to hear the answers. Saying words which express worry, but which have nothing behind them.

During the last few weeks before the get-together Gertrude telephones the priest almost daily. At first she is embarrassed, chuckling self-consciously. Later she telephones with the pretext of asking him for a cup of tea. In the last days before the family arrives she makes no excuses for her calls and gives no explanations. She reports dates of arrival, discusses the children's plans, talks about blankets she has brought to the dry cleaners and about the arthritic pains in her hands which are getting whiter and older.

Apart from tidying up, some washing and ironing, some cooking and other such small chores, she does nothing with her time. Her small garden, apart from grass, has nothing in it. She never knits, sews, reads, but only spends the evenings in front of the television. As she has no friends apart from the priest, she sees nobody except her immediate family.

She is asked to various functions in the Jewish community, but never goes. 'I was asked once', she tells Father Daly, 'to the senior citizen's

club of the Jewish community. I was only seventy at the time but
believe you me there were much older people than me there. I couldn't
get there by bus so Doris gave me a lift. When we arrived I was
horrified. Perhaps I did not look at myself in the mirror before I left
home, but I couldn't have been quite as old as some of the people.
Some I knew years ago and they looked a hundred years old. Wrinkled,
stooped, speaking of nothing but their illnesses. They served us some
tea, all very nice, but the two ladies next to me could not hold their
cups, their hands shook so, and their tea spilled. Everyone was so glad
to see me, mind you. "How are you, Gertie?" That's what they used to
call me in the choir. "We should meet soon, we'll call you." But do you
think anybody called? They're all like this, when you become a widow,
they forget you exist. It's difficult to invite elderly widows, one has to
fetch them and to have an even number one has to invite somebody
else. You know.'

She stops, thinking of the round lampshade, studded with hundreds
of tiny mirrors, turning round and round, reflecting many white heads,
many wasted lives like her own.

She never went back to the senior club or bothered to belong to any
of the women's groups. It only costs money, she thinks, and when one
does not have a car one cannot get anywhere. No one wants to give
people a lift every time.

*   *   *

Her old friends from Limerick got married and lived in their own little
boxes, far away from Gertrude and her world. The people she knew in
Dublin never got close enough to become friends. Therefore when
Daniel died Gertrude remained alone. During the first few months,
after she had sold the house, she enjoyed the sudden freedom. No more
a servant in her husband's house, but a free woman. If she ever thought
about remarrying, she never did anything about it. Once she experi-
enced freedom she wouldn't start again, mending socks, washing
underwear, cooking three meals a day. The flame that had burned
within her in her younger days was long extinguished after years of
lukewarm married life and endless arguments. With the flame, the
warmth died too. Gertrude has become reserved, controlled.

After the first few months, apart from her move to Chester, she had
been spending her days in idleness, though convinced she was always
busy. She lived like that for over twenty years, not opening her heart to
anyone. Until she met Father Daly. Something alive and eager, waiting
to be found out, must have remained in her, so when she met the priest
she held on to him, started talking, saying all the words she had never
said.

Father Daly is an average priest, but he understands what's bothering people. And he has an enormous store of stock phrases which he uses at the right time with confidence. He actually enjoys Gertrude's dependence on him. He enjoys the knowledge that he alone listens to her, that he, totally insignificant in the eyes of God, as he loves to describe himself, is sitting in this Jewish woman's house, helping her peel off skin after skin. He loves seeing her exposed, naked, defenceless.

He carries on his duties, mass, school, community work and fundraising for the new church which is going to be built at the foot of the hills in this growing parish, but spends more and more time with Gertrude Klein. He starts thinking about the Jews and doubts about traditional explanations start welling in him. On his visits to other parishioners he begins to voice embarrassing ideas.

The residents' association conducts a survey asking parents for their views of the possibility of a non-denominational school in the area. The survey shows most parents support the idea. The Church doesn't like it and Father Daly doesn't help matters by telling a Protestant woman that her son wouldn't be happy in the Catholic school. The word gets round and people interpret it as a refusal to accept the child into the school. The school board sends a circular denying such implications, but the priest is criticised by many. He is becoming isolated in his growing unpopularity. People say that he embarrasses them, that his sermons are too preachy, that he spends too much time drinking tea in people's houses and not enough time on community affairs.

One day, Gertrude tells Father Daly she heard from Henry. 'A wonderful letter,' says the old Gertrude. 'They are happily married. Madelaine is still working with Air France. They've bought a flat. They even have a dog, although it beats me to think what they do with the poor dog all day, when they go to work. But this is their business, isn't it?' She is gleaming. The old happiness when everything looks alright, the children clean and well dressed, the house shining and the clothes according to the latest fashion.

He knows how much she fears the family gathering, which her heart tells her may be the end of something.

'I don't know how we are going to manage. But they will all be here and this is the main thing. It's going to be a real festival. Everybody is planning parties, I do think they exaggerate, Father, but there is nothing I can do about it.' Her face shines happily.

She chatters with the priest about the preparations, about the food. 'The girls said to me, "Mother," they said, "you don't have to do a thing." Do you think I argued with them? Not at all. "Alright, girls," I said to them, "alright, the pleasure is all yours. You work and I play." For once in my life I'll be able to sit with my feet up and let the others work, won't I?'

She asks the priest to visit her when the children come. 'Some of them, Joan and Mike, their children, Alex and Doris and their children will be here for the Seder, Passover you know. It may interest you to see how we celebrate the Exodus from Egypt.'

'Sounds fascinating,' says Father Daly tentatively.

'It *is* fascinating, I assure you. Jews all over the world get together with their families to tell the tale of the flight from Egypt. Will you come, Father? Say you'll come.'

'Are you sure I won't be in the way?' he asks, for form's sake.

'Of course you won't be in the way, I insist you join us. Please say you'll come.'

He promises. Later he asks a friend, a priest who did semitic studies at university, about the first night of Passover. He gets himself a Haggadah and reads as much as he can. The ceremony seems very complicated and he is afraid he will arrive on her doorstep at the wrong moment. Therefore he decides to arrive early so as not to interrupt the proceedings.

He is greeted by an aroma of hot chicken soup. A tall man opens the door and he can hear the clattering of plates, the chattering of children.

'I am Dermot Daly,' he says, almost shyly. 'Mrs Klein asked me to join you tonight.'

'Please come in,' says the man. 'Mike Goldman.' He firmly clutches the priest's hand. 'Gertrude,' he calls loudly, 'you have a visitor.' Seeing Father Daly is still hesitant, he urges him. 'Come in, come in. My mother-in-law is on her way.'

He enters the living-room when Gertrude comes towards him.

She looks almost apologetic, but joyful at the same time. 'I am glad you could come. I wasn't sure you'd come.'

He knows, at this moment, that he should turn round and leave, that he should exit her life. He knows that his presence disturbs her, and he senses danger, his abdominal muscles tightening. But he also knows she needs him and that if he goes now he'll never be able to come back.

He follows her to the dining-room, where two men, three women and a few children sit around an elongated table.

Gertrude's voice says, formally, 'This is Father Daly. These are my children, Alex, Barbara, Doris you know, and her husband David Ross, Mike and Joan Goldman. Make room, Joan,' she adds, 'make room for Father Daly.'

He protests and says he doesn't want to interrupt. That he only meant to drop in for a couple of minutes, but his protests are waved aside and he has to squeeze between Mike and Gertrude. She sits at the top of the table, her isolation in obvious contrast to the sticky closeness of the rest, who have children sprawling all over them.

'You came just on time, we are beginning the meal,' Gertrude says. 'We have finished the first part of the ceremony, prayers and the like. Now comes the more important part of the evening, food, glorious food.'

Alex, a thin, bespectacled man, whose face is very like Gertrude's, says only half-seriously, 'But Mother, how can you say that prayers and the like, as you call them, how can you say they are less important. The food is only secondary. The main thing is the prayers, don't you think?'

'Of course, Alex,' Gertrude says, as if talking to a small child, and to the priest she says, 'Alex always mocks me. I have long given up taking his unorthodoxy seriously. Everything he says is meant to mock me, you know. Have you ever heard the like, Father?'

Joan frowns upon hearing the word father. But he cannot see her frown since she's sitting on the same side of the table. She swallows hard and does not say a thing.

Barbara, sitting opposite her, says reproachfully but lightly, 'Of course Alex knows that eating is as important as praying, don't you, Alex? We have no abstinence, no monastic life, so the meal is a vital part of the ceremony.'

Alex looks at her and winks and the two chuckle, as if it is a subject they have already discussed many times and upon which they are delighted to agree.

'So perhaps we can start eating if the food is so important,' says Joan, her voice sharp and pointed, very like Doris. 'Come on, Doris, we'll get the soup.'

'Sit down, girls, sit down,' Gertrude says, her voice high and clear. 'No need to get over-excited, I am quite capable of serving the food in my own house. One of you can help me, that'll do.'

'Hey, what about the hard-boiled eggs?' says Doris. 'We forgot the hard-boiled eggs.' Her voice is almost metallic. She looks the priest straight in the eye in open hostility.

'I don't think I can stay,' he says, trying to make a respectable exit. 'I meant to come in for a few minutes, that's all. To meet everybody, but I don't want to be in the way.'

'Stay as you are, Father,' Gertrude's voice sounds scared for a minute. 'I won't hear of you going without tasting a real Jewish chicken soup with kneil. The secret weapon of every Yiddische mama.' She laughs, alone.

Father Daly tries to chuckle with her. 'If you are sure I am not in the way,' he says.

'I am a hundred-per-cent sure,' she says. 'I asked you to come didn't I?'

She gets up from the chair, which is well cushioned, as is Alex's chair. He notices she has difficulties getting up, as if her back aches. She supports herself with one thin arm and goes towards the kitchen, with Joan and Doris hurrying after her.

The children, scattered among the adults, start taking an interest in the new visitor. They are between the ages of three and fourteen or fifteen. One small boy keeps whimpering and fiddling, placing his head on Barbara's knees, while she tries to caress him firmly, as if to put him to sleep with her long fingers.

One of the two girls, sitting beside Mike, stoops over Mike's knees towards the priest and asks, 'Why did you come?'

He smiles, but before he manages to answer, Mike chides his daughter. 'Not nice, Dolly, it's very rude to say things like that.'

'It's alright,' he hears his own strained voice, 'after all I am sure it is weird to see a stranger, and a priest at that, at a family gathering.'

'I am not even sure she knows what a priest is,' says Mike.

'Of course I do,' says Dolly. 'Shirley O'Brien in our school has a priest. He always comes to their house. I have seen him. He is fatter, but. And he has no hair.'

He smiles. 'Sorry, Dolly, to spoil your Passover for you. Your granny invited me.'

'You're not spoiling anything, stupid, it's much more interesting to have new people around.'

'Dolly!' says Mike angrily. 'If I hear you saying such things once again, you'll be going straight to bed.'

'It's alright,' says Father Daly.

'Eggs coming,' Gertrude's voice is high, almost shrill. 'An egg for everyone, salt water here. Help yourselves.'

The people around the table dip hard-boiled eggs in salt water. Some of them eat enormous matzo crackers.

The soup which is served after the eggs is tasty, hot, aromatic. But the main course, minced-meat balls cooked in gravy, is dull and the vegetables over-cooked. The pudding, prunes, is also over-cooked, more a laxative than a pudding. Not like other festive meals Father Daly knows.

Immediately after the meal the dishes are cleared and everybody returns to the table. Alex starts reading in Hebrew, fast words rather mumbled and muddled up. Everybody has a Haggadah but every Haggadah seems different, occasionally people get lost and ask for the place. Someone pushes a Haggadah in front of the priest, who tries to follow the English translation. From time to time Barbara, Alex and a blond girl sitting beside them sing a section, with the others looking on, bored, as if waiting for the whole thing to come to an end.

Gertrude doesn't take part. From time to time she tries to smile at the children around the table, her gaze cloudy and vague. In a funny way she is enjoying her status as the head of the family, although the ceremony itself means very little to her. She has around her table an apparently united and happy family. What more can anyone want?

'Carol,' Alex says to one of the girls, 'are you opening the door?'

The girl runs to the front door.

'Pour out', says Alex expressively, a cup of wine in his hand, 'thy wrath, upon the heathen that have not known thee, and upon the kingdoms that have not called upon thy name.'

Nobody looks at Father Daly. They all look away and he remembers, just then, the story about Jews who slaughter children during the Passover, in order to make matzos with their blood. Pour out, he repeats in his mind, thy wrath upon the heathen, upon the heathen, that have not known thee. That have not known thee. But we do know, he is thinking with satisfaction, we do know.

Carol returns. 'He was here,' Barbara says softly. 'Look at the cup.' And she points to a silver cup filled with wine at the centre of the table.

Barbara's daughter starts to sob.

Alex tells Barbara to stop it, 'You are frightening the children, can't you see?'

'It's only pretending,' says Barbara to the child, 'we only pretend that he came. Elijah the prophet is a good man, he loves children. I know it can be frightening, but there is no need to be afraid.'

'I don't want Elijah,' the girl repeats, sobbing. 'I don't want him to come.'

'If you don't want him he won't come,' Gertrude says, trying to cover up. It doesn't occur to her to treat the child's fears as real.

'But mummy said he came,' the girl stops sobbing and looks at her mother with eyes like Gertrude's.

'I said it's true, darling. But the the point is that Elijah is not real, he is someone we only think of. Like witches, you know they only exist in storybooks. I understand he frightens you, darling. I really understand.' Barbara leaves it at that, and hugs the tired child, who starts to doze on her lap.

The priest never thought of Elijah as frightening. Here again is something totally alien to him, mysterious, ritualistic and well defined. He catches another glimpse of Gertrude. Gertrude who might also have been afraid once, not only of Father Creagh and his followers in Limerick, but also of a door open to the night and to guests from another world.

The family sings now, half-heartedly, half-a-dozen songs monotonously, which Barbara and Alex seem to be the only ones to enjoy.

After the singing they slump in the scattered chairs in the livingroom. The time is almost ten o'clock. Joan and Mike take their children upstairs and Doris and David and Alex and Barbara prepare to go home. Gertrude goes upstairs for a moment, asking Father Daly to wait for her return.

'I hope', Alex says to the priest, 'that you weren't too bored. As you can see, we didn't adhere too religiously to the ceremony, we aren't too orthodox.'

'It was very interesting, very interesting,' he replies. 'I am grateful to you for having let me come here. So seldom one has the opportunity to see other people talking to God.'

'God? Don't make me laugh,' Alex says, mocking. 'No one in this house believes in God. This is simply a tradition we keep because of some guilt feelings towards ourselves and our children, who must, of course, have some religious base. Or so they say.'

'But it's nice,' says Barbara. 'Alex tends to exaggerate.' She adds this lightly, pressing Alex's arm slightly.

'Speak for yourself,' says Doris, her voice sharp and hard. 'Don't include me and David in your atheism. If you want to know, I am fed up with your mocking. It's time you had some respect.'

'Respect?' Alex says slowly and deliberately. 'What do you, my dear sister, get from this ridiculous story of the Exodus from Egypt? The facts are simple. The Torah tells us, let my people go. The ten plagues, the Red Sea, forty years in the wilderness, and in the end a pisgah view of the Promised Land. Fantastic! But the rabbinical arguments? What do you make of them? I don't say they're valueless, on the contrary. But there is nobody in this particular family who even understands what is written. Apart from Barbara, that is, because she went to Hebrew school in Canada. But we? Learning by rote in cheder after school, exhausted and blasé, happy only when we could invent excuses not to go.' He stops for a minute.

Doris whips again. 'Stop this talk in front of my children. With your children you can do whatever you want. My children will have respect for their religion and I won't stand for my own brother spoiling their Jewish education.'

'Jewish education? Jewish education you said?' Alex doesn't let go. 'Do they know anything, with their Jewish education at all, apart from a little reading in the siddur, some customs and stories from the Torah? Do they understand the significance of this Passover? Do they understand that the existence of our race depends on passing the story of the Exodus from father to son? Do they get the feeling of miracles in Passover, in Purim, in Hanukah? Do they know that the idea is to get across to them that nobody must be allowed to annihilate them again? Did they tell them about it in their Jewish school? Or perhaps you have talked to them about it? Do you know any other holidays apart from Passover or Yom Kippur? Shabbat, for instance? Do you light the candles? Does David say kiddush? What is all this talk about respect for their religion? Exactly like Mother, words, words, words.'

'Look at our rabbi!' Doris retorts. 'All of a sudden you care if my children understand the secret of the Jewish existence. Me, light candles, ha? And you, what do you understand? Why don't you pay your membership fees to the schul? Why don't you come to schul even on Yom Kippur? I didn't expect sermons from you, mister brother. People in this community have forgotten how you look.'

'Doris, Alex, are you altogether crazy?' Barbara's voice, calm, dark, breaks the argument. 'First of all, you forget you are brother and sister. And that today is a holiday. Apart from that, we have a visitor, haven't we?'

Everybody, including the children, stuck in the middle of the battle like forgotten corpses, turns to Father Daly, who stands very close to them, listening and curiously collecting the details, his eyes alert, moving from one to the other. Do they expect him to whistle, like a referee, to mark the end of the match? But he doesn't say a thing, and instead turns his head towards the stairs and Gertrude, who is coming slowly down towards them.

'Why are you all standing here, in the hall?' she asks, her voice clear but tired. She hasn't heard a word of what was going on. 'Come into the room, we'll have a cup of tea before bed.'

'I have to,' the cleric says, breaking his silence, 'I have to go. I have a busy day tomorrow. A meeting with the bishop. For Easter. I already have stayed too long.'

'Why do you say this, Father?' Gertrude sounds alarmed.

'I meant', he says hesitantly, 'that you must want to be together on your festival. That I'm in the way.' His eyes move fast from Gertrude to Doris and he adds, 'Thank you, Mrs Klein, for having invited me. It was all very interesting indeed. I have learnt a lot. And it's always lovely to be with a family. I really must now . . . .'

She bursts out again, 'You can surely stay a few minutes. I hope all this wasn't too much for you?'

She leads him into the living-room and sits down in her usual chair and he, obedient, sits on his. Thus, with Doris and David in the hall putting on their coats, collecting children, bidding loud farewells, and with Alex and Barbara in the kitchen, starting to clean up and wash dishes, they are alone once again. Dermot Daly, a parish priest, and Gertrude Klein, a Jewish woman, alone in her living-room, about to take a cup of tea together. Their intimacy does not last more than a couple of minutes. Joan and Mike come down and join them after having put their children to bed. From the kitchen Alex and Barbara and their tired children also join them. They all drink cups of weak lemon tea and eat Passover cakes. They chatter about this and that and say very little. When he leaves, he leaves behind him a much more pleasant family atmosphere than the one he found when he arrived earlier in the evening.

'What a farce,' Barbara sighs to Alex later that night when they are going to sleep. 'Your mother knows from nothing. The whole ceremony means nothing to her. Tell me, did you or did you not get any religious education?'

'I have told you already, Barbie. We went to cheder and we can, just about, read the prayer book. But it was a great big bore, and sometimes it was so boring, we used to throw beigels on poor Rabbi Goldesheimer. Who had patience for more studies after school? In the winter we used to come home in the dark, would you believe it, worn out.'

'My poor Alex,' she cuddles him. 'You really had a hard time. What can we do about you, my sweet, what can we do about you at all?' And the two, giggling like children, pounce on each other, forgetting everything else.

Which cannot be said for Doris. She and Joan are truly furious that Gertrude invited the priest to the Seder. Doris and Joan, who cannot chase their anxieties away with jokes or love-making, have, like their mother, drowned their flames, if they ever had any.

'We must', Joan says to Doris the following morning, 'do something about mother. These faints, she drives me bananas with worry. She's getting old, Doris. And this priest. I am sure that five years ago it would never have occurred to her to make friends with a priest.'

Barbara joins them and says that perhaps this friendship comes as a result of Gertrude's loneliness.

But Doris can't agree. 'She is very happy on her own. David and I asked her to come and live with us. But was she interested? Not at all. She wants to live alone, not to have to do anything, have no timetable, look around the shops. She's happy like that, can't you see?'

These arguments aren't new. In truth Barbara had already decided to give up the fight. 'After all,' she would sometimes say to Alex, 'she is your mother, not mine. I wouldn't let my mother live like this, it's unhealthy. What if something happened to her all of a sudden? With no one around? Good job she has this Father Daly, good job he visits her a couple of times a week. Perhaps we should see her more often, Alex?' At this point Alex would usually stop her, claiming boredom. But she now tries one last time to persuade the sisters that Gertrude is crying out for company, that her calm is only a pretence.

'Why should she pretend? For whom? For what? For me, for you?' Doris continues her own battle, scared to be involved more fully in her mother's life. 'When I offer to take her someplace, to come and fetch her, to be with her, all she wants is to be alone. So I must think she really wants to be on her own. After all, one has to respect her wishes.'

'But Doris,' Barbara says, 'can't you see the desperate message under all this? If she is so happy, what did she need this priest for? No one made her entertain him. He visits all the houses in the estate. Whenever new people move in he pays them a visit, but not everyone is so friendly with him. She loves having her own friend. She needs friends.'

'Friends? Father Daly?' Joan calls mockingly. 'Don't make me laugh, Barbara. He must want to convert her to Christianity before she dies, or something. He must be nagging her to such an extent, she simply cannot throw him out. You know how weak she can be.'

'What nonsense,' Barbara starts, as usual in these arguments. 'Why can't you stop looking at it from one narrow point of view? People don't always do things in order to exploit or gratify themselves. It's evident they are happy together. Both found a friend and it's marvellous. And your mother can do with someone who demands nothing, except the pleasure of her company.'

'Barbara,' Doris says, barely hiding her hatred, 'you are naive. It's clear this Daly comes here with a very good reason and mother, being on her own, finds it difficult to throw him out. It was plain last night. The way he sat on and on, without grasping that he was not wanted, that he was in the way.'

'In whose way?' Barbara says. 'Who didn't want him? He certainly didn't disturb us. On the contrary, he managed, by his presence, to alleviate the tension. There was such tension in that room last night, I was sure it would explode. What's wrong with you? All of you? What's bothering you?'

'Haven't the faintest,' Joan says fast. 'Do you, Doris? I must be the only one who does not sense a thing.'

'Of course there's nothing,' Doris agrees. 'What do you think is bothering us, Barbara?'

'I don't know,' Barbara is indeed naive. 'I simply feel the tension in the air. Never mind. But you were saying that Gertrude is worrying you. What can be done to help her?'

'We have discussed it again and again, David and I,' Doris chips in first. 'We thought it would be better for mother to sell her house and come and live with us after all. We have that room with separate entrance, its own loo and bathroom. She won't have to sit there all the time, of course. She can sleep there and if she feels like being on her own during the day, she can go there. The rest of the time, our house will be hers.'

'And David doesn't object?' Barbara asks. 'I cannot see Alex agreeing to such a plan.'

'Alex!' Doris says. 'Don't speak to me about Alex. He was never one to do anything for his family. In fact it was David who suggested it, if you have to know.'

'And what do you think, Joan?' Barbara asks.

'What do I think?' Joan tries to gain time. The subject seems to have been discussed extensively before Barbara came. 'I, I mean Mike and I, we agree to everything Doris and David suggest.'

'And that's that.' Barbara's voice hardens up. 'Your mother's fate is sealed. The house is sold for her. She is given a small room, with a separate entrance mind you, plus permission to sit in the living-room. And the money from the sale of the house? Dividing the goodies while she is still alive? And you have the cheek to say that your mother is perfectly happy to live on her own? If she is so happy alone, why change the status quo? All because of a few grand?'

'You're wrong as usual, Barbara,' Joan says. 'No one will take the money away from her. Apart from the expenses Doris and David will incur. That's all. The rest she can leave in her bank, or invest, wherever she wants.'

'As long', Barbara's sarcasm erases her former naiveté, 'as this priest disappears. From now on we shall guard both mother and her small fortune and mother and her little soul. A perfect plan.'

'I don't understand', Doris says, groping, but aggressive, 'the objection. You're the one who claims she is always alone, that it's dangerous for her to remain alone, in case she faints again, God forbid, or falls ill suddenly. I think it's a very sound plan.'

'Your mother, have you asked her already?' Barbara asks.

'I suggested it to her a long time ago,' Doris says, 'and she refused. But one can pressure her, we shall all be here next week and if everyone talks to her she is sure to be persuaded.'

'In other words,' Barbara says, 'we shall brainwash her to death, we'll scare her about the unknown future, including conversion by Father Daly, faintings, death in the bathroom, arteriosclerosis, or loneliness. What a perfect scenario for a woman's magazine. Mother in danger of losing her religion, or in danger of death. What could be more convincing, more powerful? And she will, of course, be convinced. Because we shall all work on her for a whole week, which is supposed to be the most wonderful week of her life, her seventy-fifth birthday, mass celebrations and queenly feeling. All this, Doris and Joan, is simply touching! Your worry and consideration, your care. Only don't count on me, sisters. Or on Alex. I shall do for your mother what she wants, not what you want.'

'You will do for mother what she wants?' Doris shouts. 'When was the last time Alex came to visit her, just like that, without a reason? Just to see how she was? When was the last time you got off your fanny and took her to your house to spend the day with you, or just to have dinner?'

'The answer to your last question is, in fact, last Tuesday, just before Passover. And just as you aren't your brother's keeper, I am not my husband's. I'm responsible for myself alone, and won't have you attack me about your brother's omissions. I do think the family disharmony didn't begin yesterday and you were probably no better in childhood. But that is another day's work. I won't take part in brainwashing her and I won't have you spoil her last few years only because you need the money or because you are scared, in a real ghetto-mentality way, of one little man who made friends with your mother, scared just because he happens to be a priest.'

'Barbara,' Joan says, her voice calm and deliberate, 'I am sorry to say you don't seem to understand the problem. It's dangerous to let mother go on living on her own, but it's also dangerous to let her continue her friendship with this Daly. He has a bad influence on her. Her faints started since she has been seeing him. She . . . . '

'She can tell him things she could never tell anybody else, that she never dreamt she'd be able to tell anyone,' Barbara interrupts, 'she can, suddenly, after all those years, talk.'

'There is no point in explaining, Joan, can't you see,' Doris says. And to Barbara, 'Alex and you don't have to agree with our plans. That's all there is to it.'

'Oh no, it isn't. That's not all there is to it,' Barbara says. 'We too shall talk to your mother and we too will have something to say.'

In spite of Joan and Doris's past reluctance to be involved actively in their mother's life, they are now ready to change her life for her, to save her from herself.

Barbara doesn't argue any more. But she too has sensed a change in Gertrude during the past few months. The old woman is more open, laughs more, sings to herself. She doesn't look at herself much, doesn't talk as much about shopping. Once she even said to Barbara, out of the blue, 'You know, Barbara, I am happy. As if I have just grown old, just become a grandmother. Everything is peaceful suddenly, everything is bright.' Barbara understands the cause of the change and says to Alex that these are the happiest months in Gertrude's life. After years of suppression, of mental masturbation, of bitterness, she suddenly has someone, someone who comes to see just her, to listen to her alone.

The family keeps coming. On the last day of Passover, Rose and her daughter arrive from New York to join Joan and her family at Gertrude's. Two days later Henry and Madelaine come. They stay with Alex and Barbara, but spend most of their time at Gertrude's.

The priest is far away. Gertrude cannot phone and invite him for a cup of tea and she is getting tired of the family's constant presence. The illusion of pleasure in a large, happy family is wearing off fast.

Rose never stops talking, nervously, fast, trying to make up for all the years separating her from her brothers and sisters. She talks about America, about life there, about greater involvement, as opposed to the Irish way of life. She talks about things she has discovered, transcendental meditation, yoga, communal living, air pollution, organic food. She has discovered all those, but found nothing new. She is contemptuous of her brothers' and sisters' apparently quiet life, but envies their stability.

Henry and Madelaine, on the other hand, are so much in love, so absorbed in themselves, so silent, that they become a focal point in this strained gathering. Henry tries to pay as much attention to his mother, who is jealous of his pretty, confident new wife. She is about thirty-five, a career woman, who, without leaning on Henry, consults him on every little thing, respecting his opinions.

Alex doesn't spend much time with the family, but Barbara is with them most of the time and the air remains thick with arguments, Rose and Madelaine siding with Barbara, and Gertrude appearing to side with Joan and Doris. There is a constant sense of danger, a sense of important things being weighed now.

The sale of the house is discussed by everyone, in various corners, in whispers, but no one asks Gertrude's opinion. Barbara still claims they're selling their mother down the line. In the end Alex decides to intervene and ask for his mother's view on the matter.

Gertrude is slightly lost in this so-called family gathering. She is less and less able to concentrate on what's being said to her, to contribute to the general conversation. She utters her usual trivialities, like 'the cost of living, isn't it dreadful', or 'one cannot buy anything of value these days', or 'isn't the weather awful', and they sound ridiculous when said, totally out of context in the middle of the serious conversations her children are trying to hold as they get to know each other once again after all the years.

When Alex asks her his question, she doesn't grasp it at first. 'Sell the house? And what will I do? All the houses I have seen lately cost more than thirty thousand.'

Slowly and patiently, Alex explains Joan and Doris's plan. The main reason for the suggestion, he says, is their fear for her health.

Gertrude still doesn't understand. 'I feel perfectly well,' she says again and again. 'And after all, Doris comes to see me. And Barbara. It is a pity that the others do not live closer, but that can't be helped. I have everything I need.'

Alex asks her if she is lonely on her own.

'But I am not lonely. I have friends. Father Daly comes here quite often.'

No one interferes in the conversation so far, but on hearing the priest's name Doris cannot help saying, 'What does he want from you, this Daly? Why does he come here, Mother? Why doesn't he leave you in peace?'

Gertrude looks Doris straight in the eye. Doris looks frightened.

'I have something which is mine. Mine only. Never, all my life, even when I was a young girl, did I have something which was only mine. Apart from my singing. Perhaps. And even this your father had to take away. Now I have something which nobody can take away from me. Not one of you can take away from me.' She recoils suddenly and stops. There is a thick, heavy silence in the air.

Barbara breaks the silence and says, 'It's wonderful, Gertrude. It's wonderful you have such a friend. I am sure you're happier now than ever before. You would like to stay in your own home, to leave things as they are, wouldn't you?' Ignoring Joan and Doris's hostile glances, she carries on, 'We would like to hear your views on moving in with Doris or staying here. What do you think?'

But Gertrude retreats into herself. She can't say more than what she has already said. They all talk at the same time, the room is full of voices, murkily filling her head with a low humming noise. Everything seems vague, far away, unreal.

Alex pressurises her, says he has to know, once and for all, what she thinks about the plans others have made for her. He talks and talks, crowding his mother.

She suddenly bursts out, 'Take everything. Take it all. The house. The furniture. The linen and the crockery. I don't need a thing. Take it. Take it all.'

'Nonsense,' says Alex, 'this is not what we're saying. We simply would like to hear what you think of Doris's plans. To hear what you really think.'

'Take it all,' she says again. 'All. The last six months you cannot take away from me. The rest, I don't mind. Take it.'

After this outburst they drop the subject.

Gertrude keeps having a vague sense of danger. She longs for the priest's company, for his calm within the commotion, the shrill voices, the tensions surrounding her. Apart from the arguments, there are also unending preparations, constant business. All this tires Gertrude, who can't do much but is fatigued by the activity.

On the morning before her party she escapes them all and goes out on her own, saying she will buy an evening paper, but really to phone Father Daly. It's the first positive action she has taken for days, the first move towards breaking the circle.

She finds herself walking energetically towards the presbytery. She has no time to marvel at her sudden courage. She simply walks, fast, her head high like a mast, floating smoothly on a calm sea, her back straight, her step light. She is happy again. She doesn't hesitate at his door. Three hundred and sixty-eight, she says to herself while ringing the bell. She knows they will sit inside, quietly, talk a little, drink tea, and the peace will make up for the awful noise buzzing in her head.

The door is opened by a woman in a blue nylon overall. 'Yea?' she says, her voice coarse. 'Can I help ya?'

Gertrude recoils. She has forgotten priests have housekeepers. She isn't ready for an encounter with a third party. 'Is Father Daly at home?' she hears her voice, far away.

'Had to go to Limerick yesterday, missis. There was a sudden death in the family. They needed him, like,' says the blue overall. 'Can I give him a message? Who'll I say called?'

'No, thank you,' says her accurate, cautious accent. 'I shall see him when he comes back.'

'He'll be back tomorrow, or the day after, missis, don't be worried now.' The blue overall sounds a bit kinder, as if divining the imploring loneliness of the small white-haired woman at the door.

'I am not worried,' she says vaguely. 'Thank you.'

'All the best, missis,' and the door is shut, the blue overall going back to scrubbing and polishing.

She stands, small, forlorn, at the priest's closed door. To go back home, to the noises and the commotion is unthinkable. She starts walking along the narrow roads of the housing estate at the foot of the green hills. She walks, straight-backed, wide-hipped, rolling in the stormy waters. She walks for about three hours, round and round, up and down.

They find her only at nine that evening. Alex, Henry and Mike and a couple of gardaí who have been called by the worried family. She lies, panting, near the ditch at the side of the road at the foot of the hills. Breathing heavily, her face red and her legs swollen, she lies and stares, seeing and not seeing the faces above her.

She dies in hospital of what is termed by the doctors as exhaustion. Clear cut. On her seventy-fifth birthday.

No one remembers to notify Father Daly. When he comes back from Limerick he hears from his housekeeper of the little woman who called to see him and, by her description, understands it was Mrs Klein. He goes to her house immediately and finds the members of the family, the ones he has met on the Seder night and some others, sitting on cushions on the floor. Gertrude is not with them.

Doris says to him, her voice harsh, her face swollen and stained, make-up smeared on her yellow cheek. 'You don't have to come any more, Mr Daly. My mother is dead.'

Something closes in his chest and he feels pressure in his stomach. He knows that the disappointment of not having found him at home that last day is an indirect cause of this death. 'She came to see me, two days ago,' he starts, hesitant, his voice quiet. 'I wasn't at home. My housekeeper told me. What did she die of?'

'Two days ago?' says an unfamiliar voice, American. He notices birdlike features. 'You were her friend?' And the voice is kind.

'I think so,' he says. 'I am very sorry, I feel guilty, perhaps she needed help when she came to see me and then — '

Doris doesn't let him finish. 'Help? From you? With all of us here in the house during the last week? I am sure this was not the case, Mr Daly. It was you who must have wanted something from her. But she is dead now and you haven't managed to get another soul for your collection.'

'Doris!' says the American voice. 'You forget you're sitting Shiv'a. I am sorry,' she turns to the priest, 'if you feel guilty. There is no need. Barbara told me that you were good friends. It's sure good to know that she had at least one good friend, after all her lonely years.'

'I think we were friends. I never thought I was that important in Mrs Klein's life, but I am glad she thought of me as a friend. I am sorry,' and here the priest, used to sermons, turns to the people sitting along the walls in this familiar room, so dark now, 'Please accept my condolences. She was a good woman. May she rest in peace,' he mumbles and leaves the room, walking backwards.

YOUNG MEN GO WALKING
James Liddy

Young men go walking in the woods.
Hunting for the great adornment . . .
Wallace Stevens

JAMES LIDDY, born in Dublin in 1934, for a time practised at the Irish Bar and is now associate Professor of English at the University of Wisconsin-Milwaukee. He has a distinguished reputation as a poet and his books of poetry, published in Ireland and America, include *Blue Mountain, Chamber Pot Music* and *At the Grave of Fr Sweetman. Young Men go Walking* is his first novella.

1

Stephen writes.

We wrote letters. The second letter he wrote was:

Dear Mr Corrigan,
   When you said poetry was part persuasion and part talent you were right. And they are in proportion of about 9:1. My thought is rarely in words but often in images. I dislike changing what I say. My poems have something in common with Joyce in *Stephen Hero* who is afraid of pushing himself from what actually happens into truth. I am inclined to think that the truth is in the action or occurring, I mean occurrence, rather than in the poetry I make of this. I have been living so long in my literary mind that if I were to fall down the steps into the lavatory of a Dublin pub I should say 'Grace' and pull back my tongue. I remember when I was between fifteen and eighteen years old, which was last year, I always asked myself this question: 'Do I want to be a writer?' I only had to answer yes or no to have it so . . . . I shall come on the 8th or 9th but it doesn't really matter if you're not in because I usually walk around the city in the afternoons anyway. I will bring some pieces with me when I call. However there is one piece I can't change because I don't know what it means. It is the first time this has happened to me.

               SPY WEDNESDAY
               This Wednesday
               Birds whirl like ashes
               And settle in the trees.
               And O my love that it
               Should come to this —
               Kiss of betrayal.

I hope you don't mind my unburdening myself. I thank you for
your letter.
 Yours,
      Vincent Cosgrave.

He did come, he came many times, he came the first day. I was taught-
out, malcontent, feline, back from classroom chalk, a bored lot of boys.
Attempting to teach, discuss, of all occurrence, Naiads — ladies of
class, without class. To Dublin lads. I saw girls in swimsuits in
Hollywood and Pompeii, reminded them of procession of mourners to
the tomb of Daphnis, flowers on strangest grave of chastity (his of a
differing hue, in his first letter he had written, 'I accept chastity, but
not the chastity that rots the minds of people . . . .') but those flowers
only grew for them, from the top of bus, in Palmerston or Rathmines.
Villa'd plants. They went off to the new slums unseeing.
 Teaching was not a job, just a weariness. But I recovered, ate supper.
Even the Sliabh Luchra muse knew poetry arrives after eclipse,
disguise. And never forget the fall of darkness. Eat up.
 Bell rang. Down the stairs. The white arms of the wallpaper opening
again (wider) — carpet to door — out on to the step.
 'You're Steve . . . Corrigan?'
 'Sure. Hello. Let's hike upstairs and have something.'
 'Okay.'
 Begin the begin.
 Chattings about writing, forms of, college lore of, what classes of
imagination not prosodic, Dublin dockland dawns, incipience of
logorrhea — afternoon songs, morning refrains, dead-drunk man's
snores. Hibernian nights, derisively participating. 'Hatred the soul of
wit,' we crowed to each other. The route elegantly mapped to
compromise: to the frequented, the crowded, The Pleiade ('What a
literary name for a pub,' souls said, who wanted to discuss literature in
public) — vernal smoke rings in the gilt mirrors. Talk to go with it.
Remember the fall of the second darkness. The sixties as I saw it in
Dublin cigarette smoke.
 'Have you got a fag?'
 'No, I only smoked once in my life, Vincent.'
 'Oh, I read *A Movable Feast* earlier today in a short sitting. It's a lovely
book and it makes me feel again Hem invented the word and turned his
world on it.'
 'The bitchiness of it, however platonically conceived, the butchering
of Ford and Scotty. Sorry about having no smokes . . .'
 'He was nice to Ezra Pound.'
 'They played tennis. Hem knew he was no poet, no competition.'
We were sitting at the slender red table made by Captain Hone,

father of a poet, papers, letters jaggedly opened. Bottled Guinness I brought last night from The Pleiade; sipping, regarding each other. Name the convention for this.

'Vincent, you know Dublin is either catty or silly. But there are court occasions now and then. Paddy Kavanagh's *Collected* is coming out soon.'

'The ma is always at him. Jesus, you should hear the way she goes on about him. "Kavanagh or such ilk who can combine genius with spitting, pub crawling and general carelessness and still manage to exist." She goes on and on.'

'A mother keeps her son for her . . . .'

'What they drive you to . . . I have been reading *The Tragic Sense of Life*. Consciousness as he says is suffering. The will to life conquering.'

'That's one book you could not read at a sitting.'

'The ma drives me to it anyway. Do you think it is a poem?'

'Maybe a testament . . . .'

'Not quite in fact, I think. But it does pain me to read the bloody thing. I'd love to know what Kavanagh thinks of it.'

Next time we met, a day or so later and later in the day, we began those walks from the south, south-east, from the barracks that was going to be the concert hall, across the canal by the bookshop, Kavanagh's Muses behind the window, or softly through the dray horse leaves of Percy Place. The canal smelt of all impurity except barge oil. The towpaths shivering against each other. Little room with rest where I might lie and be paper, bits of paper floating off somewhere with that message. At the corner of Lower Mount Street rain and coloured bits of paper on the kerb — buses in confusion and caravan because of lights at this junction.

'The city stops for you now and then,' I said, 'for one second.'

He was silent. Young, a student. I was full of talk:

'Nobody relates the city and love together, as they should be. It is why men built more than temples or retirement huts by the sea.'

He was stirring.

'No simple abode you might say. Where was I reading: "All flesh suffers because it is discontented with its sorrows in a single locality"? But what will Kavanagh be down in the pub?'

'Now the poet has mercifully left the potato sprayer behind. He nevertheless rises early and — as is bardic custom — consumes a noggin of scotch under his pillow. He proceeds to the bookshop on the bridge, gets a read of *The Irish Times*, consumes another noggin, moves on a less north-easterly course than ours to the pub where he drinks lunch with his friends. He decides on the horse of the day, retires to pork chops of the holy hour, back for conversation interspersed with singing. Sean Garland will accompany, he has an exact liturgical sense. Then the descent into the lower world, the jangling shades . . . .'

'What will he be like now?' he asked.

'He may not be even there. Or he may be there in his cave.'

'I don't understand. I'm not a caveman. I prefer mountains that lift up from their roots and walk, falling over themselves when they find their legs are legs of mice.'

We were going rapidly towards the cave. Within and without hollow. *Les caves d'Irlande*. Amber light of RTE broadcasting had only partly penetrated. It was still a sweet Bohemian place. The inhabitants, who may have been the last to survive on the Bohemian sea coast, lived every day without necessarily being employed or thinking of it. High breathing, a high ceiling.

A kind of virtue: yet the pint already cost two shillings.

There must be a rest. Stopping by the way. Place of refreshment, hallucination and anger. No final resolution. Up Merrion Street and by the shuttered martyr's — to Halpin's. There they were, in their sizes, graduated burgeoning servants of the public, citizenry of our Republic of Pseudo Letters. Still seedlings. Voided. Insipid gonidia.

'Three and ninepence . . . . Thanks, Billy. How's Valleymount? Any white heather yet?'

'It's grand, Mr C. Oh lots of it, lots.'

Vincent beside me, what is he? Beast, brightness, pennant or gonfalcon? It would drive people crazy. In the end would it drive anybody crazy? He would write moons beyond, from his office, 'I am being eaten by woman.'

'See, Stevie, the fellows there . . . in the corner to the jakes. One of them is one of the blokes I got trapped with in a class reunion last week. I can't stand them but for some reason they consider I was one of their group in school.'

'I know them.'

'At the end of the night one of them ventured idealism. Love, compassion, honesty or humanity I forget which. Christ and all that jazz.'

'The old middle-class revolutionary sense.'

'Social-Justice Christianity.'

'Jaysus, let's lick an old ikon, if we're going to have them.'

'After a long boring argument I actually got one guy to admit he wasn't a Christian, or rather he didn't know what he was talking about. These boys are the brains of UCD and have futures as members of Tuairim but the absolute fog of their beliefs, the warm fog of their world.'

'Yes, I know. The college contemporary, I will watch them on television, but I met them all before . . . .'

Out the door, part of the old pub, whiskey sign lettered on frosty glass. The corner of the closed Green. Barred at darkness to those too hot to wait for the morrow, who haven't friends who will leave their flats. The keepers, after final nook survey, are on their buses to rashers and sausages, bread and butter. Lovers keep out. We'll spike you. Inside flower parties: grass bending to the begetter's lily; Jesus, faun of greens and parks, flora of the Church the mother. The drunken lover, the roomless student, who climbs in on Saturday nights joins the pasturing. Protected as they walk around, about.

Will you mislead us?

My city, through thy cups of white flower. The bottles of my life sit on the branches of your thoroughfares but don't watch them, watch the cars.

Through thy pollen.

(In Tarentum once a Fulbright gentleman met a member of that many-readered genus: poet of Ireland; and having mentioned my Shannon name, redolent of Cromwell's troopers and eating barnacle geese on Friday, the ilk-genus member retreated and quacked: 'One of them Grafton Street crowd.')

Boer War Gate. The silly dead. A gentleman and a solicitor from Clones once surprised, describing as the most impressive monument in town. But there is a beautiful hero in insanity, it sees him crossing over by the other gate.

Birds signalling, squawking, in an alcoholic firmament. Come back, George Moore's Paul Verlaine, to the café table, drunk satyr and rose. We pray to you, flower-kid oblivious.

A poet's public house is his church. The collections. Moon and body together, focused among silver-coin reflections.

This is the Dublin (Ireland) branch of the connection between learning and the fuzzing of the senses. Ask at any local office of Dionysius. Review copies in a small city. Bardic bog, hinterland, tears as you sang from a hedge. Tears of the whiskey (our culture will disappear when it becomes too expensive). We should have been borne, some of us are, in toxic semi-literacy, from the briary hedges.

The coloured photograph of the Acropolis, same of Fisherman's Wharf. The punter who goes to Cheltenham, the nice fella who works in the Blackrock Tailoring around the corner, the writer who arrived years ago from the burning seaweed of the western isle. The smiling editor of the *Broadsheet*. My older colleague in enchantment of the heart through imaginative mysteries, Constantine Ryan. An elder in suit, tie, overcoat, cap. Saw me, ignored Vincent, and told me the great poet had gone to his digs, 'the ones he has now on the North Circular'.

'Vincent, bad luck to draw a blank on your first visit. Only Con is here and Sean Garland.'

'Mr Kavanagh', Con began, 'left a half an hour ago after a heavy day. His duties did not leave him feeling particularly well.' Pilgrim of delitescence.

'What will you have, Vincent, and your's Con?'

To pass what we earn and what we don't across the counter. Search of the pockets. Our lot. Altar lists.

Generosity moves among the people of Hell, the troubador knows. Roses of mother unstrewn from their vases under the stools.

Con Ryan, still not seeing Vincent, took a letter from his pocket.

'This is from David Wright. The irony about Snee . . . .'

'Indeed, Con, the worst to die from a form of cardiac alcoholism two years after going off it.'

'A whole trunkful of work turned up, poems, letters, prose, the rest of it, Methuen had commissioned his autobiography.'

'He told me,' I said, 'he had a good record: slept out five nights in two years. Leaking shoes are the worst.'

'He was going to appear in *The Twentieth Century*. And irony of ironies he will be posthumously in receipt of the Poetry Book Society Choice'.

Vincent was open honeymouthed — it was all true, the commitment of literary gents unto death, fame after it, the whole bit. It is hard to credit but it happens. Just one impossible dream a night.

'He is riding the crest of the grave.'

'The death froth,' cried Vincent, 'Verlaine.'

'That is a kettle of fish of a different odour, young man,' Con had recognized his youth, 'do you really think the late deceased poet was in Verlaine's class or mine for that matter? What do you know about it anyway?'

Vincent babbled on in reply, showing off. Oblivious of what he had provoked, which worthies had assembled. He was debating literature, despite his warning. He was assuming his place in literature. First nights are first nights.

* * *

Vincent burps.

Dark, dark, phoenix forest.

Oh come all ye Irish secondary schoolboys to a little corner of Norfolk. To these hedgerows. These box gardens.

Wheatfields of Walsingham where I dwell and delve. Our ladies. Don't starve lads. Forest men keep in their hearts. Magdalen dubh. Enterable leaf by leaf.

Stephen's thing for me a prelude, motions of contrary desire. Women everywhere: surround, enfold. Fantasies to which I am driven?

I didn't know they wanted me so. I'm not tall or blond. I'm slim, that's it.

His kind are too much fun. Is this the hardest thing you have to do — tell them you're different? If you like them. They may love you. If he knew — he doesn't want to. I have to be like him, though I swear by the lust of the ghost of John Keats I'm not.

Damn you, Corrigan! You are my friend. Your love for me has become part of me. Something I can't define is poking me — I was flying back like a bird. Initiation, preliminary unfinished bitterness.

We haven't kissed. I can't. He wants it back. He hasn't asked, he will. At home last month I nearly turned into his dreamy love. It nearly happened. You could have your body transformed. I thought I had a collapsed lung.

Escaped, eighteen recently, evergreen. What have I? Out of Eire have I come. Home, red curtains newly washed, quietness — quiet as the near cemetery where the leader and the led sleep. The house is actually in the lands of Prospect, a designation. Is he Prospero, magician with an imaginary manuscript and an island pub? If I hadn't wandered south of the Liffey I wouldn't have found — gone along with — his radiance. He has a witch-power. When I grow up and become a writer I will be called a harbinger of Eire Nua permissiveness.

Car is his cell, glass in the hand his wand.

From thoughts of him, spirit good and evil, I used to walk in the Bots. The ordinary moral lovers rolled around in the new daisies. The transistors loudspeaked. I am far and unfetchable at present. Can I help keep it so? Say my prayers to orthodox Yeatsian paganism.

In the gardens were girls with bare arms, a postbox, a man holding on to the railings with one hand.

In Dublin, sun shining on skirts across the street.

Give me the mot-watching skirt-fumble of John Keats. It's honest. It's real. Man not made to end his loneliness with another, you bet. Something different — God's plan. She is handsome, she is pretty / she is the girl from Strumpet City.

The gardens, I got away from him and his crazy renditions. Help from blossoms, breathing and giving. Evenings lowclouded, warm. I could put my finger on the scents, I can find them here, those that remind me of the Bots. Strangely enough the most predominant is the yew. It smells of death right at the height of growth, but a good death. (I like Lady Powerscourt remarking to Vita Sackville-West that there were no Irish Yew trees in her garden. She must have wanted trees that point their delicate branches towards another world. Thank God taxes are throttling that bunch. Strumpet villas.)

The Bots in certain places on certain walks, the scent of viburnum. Then saxifrage and sweetpea, and all over the air of the clay.

I feel a fear of love. Nature whips me. I have the moral sickness of the young: I glimpsed some place the perfect body, the body for me. I saw her shadow, she's in the pavilion of Stephen's Green. My homosexuality is a moment's unreality on the way back from desert acrobatics. Yes, I will take a girl to the real garden, though she is not perfect she will be this evening, that is my permanent heterosexuality. The ducks will understand.

I picked up a white leaf for her, I stuck my hand into the black earth long springs ago, touched the womb, knowing my destiny was women. I walked out with her in the rain along the cliffs. You were waiting when I came that night. Yes, you were there. I dropped the seconds like water jewels and counted them — staring at them. (You did not stay long, I went upstairs to sleep, to dream of you.)

I gave him my love too. He gives me passion, the idea of it. Romance is a necessary condition. I suppose as you get older you will get colder to yourself. Cooldown. Now I'm getting 'A Sentimental Education'.

Having to stick around here on piecework. Manual labour, horrors of. Poems can come out of anywhere, can't they, Dublin maestros? An industrial poem — 'Work the Death of the Mind'? Rain all the time, rain in Norfolk, you would think there would be something else in Norfolk. Maybe there never was. Living in a Nissen hut. Horizontal ivory tower. If the rain stops I'll go out for a jar. I'll come home making poems under the trees. Cries in Walsingham of birds in them.

The water smells of trees. Was it of the novel George Moore said it had to have a tree? Irish novels, have you your trees? Yes, sir. The houses of gentlemen have trees. They make an aviary. Thanks again for taxes and tree fellers.

My skin is becoming thin, my beard hurts.

Mind says nothing. Nothin'. 'Devoid of the usual human responses' shall I say. Dehydrated, chloralhydrated. There is ever in my fluttering bosom the unlusty kiss of Shelley. Empty touch and heart. The eye is sand . . . there are no images sprouting — if the soul springs up again, if it comes singing up to the aether . . . .

Sex the most our small savage instincts can do. Will travel, can make baby, without singing. Ethics is loving what you don't want . . . excuse me, miss, no more pure worlds.

In a wheat field under a Fabergé sky I lost my virginity. I did not nor do I feel guilty. Perhaps it was wrong (ethics that bird-speck in the sky), it was not selfish. Ah again and once more in a Norfolk cornfield and, as George Moore would murmur, in print, me hands did stray. Strain of thighs, et cetera. They but describe these matters in bad novels.

Perhaps it was lust, though don't call it that. I slept with the nicest girl among the Nissens so it was art. There has been change — not the change I expected. It was not inhuman. I made it several times and she never found out about me. It was my first. A new batch of girls arrived over the weekend, young schoolgirls. One of them fell in with Martin. Guess what he wants, in a moment? She wants friendship. Martin drops her like a stone. If he but dropped her like Biddy Early's blue bottle into the lake.

I like her, I buy her a drink. Talk a load of nonsense. She smiles at me, she's nice. Has a special body. We walk home from the pub behind the main group. She groans and collapses on the ground. She's not drunk. She's just crying. She has not heard of Robert Lowell nor Our Lady of Walsingham. She hates the world, hates her mother. She hates me: I'm a man. I am another phoney, something for nothing.

Legs sideways, face in hands weeping. The blackness of it. Pouring forth, the ear. Headlights pick us up on the verge. Ye police station is twenty yards down the road. What a place to do it. It looks like rape. You may actually be committing a crime. Life is as obscene as it is beautiful. The Attorney-General may not like it.

I'm explaining to her and being as gentle as I can. This has never happened to me before. I shiver out of control. I have one cigarette and one match left. One is never prepared. For years, no victories to count, the Irish logistics have been nil. The match goes out. Pity the sensualist who cannot stop, the sinner who can't cure himself, the cops who do their duty unpleasantly.

My difficulty lies in the profusion. I love women now. There are too many suddenly. All weeping on the verge of some roadway. The hollow, not the hollowness, of love. In a wilderness. Love haunts the country places. The easy road . . . .

I made passionate love last night to three girls. Tonight, if I wish and look at the stars, five would sleep with me. The Christian Brother boy's paradise. Heaven is weaker than I thought but continuous. Marilyn Monroe, in heaven, sends this message to poor Catholic boys everywhere, sex without love is better than love without sex. Hot gospel, and philosophical necessity. Not a fucking Socratic dialogue in Stephen's Greek Temple in Grafton Street . . . .

A Cuban girl has arrived. I have a conversational relationship with her. We exchange world relationships. It's hard to feel about the foreign policy of Ireland. There is only a foreign minister. I pretended I was Stephen, I was your instant fascist. He says anyone who believes in anything is a fascist. Its mistake was to identify its extremes with the extremes of state power, it should have been confined to the human heart. I tell her this, she is shocked, Fidel hasn't mentioned it. A fascist is the enemy of the state, her state. I tell her I am a Trotskyite and she doesn't know if he is a fascist. Fidel will dine on stars and cigars anyway.

There is Wanka, a Norwegian. She says men are good, I want to be good to men. Men are so nice to be good to. Her English was better than mine in the pub. Scandinavian English is so good. I tell her about the weavers of the Liberties. The flight of the weavers from the Liberties. She asked if these weavers had been handsome. I said they were as dead as Victorian clowns except for an old man and it doesn't matter whether he had been handsome or not. Drunk, he was. I can't avoid it with her tonight, she is so visual and men are so nice.

Men, men. My preferences are at fault. The mad cursers are the best. There is one thing more foul mouthed than two students talking and that is three students talking. All Calibans, to a beast.

Gerry, a heterosexual Genet, is the camp's poet. He is a nice bloke, I don't know whether he is a good poet — Stephen likes discussions like that. Poets only have to be good in Dublin, where maybe they never are — quite — or bad either. Gerry is an expert on house and home breaking. He steals four or five bottles of spirits from the same shop. God, he isn't even handsome. I thought thieves had to be. He left home at sixteen and returned recently for his parents' wedding. Took them spirits, he is a Rilkean angel with dirty long hair.

Gerry went to the Sahara last year though he had not heard of Rimbaud. His black leather coat much admired by the camelmen.

Keith is English. He is not going to the Sahara because you can get hash here. That cuts out travel. He's religious. Which in England means coveting your neighbour's pets. Means he doesn't eat them.

I hate girls and I love them. Are there other women, older, fertile, more cracked? Would give occasion and devotion. There is a girl. I didn't buy her as many vodkas as she bought me. I am buying more and more beer. I want to get white beer flowing in my brain. Light, homemade light. The peasants steered themselves through the dark ages.

It rains and we're not making money. The season is washed out. I haven't saved a penny. It will all depend on the last two weeks.

Gerry is arriving with a bottle of advocat, whiskey, vodka — lying on the grass joined by people on the clock. Colm appears over the tall grass with Keith galloping and laughing. Keith won't drink, he will smile. He will reach for his guitar. Age of the guitar. The muck of work multiplied by the sounds of the guitar: girls will flock to pseudo-Orpheus.

Lying on the grass with Gerry and people. Where they walked to Our Lady. Kissed her, happy with an image-idol. Taken from the . . . well, as the unreformed Don Juan said, there are two girls opposite, from

London. No less. Daddy's an economist with Courtauld's — have you seen the new Osborne? Hard on a Christian Brother boy.

Gerry gets the more beautiful one, I the bigarsed. The one reading *Finnegan's Wake*. It's super. Let's talk about death too. Do you feel it is an absolute loss of consciousness? She has walked over the Alps, seen cows with bells.

Going back the 25th or 26th. To his booklined glance, quoting glance. He is rich and buys booze. I have more taste for it now. Actually have to meet him next week. As many another Ariel thought, I might as well get drunk anyway. Study Vedanta and forget. Drinking like writing gets more like a job, but then as you get older everything gets more like a job. Pay me, sister.

*   *   *

Stephen tourists.

'Magical mystery cornfields western into the sea.'

'I wish you would stop talking about them.'

'Vince, I will tell you and John all about it instead of any of us going home to our teas.'

'Steve, I know you are an old presbyter more than Platonist but I am tired. At heart. Fit only for drink. Tell me later . . . alright.'

'Is it love you're talking about or is it fellows, I can't understand you. You're like guys that cracked up a long time ago. Do you see the window over there — across the street — yeah, the house that's peeling, the window there at the right, the upstairs one? I learnt it there.' John nods out at the window.

'You climbed up the wall? I don't even see a pipe — '

'I got in the front door. Pitch dark, Cis came out. I stayed back — she said, "Who's there?" I didn't breathe. Then I went up the stairs to the girl's room, she worked as a barmaid at the Marine. Lads, I can tell you I was green — that was seven years ago . . . .'

John is the village wencher. Vincent finds comraderie because of the ladies.

'John, Steve, I will tell you my side of it. The day I realised it: five thick-ankled colleens at mass, going to the altar after a night with the fella. I could tell from them.'

'Vincent, these were your cousins the country milkmaids.'

'Lads, I used to have to go to the beach or George's Head but now I'm staying up in her house. We were nearly caught a few times. But if she's slagging me . . . . I told her at the start of the season that if she wouldn't stick with me, if she went with another fella, I wouldn't talk with her. She knows, if I find out she's slagging me.' John is the definitive local boy.

They are getting together, I look sadly at my own case. Laspring they are. I keep the dawn different. 'It's already four.' Orphic tresses on mine. I laugh when I make love. Comic (forsaken) chirrups of first light.

The West has come a long way but it is still asleep. John puts it well:

'I have changed a lot, I'm a quiet chap now.'

'I wasn't quite quiet when I was in England,' Vincent says.

'Merry England,' I toast him.

'The English are a nice people,' says John, 'great for parties.'

'Not a night but several nights,' Vincent follows, 'you remember Martin I was telling you about. He spent three days in bed with three nurses, drinking all the time, and he was able to come back on the next day to stuff the turkey.'

Men without light. Flame women arrive to try and illuminate them. Paganism it's called, the joyful and instinctive urge. Often a failure: after three days.

'Let's go for a country drink? Carrigaholt is a nice place.'

'I'll be with you in a minute.'

Drive out the sunny West, wild and windy hedges poppy broidered. The fields sudden and white, the hay has been cut. The trams look inhabitants from another world. So this is the ex-Gaeltacht. Where are the barefoot children speaking Irish all the road? My mother heard them. 'It was nice to hear it along the way.' Did mother say that or was it Dev only, entering and departing from small centres of population?

Vincent, family background in politics, knows more:

'The Irish language has always been retreating towards the sea. That's where everything was and is poorest, and the poorest of land.'

The bushes almost come to the car window. What shadows do hawthorns invent on declining afternoons? The arrival of impossibility or implausibility?

'Fair dues to you anyway, you can drive,' John beside me.

High over village the sod wall, the vaults in a cemetery. And the Shannon, castle, pier, fishing boats, pots, high redbrick garden wall. Moat and bailey outline. Vincent studies history so I fill him in:

'That's a MacMahon later a Lord Clare castle almost at the mouth of river. Confiscation, then the big brick house. Burnt after the Civil War. The ex-tenant now owner doesn't bother with tourists.'

'Anything else?' Almost a professional note of jealousy.

'The house was ransacked by the tenants coming back from the master's funeral, before paraffin was applied. 1922.'

'But how did the bastards get it?' John's good question.

'A business syndicate moved in when King Billy after a happy lovenight in Kensington Palace gave it to young Keppel . . . .'

'Love's hot hands.'

'But by Orpheus the poets lost . . . .'

'We know what we thought of the Burtons the new Castle lords. Aodh Bui MacCurtin, Swift's buddy, wrote of one of them buried on the shore up there, mad tombs right in the wind:

> The trees of the apples that were readily respected but
> The shameless hard blackthorn firmly planted
> fallen amongst them . . . .

The English I put on it is not highclass Anglo-Irish literary dialect but the meaning shows. I am becoming exhausted, get me a drink.

'The English don't understand, Steve. They never did like the bible of Shakespeare — too much over-statement.'

'Fair dues to you both and the histories,' John cuts in, 'but I have enough of that and scenery. Are we going somewhere?' A great question.

'I'll walk over to the pier, they seem to be repairing it.' Vincent ambles to his place, in the sun. To him probably being as right, true and small as the rain. A few seconds he is in the door of Keane's where the froth for us has already departed from a pint of Guinness and a pint of Bass. The proprietor, a dark small Firbolg is pulling more, and speaking.

Night is falling, its voices have been speaking for some time.

'I can tell you, comrades, how the Free State was received when they drove in after the British left. 1922 it was. With hisses, groans, sticks and stones, with silence and from the upper enclaves of dwelling houses boiling water and urine . . . .'

Remote, endless glamour of these vast gardens of the West. The narrow space between counter and jakes. Quaffing. I like this view.

The unstoppable Firbolg. The Provider provides in more ways than one. To the day we die we get enough of the bars we spend our lives in. Endless recycle of the pint glass.

'. . . . The building by the church, the curate's house, there's a good one attached to that. We had a fine young curate here, Fr Cleary, he mixed with the people. He built the house, he worked with his own hands with the men, a thing unknown at the time. The night it was finished Fr Cleary sent word to the curate at Cross. The two of them sat in the house, there was a sup of potheen in it, you understand. They were at it a long time and something started them off. They stripped, took off the collar. They squared to each other, then they struck. In the sitting-room, the village watching outside. They could see them by the light the logs in the fire were throwing.'

Priests, prowling the lanes after starfall. Against love, for fists and screams. Dark shadows with the fire of murder in them. Bear shape on the stones of the beach. Moonlight hated them. Thou shalt not love. Thou shalt not be an animal like other animals.

'Sure it's tough at the top,' John comments.

He orders food; chicken-and-ham roll, it is sliced out on white paper. A plate of bread, butter is brought by Mr Keane. John won't take a piece until we have taken one, his village politeness. He's starving — he has been out hours without his dinner. He keeps saying how little he has been charged.

'A drink for the road, lads.'

So we leave the pastoral symphony.

Back to town through a strand, cows, cyclists, around the bend into the lights of Corrigbeg. To the cliff and my white house (through mermen in the almost-reach). Drunk from the country passing through the Victorian walls, big wooden staircase to the ghosts — sister-life who had drifted down the bogcotton, the reeds, goodbye.

I am in my country, John seems to dissolve, fade away from me. John fades beer in hand. Out by the door, along the stone seawall, back to the Terrace. A star in the sky above ambiguous. ('I'll give you a great day,' his wedding day he said. I associate the white light of stars with stage-light at the climax of tragedy.)

Vincent, talking, falling round the room:

'There are times when I understand my own existence. Dying without knowledge and an organisation to save myself — and I understand my nerves at the edges of my skin waving like seaflowers in the waves, the waves of the holy trio, sun, moon and stars.'

Around the house, different rooms, pint bottles, stained glasses, stairs, bathroom. Tomorrow we'll find everything. Buy ashtray.

'Vince, not them stars again. O'Casey's bloody stars in the skyways of the West, shining in the airlines from Shannon.'

'We are the stars exploding. isn't that a great thought now. But what will I do with this drunken sailor? Throw him into the sea or take him to bed.'

He is wrestling with his clothes. We sleep in the West and it sleeps in us. The Civil War has been over for forty-three years, our parents had been on different sides. Paradise was still only a dream of the garden.

*　　*　　*

Vincent thinks.

Back in the city I can breathe. Streets you know where nobody knows you. No cousins in the squares. A girl may need you, cities are made of legs. And it's not so bad meeting Steve in Dublin. Can go home. My bed, my bedroom nothing like these erotic scavenger hunts of his, huge fairy flotillas.

Dublin is democracy, citizenship. Demogoguery is not the point. I am my own, I am a lamp, an anonymous flower. I had a nightmare. Steve and a friend beat me up in some house in the country. They took off my pants. He was wearing the Aran sweater he had in The Pleiade. There had been a party to which I hadn't been invited. Interpretation too obvious for words. Interpretation my arse.

The slight drunkenness I have now from three public houses is the best state I can hope for because it distorts my vision sufficiently. The Pleiade at eight. He can be late, always late. The unpunctual smile. I am a camera. I fix situations in clear amber (all faces are beautiful). He looks cheerful when he comes in and sees me, hope springs eternal in the sexual breast.

The Tolka House was overcrowded. Clothing not bright, grey, blue and green, the faces could be seen in any old master, except for a child who is always with his father. I begin to hate abstract pictures. I wish I was Chagall, I could paint him (in that sweater?) staring as he does against the wall of the house or with the sea at his back. I'll probably end up as an art critic.

I am drunker than I think . . . and more stupid, thank God. Dublin sots and ploys. Dope should come here.

Harry Street: big red push door. Always an effort to push. Don't see him, head barman talking. Withered lilies of the alley.

'Between getting drinks, I threw out Brendan more times than I was snooty to the da. It never altered our friendship. Usual four-letter words, we hadn't them in bars then, at least not loud. It's nothin' nowadays, you hear a woman effin' away and no one even hears it.'

He's not here, never is. Hard to be comfortable, hard to look regular. They know who I am and I know who they are. I have descended to village status. Who's that mountain of a woman over there — beside the sunken Garland? I have seen her on the telly, in what play as well?

'Get us two large ones,' says Garland.

She arrives with large ones and soda. Garland wakes up, will he recognise me? Jay he does, staring. I wish Corrigan would push in.

'I am sure that isn't Scotch,' she says.

'Mary, that's Corrigan's latest.'

'Hello, Mr Garland, thanks for the compliment.'

'Deserved, dear boy . . . .'

'Sean, I am trying to tell you this isn't Scotch.'

'Of course it isn't Scotch, Mary. I hope none of the company, and you dear boy, will take it as proof of patriotism if I say it is undoubtedly Irish.'

'Sean, there is a possibility at this distinguished stage of your career you drink too much to know the difference . . . .'

She's going from table to table to ask the gentlemen present, she's got to Ryan. This is a right fucking mess of a place to have got myself into. Ryan, I don't know where I stand with him, I think I like his poetry. It thinks, it's not a canary.

'Of course, Mary,' Con is speaking, 'we poets know what we are drinking: Irish and proud of it.'

'Confirmed on appeal. Now, barman, two large Scotches. If you don't bring them I will wreck the place . . . . Give what you gave me to your friends, they won't know the difference.'

The barman tastes what's left.

'I am not surprised you can't taste the Scotch. You have taken too much already. If you don't want them get to hell out of here and don't come back.'

'This is not the right way to run a public house. You should be scientific not emotional. I demand the drinks, for which I have paid, be put in a bottle and sent to the State Analyst. We must be objective.'

Barman puts them in a bottle, screws no cap on and puts them on the table.

'Now would you do me the favour of fucking off.' She turns on her heel and knocks the bottle. She walks stiffly to the door sticking out her tongue. A performance for only the price of a single Guinness. But I'm cold and idle, womanless.

'Hello, Vincent, sorry to be late. Shouldn't, always will. How are you? You look as if you've seen a lot: pale and interesting.'

'I am embarrassed by having to stand around. They know me. Garland has a tongue when he's asleep.'

There's definitely a wavelength between us. He is an excitement in my life, little before. A bloom to my coldness. There is a notion of perfection around. Clear. The amber light. Sudden leaps in understanding. All the more to hate you with.

Oration otherside of bar:

'If these walls could talk there would be news of every sin in the book, invented or reinvented, of this crowd of writing cowboys. What a crowd they were. It was a non-stop affair. I could never understand it myself. It was such a limited market. They could have held the country up to ransom if they stuck together.'

'Steve, I have some money from the old lady. For an unguessable ungodly reason she gave me some. What'll you have?'

'Hot whiskey . . . how are you getting on with George Moore? Let's be there when fashion comes round again, to Ely Place and Moore

Hall.'

'He's unputdownable. He must have been the first to recognise Yeats for what he is. At that date a sign of genius. And his bad temper, what a decent exercise.'

'I like the flow, the shape of the life, extraordinary for a big house. Belief in café, division between solitude and society. The writing streaming after his thought.'

'Does he always tell what happens or who he is? Sometimes you can't believe and that's irritating.'

'Vince, we must go down there soon, to his lake.'

Ryan's restless, he is going to come this way and he's up to no good either. The cold glint behind his spectacles.

'Hello, Con. Sort of bewildered crowd tonight.'

'I suppose you could call it that. I have been inadvertently listening to your broadcast on Moore. You were saying nice things about the literary gent who lived on his property's five percent.'

'Con, it's really Moore would have been a great poet if he didn't think himself a Protestant, if he was not superior to mystery.'

'I know your brilliant ideas, Corrigan, but that is all they are as I hope your young friend realises. Hot Grafton Street air.'

'Mr Ryan, don't you think everyone finds out for himself.'

'Young man, I know what I am talking about, Moore didn't. I have lived close to it for many years. It's a perspective from poverty: thirty years to see the shallow progressive attitudes taking place, the neo-Renaissance fakery of our public artists. Between jigs and reels I have eaten their bread and climbed their stairs in the suburbs — accumulating my troubles as it were by finding the bread dry and the stairs too steep.'

Hard to take this over-sleeve, a schoolboy Dante. Steve's deflecting Ryan from me I think. Taking the heat on himself. Ryan's now on Steve's poetry.

'You've a number of click lines which are beautiful. Auden in the 'thirties often used these after discarding the others, the dross . . . you don't throw away.'

Ryan eventually goes. Steve stands, smiling talks about him.

'An elder in Apollo's priestly robe — once Con was Apollo, when a crowd of us went to visit Coole, what seemed like a country club or a golf club with the clubhouse burnt down. We saw some laurels and made a wreath for Con who carried it on his bald pate briefly and gracefully.'

False epic. Twilight of an ageing servant race, memoirs nobody will print.

'Attacked, Steve . . . .'

'The enemy is in your own country and there is never a single enemy. Look at the poets from Trinity, self-conscious in the corner. They are the same as in Dowden's day, self-content with sounds and forms, and now they are phoney-Irish as well.'

'Then there is the standing army of Irish poets.'

'Yes, the Gaelic lot crabbed in schoolmaster's pidgin, the Anglo's tea and scones in the Shelbourne.'

'Time, gentlemen please, we have to catch the last bus.'

'The city polloi who write because they have no one to sleep with after the pubs close, and the country boy dreaming of poetry flowing out of the mouth of a cow.'

'Time, gentlemen please, the Gardaí are active outside.'

'Sleeping walking, Steve, until the end of time, of night. And the child's soul taken away as his father carries him along on his horse on the dangerous way. The father did not know he was dead himself except when he arrived at daybreak where he was going. Himself I mean . . . .'

Another verse thrown away.

Concrete banks of the Liffey.

'I wouldn't have missed it for anything, not for anything.'

He goes south and I go north through our city that was.

*   *   *

Stephen plonks.

As you will have guessed this is a romance. This is a definition novel. The popular tongue, not Latin. 'A series of unusual adventures, esp. in which some particular person or group of persons are concerned, involving the actions and feelings of these, including as a rule a love episode.'

Or 'A literary genre dealing with such tales'. This (my life?) is an Irish romance. Which means it is a continuous journey over the heavy and sweet landscape of an impossible island, at the edge of a ford or bridge, creased from a kind of witch travel, crossing the stream, entering a place of people. There is the exhilaration of much drinking, some food, the constancy of branch and tree, nut and berry. Bushed from being in the comedy, not the economy.

Toraiocht. Pursuit. Chase. Planning, manoeuvring, not standing still but for it, the slavery. 'George Moore, you have a soul of fire.'

Tours of the island, to far-fetching sights, by twin or more fabulists — faunal surveys in a swift moving Peugeot. All the Peugeots of my life have been blue, as the actress said to the bishop. If love is not there, an empty seat in the car. Fanfaronade for the small villages and hamlets.

Whatever else we were, you knew what I was, we were pilgrims.

We were going to Mayo, we were going to the lakes, we were off to Moore Hall (there were photographs in the papers). Out of Dublin looking at maps. Past the chapel of Iseult and the Mullingar House. You go on the Sligo road, turn at Kinnegad. The gross effect of literature on itineraries, they glow.

Climbing up Leixlip Hill beyond the church I pointed over the wheel to a new bungalow, coloured brick and cement, carriage lamp, frill lace curtain.

'Marriage.'

That did it. At the very start. Propagandising. I tried to bring the conversation back to the Church, to holy ground.

'The Church fought against it. I think it tried another way to make love eternal and material at the same time, placing the beloved on the other side leaning over the bar, the golden bar . . . .'

'Rosetti,' a grunt from the passenger.

'Looking down on their adorers . . . .'

'Look, some of my best friends intend to get married.'

'Yes, but to quote the master of Moore Hall, I have it right I hope, "The redemption of love from the promiscuousness of marriage".'

'Neurotic, irrelevant.'

'It's relevant to the pilgrimage, keep your staff by your side.'

We took the turn at Kinnegad. Milltownpass, pass by. Tyrrellspass, passing on. We shall pass over into romance, song.

Moate: vast road surface, vaster woman area (convent).

The topic disagreeable to Vincent persisted. We got down to it. We had also gone from Moore to de Montherlant, Vincent objecting (these drives are long over a small island).

'You exaggerate a truth until it falls just short of myth.'

'When he talks of the artist and the curse of marriage . . . .'

'Steve, you know he's wrong to say the artist shouldn't marry at all, anyone can name good artistic marriages.'

'Alright, name them.'

'Brownings', the Carlyles' oh maybe not . . . .'

'Small beer, Vincent, small glasses of English ale, tavern corners.'

'Lawrence, O'Casey.'

'Better still: the Cezannes', the Gaugins', the Sherwood Andersons', Lowell's poems on his wives.'

Athlone, lump of a town. Hatching a river. Army dump, Roman cardboard church. Fem. building of macho hostraiser. They have, have to, some kind of sex to get away from the mad bread. The church (cathedral?) is like a brothel — bright plastic colours, lipstick, almost-wet rouge of the statues. And where are the poets of mid-Ireland . . . not on the bridge saluting. Too well fed I guess, they are beginning to keep out of the pubs.

'Steve, let me finish. It is not the fact of marriage, it is the quality of marriage that counts — if it lasts and makes good non-lasting experience (perhaps that should be called love) then it lasts because it doesn't interfere with art.'

Glennamaddy. Marriage hardly known here as a free institution. Its end not foreseen. Babies come. Strong inglorious prick.

'I'm reading, Steve, again Van Gogh's letters and trying to understand his life, the shape of his life.'

'He's interesting. Not clever but simple, not simple simple.'

'The woman and the child in the Hague and why he left her is fascinating. He says it's she wasn't good and couldn't even reform, which she seems to have tried, after once being a whore.'

'She was getting in his way. She was in the studio which was probably the one room they had, she was there and he was not at peace with it because he had something else to do besides being in love.'

'He also knew leaving her would drive her back to the streets again. Perdition. Terrible remorse for a Christian and a painter but the painter won.'

Milltown. Streets deserted. We didn't look, Vincent was into it now.

'Steve, if one commits what one thinks is a real sin there can be no forgiveness, no waving of a hand, muttering of a word, from a box. Bloody not even a woman can help. This is my view of the artist.'

Unhealing herbs. In the interpretership of the West. Rain fade. Wheeze cows. Here sin is fed them: clergy's gift once a week. They smashed the bottle of poteen, they ripped out the fiddle, and they kicked the mandoline into the ditch. They stopped everything as basis of discourse.

Lights between hills, gardens, an old man, children between lamps, winkled through drizzle Closed doors, faces behind curtains. Ballinrobe. Long tall street, three-cornered square, softlit pub. Powers sign winking. Nearest town to Moore's stableboy childhood.

Lined publican, nondescript pub.

'Two large whiskeys for after the journey.'

'Water, gentlemen?'

'Never for jackeens.'

I tasted, I swallowed, I looked up . . . beside the bottle on the shelf the blue and white cover, the flag of To Kalon . . . the first or one of the early editions of *Ulysses*. In a pub in Ballinrobe?

'You have an interesting book there. You won't mind me asking how it came on your shelf . . .?'

'Oh that. The wife. She often is at the reading. I'll call her, she'd like to meet well-educated people like yourselves.'

She came down the stair redfaced, crimson balls-of-malt cheeks, a lady of the provinces rather majestic drinking to extinction. A blessed creature. Night-halo'd in her shimmering.

'That's a very famous book you have there, by the foxiest poet of novelists . . . .'

'It's amazing,' Cosgrave squeak.

'A friend of mine gave me a present of it, he was a priest. It opened wide my two eyes. It is wonderful that one man can remember so much. Know so much, you know.'

'Almost everything.'

'What will you boys be having?'

'No: what will you have . . . :'

'This is our town and we would like to treat you.'

'Well,' I said, 'in honour of James Aloysius I'll have a pint of the native juice.'

'I'll stick to the malt.'

Rounds began. The garden changed it was the same. In adoration the book of liberation. We gave a paragraph from it, each of us across the counter in low voices to the publican's lady. We were listened in to by the regulars, the talk wasn't literary any more, they had been 'out', irregulars. Souls that once had fire and gave it . . . . The horses screamed.

Blaze seen for miles. Pagan pyre in godless land. The pure are burnt or are burnt with misfortune. Souls already consumed with . . . little cairn out of earth's ears. Ever blissfully self-watering lake. Gently dispelled rushes. Emergence.

'No man from this parish ever set match to it. No one around here would do that. We remember what they were like in the Famine. They took in tenants from other places and let them build huts on their land.'

'Who then, why — that destruction?'

'They say it was some lads out Ballyglass way. But you'd want to go out there and ask yourself, sir.'

Waterlilies. Small fish. The god has vanished, the path is there.

'I'll tell you what me and Jimmy here wouldn't do. We didn't like it when they brought him back burnt. Begob, we kept all the knobs waiting that day at the lake, we did sure, and they had to send to Galway for men to row them over. That took a while I can tell you.'

'Alright to burn a mansion but not the body unless it's in it.'

Shadow and shade of an island we will look at. The artist, the singer, a jealous worm banished back to the root.

Closing time again in the gardens of the West. No clang. Past — well past. The lady of the house constantly reappeared with her tray (the bisexual monster of the lake). Let there be no hurry on you. Vincent was talking to her, agreeable.

'Will you move into the sittin' room. I have to put the lights out in the bar. The boys might be bored outside. Herself will look after you.'

Smouldering fireplace, I talked to Jimmy and his friend. We were part of the alcoholic soul. Early morning: hours, powers.

'Have any of ye got ere a song at all . . . ?'

'Not even a bit of a one between us.'

'Well, I'll tell you a good story anyways. Be God it's a good one. You know Jim Dillon, a great man, son of honest John, well he was givin' out this guff one day not far from the front wall of his own Monica Duff's but be Jaysus there was this joker in the crowd . . . .'

Vincent was gone some minutes to help with the drinks. I went out to the jakes, stop . . . a gasp, pantings. Peer over the counter: Vincent was nuzzing her, mouth mouth and lower motion, stop panting, stop the panting.

No one was there that could be made user of, not angels, not men. I was for the high jump. My mind for the ditchwater.

Another one. The tray staggered. Slightly slopped. We wanted to lap it with our tongues. Vincent to the Venus person.

'Here's to all.'

'Have you any place to stay for the night. You could bunk down in these chairs if you like. I know they're not very comfortable.'

'Actually we're booked into the hotel,' I lied, I don't know why. 'I hope we are able to get in.'

Cold air to beast-flounder in. To be a licked shape. Key fumble, car spurted and lurched, lucky wide street. I know the way to Moore Hall just because I know it. I also know the way to hell.

Kiss, kissie kissee . . . ee . . . e. I must do it now.

He jumped on her, me he gave the cheek, gave nothing. Cold fish, cold slug.

'Fuck you, all I wanted from you was a fucking kiss. You know I love you, you know how I feel, you fucking bastard . . . .'

I poked him somewhere. Wildly, inaccurately. In the neck, shoulders. Strong blows like dogs leapt at me. Tearing, thumping, my nose. Pounded from the side, straight. Hard. I saw the new sky. Stellar consciousness. Luminous heavenly bodies no longer distant. And very yellow, almost orange. A squadron danced into me. Car lurched on.

Stopped somehow on the road. Door slammed.

'That will teach you to have manners.'

Epitaph. My love to the dustmen. Moore-island dust.

I am the soul of evanescence. Etherised by this. Drive me to the lake for funeral oration of myself. Let silent swan cortège me. On this menu of tears go sleep, the sleep of the bust.

Narrow Mayo road. Long range of blue mountains. Streak of bog, scarcely the white blot of a cottage. Plover rising. Larch. It was so painful. Aching face. Hangover clipped its hand of steel through my brain. Shut eye, peeped out of the other. Same menu: breakfast on tears. I looked in the mirror, I knew it, I knew it. The left one. It will get blacker.

'Good morning,' man cycling by.

'It's going to be a grand day,' another one. Where are they going at this hour? It's Sunday, eejit . . . (A good one for Moore).

I was stopped by the demesne wall. Plaque on it. Naturally. 'Moore Hall the home of John Moore, President of the Connaught Republic, who gave his life for Ireland.'

Up overgrown sidepath alongside government trees obscuring undoubtedly mansion from lake. No profit in classical timber. Gentlemen's trees all cut down, hope they left one in front. A wide dark passageway, tunnel, for carriages or rather tradesmen, scrambled through window, out to façade. Huge house, lovely, superbly Palladian in bog and mountain. What an imagination. '1796. Fortis Acere Cedere Potest.' The pillared door. Ivy. Empty. Gutted. Outlines of fireplaces. Decaying nests. Cathleen the daughter of Houlihan walked to the house of the writer with foul rags in one hand and cans of petrol in the other. Neither the lake nor the writer of the lake could save it.

Talking of Kathleen, her sons, and her ruins, Vincent came out of the door, on the steps.

Staring, harmless as a little altar boy.

At what point does one say anything?

'Oh, Vincent Cosgrave, now that you have returned we might as well hold the communion for what is lost. Here is the passage I was going to read. Will you, for me?' My voice as shaky as the great chimney.

'"Moore Hall blazing amid its woods, casting a fierce light over the tranquil lake, lighting up the old ruins on the island. The lake, I said, is several hundred yards distant, and the water that will be pumped from it will not avail to quench the fire. My house will burn like a torch. Moreover, even if the villagers come to quench the flames, the Republican Army would not allow them to do so. Everything will be lost; and I doubted not the fulfilment of my dream; and my thoughts turning to an eighteenth-century Dresden tea and coffee service, my heart began to ache."'

'Well?'

'Steve, I can't read any more. It hurts.'

'Let's go. We have seen enough.'

'Yes.'

Vincent wrote me a note a few days after we got back.

Dear Steve,

I'm going to the sister's house to recuperate. I'll walk
around the lake and look at the water and the grass and I won't
talk very much to anyone but myself.

I often wondered had I the strength to hit anyone hard
enough to do damage, but I'm not sure it is a gratifying thing
to know. Yet, it is, one might say, effective.

I do hope you're well.
        Love,
           Vincent

*   *   *

Vincent blinks.

You pay an honorarium. You count it out, Cosgrave. Blood and
Guinness stains. At least in Mayo: you spread it around (Mayo was
once under trees I suppose).

We both did doff out as ferngatherers in that country turning it
believable to the east, the lakewater, the violence through it, fish and
boat slap. Rub-a-dub. Smack across. Rubric of fuchsia. Priest's hole of
bog. Our names are there muttonable. As real as sheep of pasture.
Whether they ride into lake water or into ditch water under half-
bending trees, their mouths are full of grass and purple clover.

It's Pleiade time again. Get your shattered breath together.
Planxties. My face for their faces (it will be more revelatory when we all
bunch into monograph photographs), I think I am beginning to like my
face, spots of suffering (candle grease of post-sober midnight) — youth
and suffering, what a combo, should go places. (Your damp dark
chattering crew in Kiltimagh dawn, Davittland.) They aren't too bad in
the Pleiade either, at least they are crazy about something. I don't
know what it is, but I will join anyway for the crack.

Warm today, showering sun and rain. They're crazy for drink. Life.
Out at home a bush of dogroses flooded over the grey concrete wall.
Earth is full and warm and heavy. Profusion not enough perhaps.
There must be darkness, madness. Thank God I don't take the aspirins
of reality except rarely. It's early days.

The old lady was waking me with what I thought was a very bright
moon shaking in my eyes — there I was in broad daylight reeking of
drink and still wearing my clothes. Fool, fool, fool. That's a good
thought to go into the pub with. I'll wait for the dawn on me oul'
Cleopatra.

Trinity scholars more than one, Ryan, Stephen perched uneasy at
one end. Tonight he has the waiting look. Buzz of bards before bards

fuck each other off. Half-a-crown buzz.

'I just heard it on the radio,' one of the Trinitys. So here is Revelation.

'What?'

'Ezra Pound's in town. He's flown the coop from Westminster Abbey. Mr Eliot's funeral. I suppose he made up for the Government not being represented.' There is excitement in the hive, nine queen bees in a row. Peace will drop its slow seeds.

Ryan listening. The day's publications in his lap.

'We must make an official welcome.'

'Though he reproduced Arthur Griffith's guff in *The Cantos* he probably won't go in Leinster House.'

'Griffith didn't get much chance either. I wonder where he is staying.'

'Maurice O'Doherty of the six o'clock news', piped the Trinity, 'said, and he doesn't know who he is, that he is staying with Mrs Yeats.' Lights of Knocknaree.

Stephen tells the old tale of Kavanagh mystifying the Americans in his lecture about the question: 'What great poet was Longfellow's great-nephew?' Stephen looks at me as he tells it. Love still floods. Should I write an ode to dam builders?

'Vince, no hard feelings, alright?'

'Okay.'

'I have to see Christy Brown tonight. Out in Kimmage. Promised two weeks ago. Will you come?'

'Okay.'

'Corrigan,' Ryan is breaking in, 'that's a conjunction: an old god talking to an old muse in the museum of Palmerstown Road.'

'If we could get Ezra into town,' the gleam of unintelligent youth.

'Not an earthly,' Ryan in command, 'E.P. belongs to that generation that didn't consider, with the exceptions of the Americans and Mr Joyce, that imagination was helped by alcohol. Our experience is strikingly different.'

'Could we go up there — I am sure Steve has the charabang outside.'

'Not proper. George has kept her distance all these years. One of the few dignified things in the country.'

'Yeah, she puts them in their box alright. She calls the Yeats Summer School "The Sligo Racket" and the proceedings at the tower "The Gort Racket . . . ."'

'She did more: she folded up the Cuala Press because there was nothing worth publishing.'

'Bless the lady.'

'The right thing to do', Con adjudicates, 'is to send a telegram. Who has tanners?'

And after Stephen buys a round it is duly sent. 'Irish writers say with pride a welcome to Yeats's and Joyce's city and ours.' It is dispatched over the phone, it will not be remembered. The words flowing and sizzling in the grail chalice of no legend. We have all done our duty. Another round. The copy will not be kept.

Sean Garland wakes up when it is over. What a drunk son of a pedant he is, in ways delightful. Perfection of the type and he smokes a cigarette as elegantly as Cocteau.

'My Cherubs, he has the taste of Italy and the whole of antiquity in his mouth.' And such forth fountain splashing.

Stephen is whispering again. The whisper an Irish vice. Something on the lines, I can't hear it all, that when you are my age (Oh my education) you forget everyone is going around trying to stop poetry, you become a self-communing spirit. For some reason I think of my poem, 'The Poem on my Table'. Ryan rattling on.

'That's what Yeats said about him, interestingly enough, and W. B. was a wily old bird, "A sexless American Professor!"'

'Oh, Con, that is only a clever phrase. The masculine fire of *The Cantos.*'

'A greater stud,' says I to back up Steve, 'than any languishing stud on this here stud farm.'

Ryan is really going to go for us now.

'What a deception. They are not studs here at all but queers and pansies.'

'Right enough, that's not a bad stable either.'

A Trinity backs him up. Trust them. Con has been waiting for this moment. Life is good. Maybe.

'I have nothing to say about it except that because of them The Pleiade has become a boring and vulgar place. For you learn nothing from queers and pansies except death. I want to live, be happy, feel rapture in the morning, mornings of the race, not this desperate playing around with sterility.'

'Excuse us,' says Stephen, 'we have to go out and see Christy Brown. Don't expect us back.'

'Oh shite and onions,' I conclude the proceedings.

Out on Harry Street. Two suave studs, a blue car, the future. But I don't want to drive through the stars tonight.

'Con will never be happy, Steve. Will Brown be a relief?'

'He's nice. I met him through the magazine. He boozes, the black waters. I have pushed him down to the pub where his brothers are.'

And Stephen knows his way to Kimmage, not bad for a hungry culchie eh . . . .

'Curiouser and curiouser it's getting. I'm a conservative really.'

'You don't like being taken for my conservative wife . . . .'

'Fuck you, mate, if that is what you think.'

'Fuck, Vincent, if you think that's a reaction. I was being ironic. Serious also. That metaphor of affection is not totally hideous. Specially as it's not legal. I could love you as an osprey, a gladioli, a wife, a beautiful stone wall, any damned thing.'

'Look it, mate, I'm not your wife. I'm just a guy you go out drinking with. We are going to see a fellow writer. I tell you I'm a conservative and you better believe me.'

'What I am saying is, it is a part of forms turning into change. Society is changing faster than rape, psychic underlay, the surface doesn't matter like it used to . . . .'

'You are ignorant, Corrigan, you don't know about women, you don't know them. You have never looked at them. And I have heard it from you — the revolutionary mind. I hear it every night going home, the whole thing; down to the orange canal lights. And you never touch a woman . . . .'

'I have carried the revolutionary torch under orange . . . .'

'I know your great lines by heart. Will you stop repeating them?'

'If that is what you think, if you don't know I begin again with each line.'

'If this is the way you want it, mate, then it's the way it is to be . . . .'

'You always go on like this because you know I love you.'

'If this is the way you want it I am getting out.'

'Then you better get out . . . double quick. There. You fucking little bum, I will talk when you apologise.'

Bang, bang, I am getting used to his door clang. The pavement isn't bad, at least it's free.

It is wonderful but I can't stand it all the time.

Ireland the only country where fairy stories are for fucking kids. Kids are the only people who live here.

Back to the G.M. 'In Ireland men and women die without realizing any of the qualities they bring into the world.'

Osseous.

Oh good, here's a bus going to the Pillar. Walk up to mother and Glasnevin dead.

*   *   *

Stephen is tired of all the driving.

The West of Ireland swallows up a car like drainage money. Weekends in ghost towns take your car and bar money to eternity. They usually drop your wallet in some lake before you ever see the beaches. We

opened more and more sergeants, pint bottles of the brown stuff —
Vincent said, 'What we want are statesmen, where are they in our
country?' Names are there, I would answer. We argued about the Civil
Service which he'd like to enter. He kept quoting what someone had
said about it. 'Unless you're part of it you can't begin to understand it.
Even the people who are part of it don't understand it. There's a princi-
ple behind it all somewhere but no one has found it yet.' Already a
citizen of the actual occult state.

Evenings in town when it is almost invisible. But I can see it by the
moon in the afterpub. Out of sight, whispering that we won't
remember it.

Every night with him in town. Con staring at him. You don't want to
be mauled in your first year of literature by an elder in Apollo's priestly
robes but you are. Like graduate school only more dedicated. Training
. . . I see him every night I can. I am driven by compulsion: ultimate
kind of love. For instance, my time with Kris. A casualty in the hot civil
wars of magazines, became a friend again and a good one. As we drove
back from the store I autographed my book for him, wrote it on the
doorstep, 'For Kris, because we lie at the heart of a romantic legend.' I
am an eejit, like it like this.

> These fay
> Pillars will never cool us
> But my uncouthness
> Will not speak it right.

I repeat this scene on average about four times a year. Reunion, no
reunion, Kris wouldn't come over to hear Kavanagh on the tape that
night: Liaison Ratter.

Somewhere else to go besides the twisty roads of the West. We haven't
visited the eastern parts. Province of Leinster, trading coast, gold,
permissiveness. Nearer to these, England. Lovely unstriking coastline,
small thin strands, slightly indented bays, coves where the sand now
echoes to the barmaid's voice outside the window.

> It is not a favoured land
> Just a good one.

We are going there for a pastoral weekend. Uncle bought a
schoolhouse, I wrote a screed and got it from him. A doctor in Birmin-
gham, loves the IRA because he cannot love Ireland, the Brit. intelli-
gence cars outside his door (he hopes). So to warmer sweeter corner of
Ireland, the county with no lakes, few bogs, only pretty corners of rush

and fern. Barley by tractor load. Last chance. Luminous country, I have been through it. Grows lush in summer, clumps of green greygreen and blue, many small Protestant churches, neater, smaller. Amor vicit in wink of eye maybe, aye: garden, stairs, behind curtain, quake of floorboard.

To get to the Model County you go through the Garden of Ireland. What a drive. Through civilization (how I praise its botanical sturdiness). Tom Moore christened this expanse, made rivulets flow through verdure, planted fat trees and pubs on its banks, makes buses roar and stop — uprooting bushes for carpark. Lovely lady-voice of the bard cooing through the thorns. I hear you pricking me. Virgin laurel tree. Brittle hazel. By them your lyre. You make my heart turn into viburnum. The heaven-descended bard came down and sang his low melodious whisper. The ditty of the little gentleman. A pity the Prince Regent hardly saw the place. Might have shat in an Irish palace.

Moore is a great poet. Wicklow is beautiful. The siren county. Christ, keep your murderously beautiful angels locked up so no one will be seduced in the garden.

And at Glenealy a hitchhiker. Lusty eighteen-year-old wrapped around a similar of the opposite. The intense wrap. They hop in, we're off. To an historical ramble.

'I love history, it was my favourite subject last year. I want to study at the uni.'

'This is Parnell's road. His house is up there, a dream house, different kind of dream.'

'Steve, you love the dream house as long as it is big.'

'Have to admire the way he divided them, the liberals and the conservatives, at home the Fenians and the Constitutionalists.'

'But after the early eighteen-eighties . . . .'

'I don't agree with the Cruiser, he was running parliamentary strategy as brilliantly as he carved up the League.'

'I think there is too much sentimentality about him.'

October mist, Ivy Day, beginning of arrogance and cold, going back to College. Walking the woods on Ivy Day. The one you picked from the hedge at the end of a wooded walk, you forget yourself thinking of romance. A sprig of ivy in the shape of a shamrock. You wore it to mass and didn't stay near the door, walked up the aisle. You were a guerilla then. Kitty never came to the garden, she used to put socks in his bag for it. Commonplace this green: psychic land of hope and bullet.

> Home Rule Muse.
> Accompanying his words with the music of politics.
> Conquered by the song the wet cheek.

Cosgrave finds Parnell ivy and wants to turn him into moss.

'The house is by the old gate of the cemetery, the gate he went in: Prospect Square. There is a pub there that is for mourners. It's an old place: you should drop up there someday.'

'Still,' says the hiker, 'it's not really their lives that interest me but how they coped with the situation, improved the lot of the people . . . .'

'Aye, you'll rue it lad if you take up the common people. Harken rather to Master Ovid: vicit amor.'

'Old ravishment is best,' I coming from the Avondale dream.

The car goes over the bridge at Avoca and plunges into the pub. Pure Smithwickian moments. Three pints and for the girl a glass of Smithwicks. Rush to buy, emergent nation, we all have money. Three times three. Nice to be with lusty hitchhiker, he does all the talking, she wants to get to the beach, the sandhills, I can see why. She's seven miles from it and nine pints.

At the second pint I ask for his address, at the third he says he will write first because he never had such a good conversation. I will write first.

I fail to see what has taken the place of vitality and rough beauty. Vincent buys it a half-pint. The gnarled takes the empty chair. No romance, toothless. Ears drool.

'In this country today they're all for heavy industry but I've always said the basic industry of this country is agriculture . . . .'

'Feed the British . . . .'

'And do you know what I will tell you, and you won't believe me, there's no work like farm work. I have tried every kind of work . . . .'

'I never did a day's work in my life.'

'. . . and been in everything and the best days I had was following behind two strong horses ploughing the land. It gives a great edge to your appetite. If you're at it for hours you like a cup of tea, I remember they brought it to you in the fields and you'd gulp it down it was so warm.

'Up Dev,' Vincent this time.

'The biggest industry around here was Kynock's. There were full trains from Gorey and Enniscorthy. Felie Rafferty would sell more porter at dinner hour than would be sold at Murphy-Flood's in Enniscorthy in six months. He would have 200 pints up before they rushed over the bridge. Do you know, I never got in though I applied many times. Thinking back on it now I think it was Sergeant Collopy for I was Sinn Féin . . . .'

'Vincent, let's make a run for it. If they want a peasant Ireland nothing will stop them. None has.'

'How many times does he turn over in Glasnevin . . . ?'

'Let's get away somewhere, where we can resume.'
'As long as it's not about love, Steve, I prefer peasant politics to that.'
'But not folkmummery.'

Back into car. When all is kissed and pissed over I'll say for me: the best you can hope for is to have a poet as a memory driver. Ghost cabbie. It is love beyond love. Steep path: clouded.

'Grainey' yes — hill of, shack of uncle. Hill of the sun, worship, acceptance hymns. Lush people in bar also called Rafferty's, cousins? Must ask. it grows high in summer. Must travel on sunpower. God of the upper air.

In our mouths fields of poets. Our tongues must go in. The sun the god dancing in the sky. Sunday: 'Let them talk of orgasm, this is love.' Hop: into your basic room.

'Well, Vince, we have drunk a barge-load tonight.'

'Gosh, Steve, it seems like a whole fucking canal. I'm tired of the drowned condition.'

'We'll just have a little ginsy and tonicy, a nightcap with lots of baby ice.'

I am rapidly in heat with Parnell.

'It's four o'clock already.'

And then. Someone has dropped a rose from the carriage.

'May I just this night . . . just this once . . . . Tonight is it . . . please . . . love . . . get in to the bedsies.'

At last Rose leaves. You enter into paradise. It's as great as that. Slightly moving you. You shivering. Still-beating bird. Cloudy closer. Tight. We're moving, moving. Music. Into me. After shivering the beginning sweating. He tastes like an apple, the garden memory. Warm paradise, cider in the sun. Adam and . . .

Apple. Apollo.

The orchards outside, the walls outside. Before rest, peace.

'Mr Parnell, did nature flow?'

'Yes, your honour, but not for Ireland.'

On my honour, for another country.

2

Dear Stephen,

Resting. But having bad dreams. In a building like what is known as an air terminal a middle aged woman (no resemblance to the Ma) stood, sat quietly for many hours so that I eventually noticed she was mad. 'Lie down there,' she said, 'and throw blue flowers at my feet.' I ran to get help. What does all this dreaming mean? What has it to do with Spain?

For a long time I have been incapable of any feeling during the day, except incalculable disease or dis-ease. There is no reason for telling this, except in the telling. Self-pity could not be further from my mind. Or perhaps it could, I don't know. But I know why you went to Spain.

Love,
Vincent.

Dear Vincent,

Why I asked you to write first is one of the questions I ask myself resting. That is a minor aspect of un-rest. I think of you — it is a reproduction not an image. Or could be said, I suppose, that Spain is my dream. They slap each other around the neck during the paseo to wake each other up. You cannot be awake in Spain or perhaps secretly, in their half purdah, the women keep their eyes open. The Civil War fed on dreams. I try to arrange photographs of you but it is hard. I had to come to do without you, I am glad you came to the mailboat, I keep seeing you in the pier wind.

Love,
Steve

Dear Stephen,

I was in The Pleiade Friday night. Very drunk and a fellow a little older than me started to nark me, as you often did;

when you started talking about women, for instance. I hit him. He didn't hurt me and I don't think I did him much damage either. Anyway we were both thrown out and fought outside and were soon separated. No point of course just pure stupidity lashing out at each other.

Did you or did you not know that Paddy Kavanagh is finally barred from The Pleiade? He simply told old Pleiade himself what he thought of him and I believe was quite expressive and expansive in the vulgar English and bad French. He is now in The Heavens across the street where I do not imagine his stay will be protracted as that establishment's policy is to seek a nicer type of clientele. How is Franco, that crummy poet?

Love,
   Vincent

Dear Vincent,

Just to confirm I have left the American Express (no letters yet), too many pre-New Dealers around and me mammy brought me up to think Roosevelt is an aspect of the divinity. Ironically, my address will be de Montherlant's Our Lady of Communications, the Cibeles, or just say for the confidence of Caesar's postmen — Oficina Principal, Lista de Correos.

Living away from you as if your presence wasn't symbolic. In mystical literature the expressions of love are conceived, structured as a drug experience. For centuries love was the dope of clerks whether Cathar, Renaissance, Bourbon or nineteenth-century. Love a secret religion. I belong as you know. I suppose I will never get out of it. What will happen to you?

Old Lust gone south,
   Steve

Dear Steve,

You've heard by now of Nelson's demise. If there's one thing the Irish detest more than a phallic object it's a British phallic object. So there it stands broken in its sex and surrounded by policemen and conversation — the local symbol.

The rain is falling through the sunlight like warm soft needles and the clouds are flapping in the wind like the washed sheets in the line. The clouds have frayed edges for the world is very old.

I hope this doesn't sound like literature because I'm sick of it. And the radio has said 'To get love you have to live it'. I'm

glad you are away from the English radio.
   Love,
      Vincent

Dear Vince,
   You don't have to tell me, I saw the fucking thing. Somewhere off the Carretas in a bar so old I was enduring the low telly — suddenly the stunted stone animal comes on the screen. The death of Nelson and the death of stone. I used see it from Henry Street, Talbot Street, sloping over the merchants.
   Lovers of the town who waited underneath, lovers of the town's writers, sad.
   The ivory tower, where we rent a room, will be hacked down. We must record its demise. The high stone buildings and our feelings looking at them. Dublin has not died, it has passed through us. I'm so mad I'm glad we're just writing postcards. But you said you'd write letters.
   Love,
      Steve, sending poems.

Dear Steve,
   There have been letters from me. It is as difficult for me to suffer your blasted impatience as it is for you to feel it. There are letters in the post office.
      Vincent

Dear Steve,
   Yes I liked your poem and the last image of the moon over a Killydysert wheatfield. I am walking *The Hidden Ireland* with it.
   Beautiful weather here for the past three days. Lovely light and everything in blossom and the grass green and full and scattered with daisies. I lay down for long hours — Kavanagh was so right when he said that after all a great deal of our life has to do with inanimate nature. In fact the happiness was so large that I became restless to the point of madness. To do something or say something, but it is a long poem and I can feel it modifying all the time so I wait. Perhaps it is not good to write enthusiastically.
   Things otherwise very quiet. Barker reading his elegies on the Third, beautiful stuff, *Dreams of a Summer Night*. Haven't seen the people, the chosen people for some time. Walking

your Dublin, feeling the kisses.
    Love,
        Vincent

Dear Vince,
    That field is within three miles of the biggest river of these
Arthurian isles, the Lord Oliver put us there for three miles
around the water — to kipper the natives into their hovels. We
began taking the love-dreams potion with the Papish in the
unmown field. We saw the meithal moon over unscraped
stalks. I saw you by the same moon outside The Pleiade — you
were livid (burnished?) with Eire, thrombotic with escapes
from it. I can give you but a sensation of these things which is
less than shorthand. I belong to the blind race of Irish poets.
But I can feel the dust, the heavy noon, tramp of feet. To de
Montherlant again for my sensations now (and why you must
come here): 'At Hendaye he heard Spanish being spoken, like
the voice of the woman he loves.' Franco never wrote like that,
Lorca did.
    Love,
        Steve

Dear Steve,
    Phenomenal weather for a couple of days but the broken
clouds have come again — phenomenal in that though we
sometimes get warm days it's very rare to get really hot ones.
It's the sort of weather you don't really enjoy but which you
pursue, soaking in the sun as hibernating animals store up fat
for the winter. So hot I could hardly look at things, a blindness
of a different order from yours. I sat with objects, they were
intense. The nights are marvellous, cool and blue and starry.
I hope it is like this in Spain, then I would understand the
temperament. In the north we agonise to keep mentally warm.
Don Quixote is so strange a figure because he insists on charg-
ing through the heat. There are the sort of aesthetic theories
I like — isn't it funny to explain everything by the weather?
Whether you sit in the green isle or the golden red desert.
    Love,
        Vince

P.S. Franco is 'dead', why flog him?

Dear Vince,
    Can the two of us get on when you come out here? Your

letters confuse me. The ten years between us is the hell of a love machine.

This stuffy crummy room of a pension — packs of retainers, cheapest in the Carretas at 20 pesetas a night. Bisexual old-agers wash, clean patter and putter. There is a big beautiful wooden table in the kitchen. And a nino: all passion exists for this child. Seats and Renaults noising in the streets — what great sounds of machines there are in the universe, child. I will confine Franco to the Prado.

Love,
    Steve

Dear Vince

Went to the Escorial. Tomb city of Bourbon and Hapsburg. Schoolboys milling around the façade, some of the older holding rugs against the cold wind. In a dream I saw Lorca's lost *Sonetos del amor oscuro.* I picked it up from a stone street and ran away with it. If I could find it again and read it to you, you would love me forever, poem to poem.

    Steve

Dear Steve,

All the world holds silent. Only the weather cracks at all.

I'm trying to think of an event worthy of note but it seems there's not a whisper in our green and pleasant fields. For my own part I seem to be happy. I find I can read poetry much better than I can before, could, I mean. I seem to understand the language in a finer way. So much so in fact that even without thinking a poem or a phrase I seem to be able to see the language and its proper use, as a world separate from its use. And I can imagine your streets and squares, they take over from the history page, and I follow fantasy which is always unacademic.

Love,
    Vincent

Vince, like this card — El Pardo one of the most unimportant royal residences around Madrid. Yellow and white, people in uniform. Caesar was a-hunting. Stevie Boy

Dear Stephen,

I'm sorry if this letter isn't as long as it should be, considering the event. This place has little justification for existence, a salt city. No more Zosimus for me . . . . Paul and I saw him laid out: very massive and looking as if he was thinking of something else entirely. Dickie was with him all the time and said he died peacefully. At one stage he was asked if he would like the last sacraments, to which he replied: if you like, I don't mind. Later Dickie thought him to say, a little before he died, I believe in God.

The funeral was plain and simple. Later we were in the house, later in the pub.

But I resist the history of suffering I hope (the cod of it). Kavanagh's in peace.

    Love,
        Vincent

Dear Vince,

It is goodbye The Pleiade: you and the city were real and comic flesh. In a city, in the one pub of a city, there was a man. Altogether different from the schoolteachers (in whose hands he will have no rest). You knew him only for a year or two, I was luckier. Ten years' mortgage on grace. The future will be technicians.

I took from him the surprising absence in the Irish of manners and education and possibly of humour. Paddy was the Just Man.

I lit a candle in a church, went to the Cerveceria off a little street of the Plaza Mayor — it is a canteen, no seats — and drank so much beer the barmen laughed.

You may be of durable stone in the circle of suffering but I stand on the periphery a tree that feels the winter, the cold.

    Yon tears,
        Steve

Mine Dear Steve,

I resist the history of suffering because it is too easy, too comfortable to identify with. I could become tears and vomit like everyone else. Stone is habitable by the way, a lady or a man. And we are set problems, situations, jobs if you like, and we are alone. I mourn Paddy but not the death of the poet.

The wind is cold and lonely tonight, I know you are over there, love to you and around you. Now it is raining.

    Love,
        Your Vincent

Dear Vince,

I can't get over the loss of human beings I admire. That's all.

It is not something that happens often. I got the *Herald Trib* on him: 'Eccentricity said to have barred rise to fame.' Cribbed from *The New York Times,* what an honour.

I wander in old Madrid by the Ayuntamiento, wood-sellers in the streets reminding of chestnuts in prints of old Gran Via 'Calientes' . . . the length, soul weather of the country. 'Pisando la dudosa lux del dia' treading the doubtful light . . . the poet dissolved into his loved nature. I could talk to Con about him, I wander the cafés, — the marble-top tables, the white waiters, los madrileños accept it all. I am leaving Madrid, but come.

   Love,
      Steve

Dear Vince,
   I am sending this card of Zamora, the most interesting town I've seen. The banks of the Duero — the soul on baked earth. Burros. Barefeet. Am leaving for Portugal, will have to walk as there are no connections.   S

Dear Steve,
   You never said how long you would be away but presumably twenty quid in Portugal lasts longer than twenty quid in Portrane. I am armchair-traveller hungry.
   Zamora looked lovely in the card and now all Spain seems like Valhalla and why wouldn't it, after these past weeks of UCD, Europe sliced up into ridiculous pages of history. It begins to look like a play instead of a boring series of disjointed hated sentences. I'm surprised how a great deal of my opinions agree with Burke's conservatism and how much less I like Trotsky's permanent revolution.
   I saw Con last week and he is going to the US of A. The first shoots of Kavanagh deification. Con wants to miss that, it hasn't much to do with anybody. Con will be the biggest fish they've had in some midwestern town or little sea.
   Where are you — I have my moments of nostalgia.
      Vince

Vince, this here Bragança is Anglo-Saxon, red buses and pillar boxes. They are opening the new Tagus bridge. I have just seen Salazar on television in a crowd of girls, one dark. Yeats' 'The poet is always surrounded by beautiful women'.
   Steve

Postscript: Write Lista de Correos, Valladolid.

Dear Vince,

In Zamora I went to a bar up a dark path. A huge wooden table with wine and spirits on it. I asked for clarete but he mixed something. Groaning from another room, someone on straw. Goya. Found him at last. And Machado's Spain: very old quiet cafés, shoeshiners, papers.

Now Valladolid where Felipe II was born and Columbus died. Besides history and a medical school, Renaults are made for all Spain. How long shall we last in this jewelled-peasant world that holds on Caesar's breath? At least as long as the money lasts, could be two years, could be shorter. Do send the recent UR. Do send yourself.

Love,
    Stephen

Dear Stephen,

You said something in a letter about me coming out to Spain for a year or two. You know I said to you before you left that I was coming out for a month or two. I hate to seem the beast but that still stands. This relationship always seems to have you asking too much and me refusing. All in all it's made me very neurotic. I have no words to make this sweet and less than it bluntly is, for the Blue Bird must fly its way as Augustus John says. Between you and my mother, who wants to get me a clerkship in the ESB, I'm rightly lumbered. But I'll not bed with you. I'm a stark het.

Having a go at your chore. What in the name of the sweet lamb of Jesus is UR? It sounds like something from prehistory.

Love,
    Vincent

Dear Vince,

I am going to have a little say. You are wrong to limit your stay in advance on this shore, cities, old rivers, wisdoms, culture collections. You want the record on and the TLS in the chair. How can you? Have you a puritanism that cannot enjoy the olives, the sea, the scribe in the post office. You will prefer the non-event paintings of Augustus John, you used talk about mawkish drawing-rooms of pre-intercourse, and you don't even see it is not painted, it is just tubed on. And you don't understand UR is actually decent university history —

which is rare — and you would discover that Lorna Reynolds is its editor who does wonderful translations of d'Annunzio. And you would find respect for sun, visit sun and love.

Yet not hate,
Steve, much more later.

Dear Steve,

Firstly an explanation. Two months was a typing error. I meant to say four. But I don't think this would have made much difference. If you look at it without the moralising and the peripheral definitions there is no disagreement surely: I must come and go as I like and you as another human being accept that. Otherwise you would be less. It was you yourself that brought up one year, two years, and you know how dogmatic you can be. The point is made: there is to be no dictation.

But the tone of your letter is more interesting. The thing is a lecture however brief — to a small boy and he's promptly ticked off on all points in the removed parental manner. One note reminds that I may think UR is prehistoric but that Lorna Reynolds is its editor. I will remember that a Reynolds edits it. Also you point out that Augustus John wasn't a very good painter. Thank you. There are as yet some blind spots in my education. It is beside the point to say I have always liked John. I am always grateful for potted cultural history.

Your remarks on 'love', I suppose you mean the unity of love, would apply better if you were writing about unity of being. Your Mediterranean is a Robert Graves subutopia which beckons to no one but the tired and lunatic (hands off my effin' moon) or an encircled James Joyce, a domesticated Rimbaud, all handicrafts, beaches, beautiful boys, gitanos, and old walls. At its best we know it's best.

There are certain places in the heart that we do not realise exist and into these places enter suffering that we may realise they have existence (Leon Bloy). My eccentricity and yours are in conflict. The trouble about eccentricity is that one eccentricity rarely agrees with another. I am sorry about this.

Love still too,
Vince

Dear Vince, dear vicious angel from the wet glistening city,
Howdi partner.
Thou whoreunhung.
1. Thanks for the extra two months. Typing error my arse!

2. Democracy is établis: go and come, please come.

3. Give us a break, barney.

4. If you wish, you blue angelyou, to fly over the Augustus John territory, bolloxy legend, lush eyebrow raindrops, please do. Fly forever. All healthy sex is yours.

5. Even Shelley drank wine on the shores of the Mediterranean.

6. I have no objection to expatriate villas or being your Pre-Raphaelite bride. I am quite shy actually. Not just a wallflower but a pressed wallflower.

7. You could be a murderer, a killer of love, the one by yourself. Alright. El fin del Mundo. Todo va a terminar. But I am waiting for you in the railway station of Valladolid, it is open all night and occasionally I sleep under the framed portrait of Caesar as I wait for you.

Love,

Stephanus the Steam-Engine Martyr

3

Stephen waits.

Heliotropic curvatures. It seems I can go to the sun from the train carriages. Step off or on for a brief moment which is time — the track, moving off. On flanged wheels. Upwards. Superelevated, the blind put up so I could see the bleached stalk, the burning stone. Time sizzling. Let there be no firescreens between me . . . and what is there. I must never reduce speed.

I trip in quickly from the steel-blue night through the high foyer of the imperial architecture of railway, through the door.

Adding machines, power augurs forgotten — monster, thumping, beautiful: el tren de vapor. In its last months. Shunted. Stationary. Pistons steam in the cylinders. Connecting rods. Closer — the melancholy coal of the Asturias shovelled at the side of the stand — cinders from the stack — escaping gas and ashes. Hot midnight air rush. Unfrictioned. A *loco*motive.

RENFE, Red Nacional de los Ferrocarriles Españoles. Dating from early hunt-proud days of Caesar. El tren a rose de sangre, a rose of sparks and blood. Helpless, I buff away.

Ungleaming steel rails behind. Flying glare in webbed darkness. Spain travels in carriages climbing — winding — through granite Galician hills (with a keeper engine), solitary light signal of Old Castille. Adjusted smooth speed of the new lines from France, charming puff cleaving the mesetas, dinner-table land. Wheat, short tunnels, maize, barley. Iron bridges, small pueblo with lanterned mozo. Oats. Crossing signs. Hemp, flax — whistle posts, mileposts. Vines. Purple, red and orange madder. Sheep fences. Masses of olive trees. The megalithic barn.

El jefe in his control cabinet within the nineteenth-century building intoning. Caesarion. Empty otocrane. 'El tren rapido, procedente de La Coruña, con destino a Madrid, andén primero, via segunda.

My Wagnerismo is bad tonight.

'Buenas noches!'

'Buenas noches, señor!'

'Uno coñac, por favor.'

'Si, señor.'

'Me gusta más el veterano.'

The small bar would be too crowded. Campesina women with chicks in crates, old men from where — Peñafiel? Palencia? Faded overalls and wickerbaskets, food, dining before the public like the kings used to. Tapas on the counter, too expensive. Guardia will come in, leave their rifles on the few tables, they have bits of paper not bullets.

On yellowing wall the Retrato Official. Stare down, cow. Caesar is a Gallego, they are like Bretons, they run the restaurants around railway stations. Hearty food. Next train from Irun can't be long. Little Caesar never sleeps. He watches everyone from his boots. Never unstraps. Spain sleeps in café, carriage, but he never sleeps. You ran on to the platform coming here, Medina del Campo, at 4 a.m., lights in bar, drowsy waiters — knocked at the glass, voiced, they opened up and two double cognacs for you, scrambled back. You had pesetas, you always had pesetas.

Arriving, taxi rank, clutching typewriter, genius at the bud. The memorial to Colon, like Dan O'Connell on the bridge of the fair city. Dreaming of where you had been true: the almond tree becomes whiter, the white mountain almost an almond, resembling a peach until it grows to maturity. The Barbary touch.

Remember when you took Vincent down after the great night at The Pleiade, to the wall at Trinity — to hear unspoken, blessed, the nightingale in the Fellows' Garden. Full-throat pouring. As godly as you like. It is modest of the nightingale not to require anyone to listen to it. Pride of the nightingale not to care if anyone listens.

First morning in Valladolid of the burnings, Edwardian Spanish glass windows, a little sandstone mixed. Broad pavements, cobbles, dust. Dirtied. Park, earthworks, bandstand. Parks the sweetest of this belovedness of Castilla, lamps flung in branch and leaf, elfin radiance of shaded fountain, people haloed through shrub and bower — I heard later that out on the centre paseo there are obscure jungles of male magic . . . . Garcia Lorca walked through it in the 'twenties, toad inside prince, what jewellery, what paint after evening of winks at the Ateneo. You bump into lean officer like tall greyhound, green uniform with white gloves, a señorita on his arm. Ye old fake Moorish façade of the Cavalry Academy where these lean greyhounds come from. They drill by morn and paseo by angelus with daughters of good families, eyes cold as icefalls in café.

'Una copa mas con leche caliente, por favor.'

'Si, señor. Hace frio.'

'Especialmente en la corazón.'

'Si, señor.'

Banco de Medina, Banco Hispano-Americano. Banco Industrial de Leon, Caja de Ahorros y Monte de Piedad de Salamanca. Heirs of the Lombards — remember the clerk back home with lady-clerk friend tough and gracious: 'We should not live for money we should live for love but someone has to plant the spuds.'

'Uno coñac y una leche mas . . . .'

New faces blacker, heavier luggage. An old peasant in vast scarf having coffee. Stacks of mail in the breeze out the door. The moon never seen by Protestant eye, up over the dawn train. Windowlight and life. Brandy is dog sorrow: I should go on to pernod, joy and joy in strength, white flame, the dash around my throat: remember Vince and the pernod drinking, when we woke it was all over the house.

*   *   *

Stephen hangs around the city

They love poetry here too. High-school land. All learn the greatness of the same poet and believe it. Lorca second-class. Manolo in Bar El Titulo, swarthy if he isn't handsome, knows Machado is the one, everyone does. Go there for my literature class before I come up here. Manolo is waiting to do his merchantile examinations but loves poesía.

'Estudio ahora mucho . . . .'

'¿Quando? Los examenes . . . .'

'Entre el 1 y el 10 de mayo en La Coruna y como el tiempo pasa rapidamente, en la electricidad y el inglés . . . el poema 'Vasteland'. Es mucho católico.'

'Uno anglo-católico.'

'Le mando una pequeña antologia de algunos ensayos y recuerdos de el.'

Fernando always comes in, sends down a chato by Manolo, one peseta — Caesar's prices are sweet yet they run to turn off the television before the Royal March sounds and his image glares.

Pablo is the one in the bar I fear, it takes a poet really to be a bore. Met him standing in state at a posh bar in the Plaza Mayor. He keeps on catching your eye and then you buy Felipe II while he recites his latest. You don't mind your pocket, it is your brain. The night we sauntered to San Pablo, he simpered in wounded language among the Isabelline-Gothiceries. It was the day of La Ley de la Prensa. Pablo was gracious to Caesar who had been so kind by stroke of pen to restore freedom to the press. Pablo babblo: 'La libertad de las parábolas, la prensa es, es nada mas una virgen.' Rage of an Irishman, rage of Aodh. Red rage. Piss off Pablo.

I begin to find the bearla about the town. Robert runs a language school, cold tortilla for supper every night, northsider Fianna Fáiler, tribe of Vince. Perran, a not so drifty Rupert Brooke, sweating through his freckles in the heat, leads me on a little, tells me in El Corcho that his father had hunted Roger Casement in Connemara in 1916. That English look, medallioned. He said he might come to the station, with Jesús, one of his pupils and student friends, may be an amusing night of dance-the-trains — a malversation of de Falla.

I feel I'm out on a treelimb in the tierra del campo among the sprinkle-tinkle worship of Ceres rising deep green in spring, where no trees except olives grow — how many trains are belching and cleaving through them to distract me from melodising my creaky soul into something useful?

'Uno más de veterano,' railway stations forever.

Valladolid is like Limerick, shady falling down wonder. Decadent, ringed by madonnas and cement. Their clusters of church are all miraculous-wrought early-Renaissance or good eighteenth-century. Our form is structure, building, girders, what shows, it's not invisible. Please explain your poem, how it works. The moonshee's Jamp, Mohammed's angel-call is different. Self-contained form important as castles and towers. Tectonics. Fillet, arabesques. Stars, rosettes, garlands, starettes, palmleaves, pinnate leaves swimming curving. Vaulting and twining in the hunt and heat. Oenophilious sentiment of courtly youth shall be strung to never-ending cobalt blue spread of the heavens. Faience of tongues. The loneliness of my brandy mouth.

I like where I live, the centre of a little traffic plaza. I have a little stone balcony opposite nineteenth-century solids with a photograph street-level in one — shop of souls that encourages sale of white bread and white clothes to match. Sloping red tiles running away to the river, old convento. Pity Vince probably won't be here for Semana Santa, it's one of the routes. The room: with Woolworth chandelier, for which there is one bulb, beds in corners. Pensión Fuentes crumbling like the convento, pillars, yellow plaster, casa with wooden door — up shakey stairs to second floor where Madame Antonia, big and rouged and blended dreams of Paris. Has gone there entranced, but one fault, 'Perro ni hay churros en Paris.' Dreams of Paris, goes to Alicante. Clapping for the serrano who's in some bar and dreaming of feminine elsewheres.

'Uno otro . . . .'

'Ah Jaime me boy, hard at it aren't you. You'll not be afraid of things that go bump in the night.'

'Perran, you've come.'

'Here's Jesús, Jesús Hernandez, mad Irishman Corrigan, and Francisco who's interested in Shakespeare, and Pablo Ares Torres — El Gran Poeta.'

Christ. I feel the hole in my pocket.

'Mi amigo irlandés. Quel felicidad. Irisacion . . . .'

I am abrazod to death. What a cemetery.

'¿Perran, Pablo, Jesús, Francisco, que quiere tomar?'

Dos vinos, una cerveza (Jesús doesn't like wine), una ginebra con tónica, and a copa.

Pablo does not stop. Nothing for him but the final trumpet which will have to scream at him.

'Quel visión: una reunión de poetas. Una conferencia como en Madrid. Tenemos una poetica lectura . . . .'

Pablo is organising the hollowest of occasions: a reading. To start with the great visiting poet across the seas. Fucking poetastro.

'Pablo's a good fellow, great fun . . . .' A settling and literary arrangement. Cough mixtures.

Unfortunately I have my music on me, what the muse bade me scribble in hot pensión room from the poeta of *Nueva York y Odas.* Another quick copa, a gulp, and a low voice:

> The women were singing by the wall of nails
> When I saw you strong God in the Sacrament
> Naked catching your breath like a boy who is chased
> By seven young bulls good enough for a novillada
>
> You were glowing God within a palace
> Pricked by your Father with needles of light
> Throbbing like the poor heart of the frog
> Which the scientists put in a flask of glass
>
> Stone apart the moaning grass
> And the dark water that loses its three accents
> Life your column of spikenard under snow
> About the world of wheels and phalli that goes around
>
> I was gazing at your delicate floating outline
> In the ulcer of olives and pants of agony
> I shut my eyes to give in to the sweet
> Flight of white insomnia without a blackbird . . . .

The meridian fruitfulness sweeps over me: the Christ-boy passion comes shining: hot. None of them can say for that moment that Machado was greater than Lorca. I have silenced Spain on its own ground. Undaunted Pablo takes his book of poems out of his pocket where he always carries it. There is also another poet to remember: Spain like Eire the mod-land of the memory estuary of poets.

A Juan Ramon Jiminez
Poeta delicado de las flores
amarillas y cielos otonale.
y de dias también primaverales
de párajo y flautas y tambores.

Amigo de los mas puros amores . . . .

Vincent comes in through the door.

Chill has come. I am a child shaking with the cold. It is cold tonight.
Banging of real bottles. The evacuation of libraries. Cuyo? The train:
procedente de Mountjoy Square con destino La Giralda. Por los
alrededores de . . . mi corazón. I am being plucked: still shivering. I am
afraid of my own shit. Balkanisation of the heart, Bakuninisation of . . . .
   'Well, what can I expect to drink in this country?'
   '¿Tiene usted una poema?' cries Pablo.
   Pour for a live infante.
   'Gentlemen, there is a druid in this house with a druth.'
   'Dos grandes copas de veterano . . . .'
   I am dropped laughing, opening my wings around. It is true, story of
paradise, walking under trees crunching cones, laid-out trunks we
clamber over.
   'This is my compañero.'
   Champán to follow. Federico under the low branch glimpsing the
heavens in a new face. Where tourneys had cracked, rode against for
skill and promise, pretty adolescents dressed up, for the king: the
queer poet in the king. Invisible times, gardens. Parks.
   The lion chased the unicorn around it: but he wasn't chasing him.
The deer was his friend and the lion had some use for the deer. The
unicorn tripped, into the shadows he disappeared. His was not the
cemetery hated by the moon.
   'Steve, you've no idea what it was like at Hendaye. Everyone stream-
ing the platform, no one to ask, there was an American on the bench
and he said, "Son, I have been sitting on this ass for two days, I can't
figure a way out of it".'
   'How did Irish lack of logic work?'
   'I went to the bar, had my first wine, it figured it out.'
   The issuing out of el Estación del Norte, down the paseo campo
grande, by the fountain and the academy, by the theatre of Maria de
Molina, to my snug plaza. Took the luggage, brought skin nostalgia the
chill air of the Pisuerga . . . . Grab the bottle I had kept.
   'Let's go to my favourite square and finish this.' A corner missing
already yet the remaining houses solid. Little ancient park, unnoticed:

San Miguel, dustier than any doomed for development, its time is up.

Please in the name of Jesus and all saints who dwell in plazas on grass like this: I am the grass waiting for its eternal dew in this countree of harshly varied hue, let us be prophets and concentrate on our lotus. I get it up too quickly on earth, that is the lower testament. Bulge quicker than puff puff.

'Steve, so many strange thoughts coming and going out and sometimes staying overnight.'

*   *   *

Vincent sinks.

Spainyards (is that how you spell it, I have only just graduated) — the space travelling really fascinates them. Satellite showing all day, even the corridas go off the screen. Old men so astonished at the pictures their coffee cools. Technological herding in the sky, lunar heading in the press. Americans have met in the suburbs of moon. All on my first day, breathless. Steve takes me to Madrid for the old sights. Back on train.

No limit to clerestory, there's no limit to celestial wounds as Pasternak says.

Tomb Spain stretches. The big, Escorial, really arses up. Encoiled to see from the train window, waking up muzzily on the seat, wine bottle rolling on the floor. Clothes of the grave. Finery-spidery. Fine for mausoleum viewing. Mist of the dawn in which you can see Killiney.

A mattock to weed out the garden: nothing Flemish or flamenco to appear.

The portcullis, gate, bridge, last hillock, fancy villa with pool, river near and under. Sierra take, a little snow at the centre of the world, past an old church incongruous. The consuls with their wreaths of witheredness enter, one pale from drink, one paler from drink and unrequited love. Very damp corollas.

We shed our unwashed armpit fragrance through the capital. Taxi, fountain, seedy railway hotels, for Christ's sake a behind, a girl's. Good — Stephen wasn't looking.

Find his old pensión, fumbly ancient of days, washing shaving crapping going out. Puerta del Sol where people gather for the forgotten madness of revolutions. Not for thirty years, officer. As the man said who hadn't much to meet with, we haven't met since before the war.

Lamps in tiny squares which act as intersections (a boy counting pesetas by a lamp — don't nudge Steve, he is not interested in 'social questions'). Must always have been one-way horse streets. Crooks behind the toros grill, cigarette women at the bar doors, stumpy smile over stumped legs. Lotteries: can any war have done in so many limbs, organs, eyes?

Jakes, the Moorish way. Fifteen-watt bulb. Medieval. When our scrofulous chieftains frightened and disgusted the elegant and culti-vated English, when our bards operated a closed shop for families and friends and praised the prince in strictest of assonantal verse — as now you must in Steve's strict and free — when the farmers sang songs that were never written down, when Shane O'Neill codded the lesbian Lizzie, put girls up the pole and drank like a Scotsman . . . fine times just like these. Natural diet and defecation.

Breakfasts in the Café Lavante. And at night to night-cap it. The back part was full of a crowd, people standing up in the chairs. Leather chairs, boom of voice. God, strange thing: a real poetry reading. Poetry reading sweet poetry reading. Older men too, berets, maculated raincoats. God, poetry must be subversive.

Bar Alemania is a different proposition. Up beyond the Carretas, poor chewed up plaza like the underground parking in Plaza Mayor with statue of King Spider above. Café — surprise surprise — full of Americans in flight from blight of Cochin China, with followers in shawls and long dresses, basic nonconscriptables. Steve perks up his pecker at the sight of so much bejeaned flesh — personally I can't stand well-washed jeans. Steve sees them with their arms around each others' necks (and his) as the States in Whitman's homo-hungry poem.

There's a much older guy who comes over and Steve stupidly encourages him and there's another nice mess you have got me into. The guy says he helped drop the bomb on Nagasaki — I want to hit him, Steve just chats. It was all bluff the old guy declaims, Old Harry hadn't another in the cupboard. Sure he had us all fooled. He is the 'Mayor' of the bar. The self-proclaiming ring on the little finger.

'Vince, he is so bent he is a double agent.'

Bent I can take but not all the talk about it. He'd say it is not an obsession just an interest. I have to beer and bear it. Nature of homosexuals is to pretend to themselves to be in love, to talk about it. They will soon be the old-fashioned type. But they want while they wait. Cross off straight guys like me. King's darlings, the place of favourites in history. They had no choice. Attracted, yes, they were attracted — to friendship, to curse to see it blossom intolerably into imposed lust. Briefly you might fall in love yourself, maybe there's a man-to-man thing, a kindling. It would be primitive and short.

The Mayor telling us where to get a fourteen-peseta soup that's a meal in itself. Steve is excited.

'Spain has extraordinary cripples, deformed people. I don't think it was only the Civil War, it is a spiritual psychosis over centuries. The

love of God is beautiful at its most masochistic. Spain has been a cradle
of the God-songs.'

Steve is blueshirting again. Half drunk, partly to tease. He starts on
the man we saw walking on pieces of stripped tyre. Says it reminds him
of the strange creatures all crutched up or legless on the way into the
races at Listowel. Steve says it is God's intervention — racegoers cross
the wall of eyes of shame to sin by squandering their money with the
bookies.

'That fellow over there is probably only eighteen. He has, I bet, been
showing the nomads in southern Tunisia how to live. Imaginez vous,
teaching them to smoke cigarettes. Eighteen-years old and accepts
hash and humanism. I am sure it is disgusting.' Fucking blueshirt, at
least my people didn't despise.

Airless room, nothing but the heat of darkness. Hard mattress, Steve
slops and slops with the wine bottle. Talks, looking at me. I don't want
any. Gazing at my chest, he's glad there's no hair, pull up dirty sheet.
Carnivorous glance. It seems . . . . He doesn't jump on you though.
Verbal type, that's how he gets so far with the likes of me. Chats us up
for months. Spiritual eh . . . .

'V-i-n-c-e . . . V-i-n-c-e . . . .'

'So go to sleep.'

'I love you so much. Can I go . . . over . . . over . . . to you?'

'Go and dream.'

'Please, just for a second.'

'I told you I wouldn't. I came out here on condition I wouldn't have
to.'

'You don't now how much — rather what ways — I love you. You
have no idea, it's real love not sex — as such.'

'I mean what I say, Steve, just now I wouldn't even say I love you as
a friend.'

'Let me just get into bed with you. I won't do anything except hold
you. I love you, for God's sake trust me.'

'If you're the gingerman, I'm not Miss Frost.'

Morn: rolls, coffee.

Brings *Arcadia* to breakfast. Smiles over it. mildness mollifies, a soft
cheek can turn, faster a soft wet cheek . . . .

His quote from Sidney's book, 'Though he were naked his nakedness
was to him an apparel . . . .'

*   *   *

Vincent runs.

To the Atocha station. For that beaker out of the old south. Soft seat, more expensive train. Vine windows, a tablecloth stained with the deep south, trellised views. Off-colour, look at colour of dogs — trek through it. Bright toy lights which are not artificial. This northern islander never seen the like: wearing dark glasses a long time in a good dream.

Bang, drum, firewash, flare works. Cordoba. Bodhran missing. Explosion without it. Raphaelwings. Bridge of bridge — bladefire, they make angels' wings like swords. Flowerheads or green (pointille) pots. White houses stay here. Rocks streaming into my distances. Through grills into mossy parlours, you notice the dust, the caked world when you get to the river. Little bits of a brown god who makes mud pies. I never saw nothin' so beautiful.

Square of the sorrows. Christ pinned up amid cobbles and lanterns. He wept over Jerusalem, he silhouettes for Cordoba. Almost pouts. Soft figures pad through. Women cross themselves and pass, lighting candles; Christ, neurotic husband-replacer. They want to touch the beyond-mere-man.

Men don't pray: the noise in the streets is their god.

The desert laid out in the intricate body of a girl. Roman bridge, Mezquita (soul comes from the soil nomadically), perhaps a market, many semi-glitterers bargaining and pillars a-gleam. Most of the tiles are gone. (The girl becomes history, becomes a new city plan.) Lovely to pass the thin orange-trees — they seem to grow at random in the court, not Christian-planted. Through the door into a forest, labyrinth of red-white striped columns inordinately slendered. Zebra crossings. A wilderness of marble: vast are the distances, the universal rays browsing through. Steve took me to a wall like a small January crib to show me the names of priests murdered by international agents of atheistic Communism. Black crows against a wall of once-free Spain, waiting to be shot. Was it sunny that day?

Sundew on your face outside, you keep it as you go back through the Jewish Quarter. White walls, roses and dahlias. Pebbles on the floors of the patios I hadn't noticed before. Azure sleep, palm and plantain, like a stream of lamps.

Bring me a tablet whiter than a star, I think of Keats.

That word I am stumbling over 'sensuous'. The teacher in school said it was invented by Milton to get away from 'sensual'. It is alleged the latter went deeper into froth and foam. Cordoba's like the end of a wave. I plunge in but I am part of Steve's will. I am the complete aesthetic object in it. He looks at me twice for every once at white wall or orange bough. Sky Keatsian autumnally summer — yes, he came again last night and I let him. What it was like I don't remember, the vino a thick sherry from the tap was so strong. Montilla is down the railway track. He was surprised I let him and I couldn't do it very well. He started talking about apples I seem to remember. What a bourgeois, he likes to talk when he fucks.

I'll be sick tonight, summer is over in a week. He's neither sensual nor sensuous, maybe the few times will satisfy. Joyce's thing about love between men and friendship between men and women being impossible is in one sense comic but also tragic: 'love' and 'friendship', I don't understand these words.

Unlike the sequined gent whom Steve calls Freddy, I arrived in Cordoba lonely and far from seducible. But we found the most perfect bar in the world. The Calle de Munda (Caesar's victories always yielded material precision — the murage created something more beautiful) old and open to the sky, wooden booths on two floors, corrida posters back a hundred years: Joselito's last fight and a photo of Mejias, gored; Papa would have the bar open all night, dancing. The proprietor an old man with wiry white thatch, silently traying chatos. Steve likes him because another old man in an outer barrio said he was a Falangist, pulling fingers across his throat. Bar next door has a jolly bore in it, claims he was a pilot at the bombing of Teruel. Last night he grabbed the Penguin Lorca Steve took to the bar — 'creyendo que era mozuela . . . .' Laughing, Steve had taken it because: 'Fue la noche de Santiago.' Flowers of wine, halfmoon waterfalls. Bye, bye.

Seville is different, she ain't a lady. Keats wouldn't fall in love. And the food is oily — Steve keeps on talking about Christ dining with whores. Also he's mean, we go to the cheapest restaurants. Me and my stomach won't stand it.

To turn to Miss Seville, oh she's a grand mot. Castenets, flowerdolls, other hideous dolls of the lotteries, bad change for which the tambourines make up. Fuckalingaling. Scarlet variegated azulejos. A sweet tongue sleuth. Girls, the greenest light, parks are not just for girls to mind babies.

Stephen's Green with Steve, beds and flowers.

'Steve, remember eh . . . what Liam O'Flaherty said in the pub the day we walked through the Green?'

'Can't . . . .'

'What I feel now, "I am a pagan".'

'Yea, but remember now what he said after that, "You look at me as if I owe you some money".'

'Ha ha. Best I thought what he said about Jack Lynch: "He was a serving-boy for Christy Ring".'

I try to put down my feelings about Spain.

'It reminds me of feelings, I dunno quite what they are. It's like Tschaikovsky's Fourth played by a Russian orchestra. At the end of the first movement there is a dark almost suicidal moment — a muttering.'

What a madonna of the grave you must have been, Maria Louisa. My favourite museopause. Steve doesn't like it as much as the huge old Victorian ramble of a hotel here, the Alfonso XIII (he loves that handsome stamp and coin-curley boy forever), crazy about its plants and pots inside its huge yellow barrack shape. We have to walk around it — two tieless spalpeens couldn't get in — he relaxes and we go to a little place for blancos: to drink to the memory of our kidneys. We stay, we settle to think against each other. My park, alleys, grooves, nooks, shadiness. His palaces, theatres, tiles, cafés, benches, fountains. Nature against people — instinct versus artiface is not quite right: man touches my grass and shrub and nature contributes to his buildings but still a wide distance, an airy space outdoors against hanging from ceiling in from window.

Steve in the Alcázar. He was stunned, lost. I admit to the effect of a little tracery myself but he's showy with delicacy. Whimpering to himself, under the Torre de Oro: 'God's gold.' A nice how do you do.

If we hadn't such a shit place to doss in. Fault: his Celtic mania. From the station, proceeding by the foolery of a map, to a street of the ould name, Calle O Donnell. Red Hugh his confirmation name, that madness over again, the hero died unmarried almost a boy. The streets of the roaring boys on cycles. How much Ulster truck power can you stand? When the curtains have nerves. (When the collateral descendent serves the little fat fucky queen.) It is a route out. My first case of juggernaut shock. Not as bad as his monarchy vulgarity. The pensión is otherwise non-controversial, huge hall, long staircase, rooms around the patio, actually nice beds. Parrot in a cage as you mount the stair.

Symons' *The Cities*, I borrowed it out of Rathmines library, nor back to Dublin will it go. Great on·the vixen city — city of pleasure I haven't the dough in my pocket. City of pain, carousing with him, I have given it to him as he has given it to me. He insists on calling it love but I wear the amulet of innocence around my neck, difference is innocence. I want a woman. I am never far from him, I go for a walk but he tells me the café where he'll be. Waiting like a guerilla captain of perverts with a newspaper in his hands.

African dwarf-palm I believe. Roses that blossom like old Hollywood heroines. Me chestnut at every corner, me sweet chestnut. They will make a maneen of me yet. We are by the Moorish wall, this is the Quarter of love, pilgrimage can be peril. Scholars of it, us sparrow-haunted poets, we have to discuss the patron.

'Have you read your Byron?'

'I have on me nanny, you have to be in *The Sunday Times* Monday lunch club for that.'

'Get on with you, Steve, you must have read him as a UCD student.'

'Don Juan is it — how are you. Don Juan that was for Jesuits in private, besides the story is so ridiculous . . . .'

So his brilliant mind has to condescend as usual.

'Here, Vince, Church as well as State hand out application forms for virility. He's a satanic heterosexual lover — that makes it real. Something blacker than virility comes into it. Despair with cunt — "After real love becomes an endless impossible novelty".'

Feminine city I begin to like as long as Steve doesn't. Triana across. White, semi-porcelain. Up and down the river. I am thinking of the — the shape of the Venus shell. It's not pathetic. Baked I am on this riverbank. Queers can't say what they want to: your tiny hand is frozen.

Pottery, that's what they do here, women potters. Sweating in their muslin. Semi-transparency, followers of Juan. The heat's on. Another bar. Shivering in the heat. Another surge. We can't stand each other. Confrontation philanthropy.

Theme of the breakfast debate today is his new enthusiasm, J. R. Ackerley. There will be temperature in it.

'Look, Steve, the party is over, the camp is pulled out. If you must know, Ackerley is the enemy. Empty, correct, all manners. Polite and civilised of course — like Forster underneath. Hollow and two centuries old. The English honestly thought in the eighteenth century they were living in the Roman Empire.'

The next bar and we get to the heart, the nitty gritty. No more gritos for me. He'll be blue after it is over.

'From the very beginning Franco has been terrible. The reason I can't stand Spain is that people are cowed. Franco gave nothing. No structure, no adventure, no contact with reality. There's nothing to come after him. He set up nothing. The Spain you like, Azorin, Jiménez, the club of Alfonso Trece, is the king's only. Oh it survived, what was left of it, into the first part of the dictatorship. It still lives on Sundays in ABC — photos of the bearded literate who have toiled at the tertulia . . . Padraic Colum, Monk Gibbon.'

Steve comes back with some Walt Disney, the country is a museum piece, its culture has been frozen — reanimation soon. And having escaped time it will flower. Course it's bullshit because it's not true. I made him look at the jukebox, the telly. And we mindfight back to Ireland.

'Anyhow, how could you live in that coldness?'

'De Valera did, lads and lassies in mead-serving costume, the wise and overflowing Gaelic even flowing beer for breakfast, Ruritania in Rosscarbery . . . .'

'Corrigan, right Dev had a museum, Gaelic as this is Castilian, both Catholic, but there was mobility. We were isolated but we were kept alive somehow. Because democracy continued.'

This river: why do I have to walk beside you like this? I can't get time to debrief my angelicity. River tidal like ghost, docks like it too. Victorian dream cranes. Spectral trade union even. Tourist cruisers, stone and seagulls. Tins of olives they are stacking.

I have enough pesetas to get to the embassy in Madrid. I wonder where it is? They will believe me there. Mother known. Only a little troublesome, I have nothing to fear.

These last rows are simply technical affairs. That redness in the face because in the morning I drink coke not wine. Two horrible grimaces when I strike against his custom of leaving the bar when his glass is empty and he doesn't want another. I stay: he comes back in the door choking.

While he is still speaking I rush out and get a taxi. Collect passport, few clothes from the pensión and off to the estación. The one railway that does go down the quays. Through a line of carriages, traps, laden burros. I remember yesterday's conversation.

'All the donkey panniers, Steve.'

'Yes, West Clare — the turf creels. The morning outside the cream- ery chatting.

Rolling the window down, dangerous moment. When things can go wrong. Look down the platform to see.

I'm shaking with anguish. I recognise what I have to do. Survival is not perfect by any means, it will have to do for now. Cancer is operated on. I have lived in a half-world with half-sight, my heart and life withers. I become a wreath. Elegy.

Not any kinder to myself than to you.

Why couldn't I take your tantrums? I disliked them — yet the fact is I have fallen out of all love with you. Fuck you — you are genuinely saintly and do what you have to do quite naturally. There has to be a great effort before I can live the truth.

To go back to my own country: to understand, to measure it.

*   *   *

Stephen lingers on an island.

Between friendship, 'the noblest emotion of man', and sex lies the valley of tears. Tear fear. Troublin' wraiths of fog. I have been obscured. You were brought up in the West, you read novels, you learned the convention, you cut the leaves and found it the common sensitive plant.

Posse, posse on what plateau are you riding? Alcalde, here's my fucked out heart. Red soil of the Balearics: blood. Making the earth rich, what stands out. This island is an escarpment of my farewell. I am Eurydiced. I maybe won't have it again but I know all about it now. Smiler waver through carriage window. Staying, lingering on platform:

tender performance. I was Hamlet to his Hector (he will become Hamlet writing poems all night when he is rid of me). Eejit me: womb-fooler and fooling. I need balm, calm of the blood stream. Forget stupidity, deliver yourself into this yellow sunset. So crayon. Windows divided by terracotta colonettes. Today a panegyric for what I see, scarlet, green or turquoise.

Doubly foreign, Germans to the right of me, Yankees to the left.

'Give me a full nelson, man.'

'I play pool when I play pool.'

'Shit, man, you make me feel like Hemingway when I haven't any money.'

Don't listen to the bums, I must understand the morality of love. Though angels fear to tread through it. Love water: was Venus unhappy? First proposition from the *Arcadia*: 'The bloodie shafts of Cupid's War, with amatists they headed are.' Second is, write it down on the napkin: 'Brains turn to sawdust in the presence of sex.' The third I figure out: 'Even in the sawdust world there must be one who gets tired of it'.

Morality turns to music like everything else. The series of sounds crashing on the other shore, the pier's slithery green stones the continuous gap in the limestone wall over foam — how did Vince migrate all that way to Judastown? The letter duly arrives.

Dear Steve,

This is the most difficult and cruelest letter I've ever had to compose. I'm shaking with anguish. Despite trembling the time comes for the truth. To live with a lie, a deep dissimulation of the soul is deforming and ultimately fatal. The truth is like a surgeon's knife: to be a writer or any kind of human being this pain must be borne. I ask you to see that and to acknowledge it.

As you made clear yesterday, you understand what has been the trouble since I came to Spain — the lack was definitely, as you said, not on your part but on mine. I couldn't communicate what I didn't feel. The first night in Valladolid, in the early morning, in that square, my heart closed like a fist when I realised my mind hadn't changed. I could have stayed in Spain a few months, perhaps simulate a more communicative relationship, and finally left to simulate further from a distance. But it isn't the truth. My heart would have dirt in it and I believe it would have killed my soul and my poetry.

I fell in love with you in Ireland like a child. I didn't swim in the sea of love, I dived down deep to the bottom. You have to come up for air, I kept coming up. I sought to reduce the

relationship. You remember when you'd ask me to say that I'd
love you always, I'd say that we can never know how love ends.
    If love fails then it turns to hatred. I'm escaping that at least.
    I love you in my own way but not the love that should be.
        Goodbye,
            Vince

He left the house, fled the hearth the images the glasses to be filled, he
will not descend for breakfast. He has departed the village where
people live, he is a loner a liver for himself, a diner solo, maybe
ultimately even a womanless man. An insurer, an usurer.

    Is the moral tale as simple as I allege it to be? I'll take my chances on
it. I'll say: love doesn't end, is remembered, like the cup is Remembr-
ance in the Church. Do this in remembrance. Of me. Of thee. Only lift
it, it is heavy. I promise. I promise to keep wine in it.

    If your heart be not ritual.

    And destiny comes. Kerrigan wrote the day I got back. Offered his
house in Palma for a month or six weeks. Anodyne of a friend's house
when he is not there. I came to a golden or yellow luminosity which
clings to many classical sights. I came, I see, I pray to Remembrance to
recover.

Up and down the smooth street for a sign of Castilla. A barsign has: 'Se
hable Español'. But not very interestingly. To the jukebox and
gimmick stares of the officially and definitely queer — the expatriate
decloseted. In El Tereno of American bars.
    'Pardon me, what do you do for sex.'
    'I think, I write, I eat, I drink, I pray for recovery.'
    'Who are you?'
    'I am the stranger who ate a virgin . . . .'
    'You are observing us.'
    'I am having a drink.'
    'Who are you — are you Margaret Mead in disguise?'
Some nice looking kids come in, maybe the first wave of the made
bisexual by record player. Play your own bisexual kit. David is a special
beautiful one who sits for hours, a beer narcissus. My previous inquirer
was over, gazing at David talking to me.
    'And what do you do with beauty?'
Annoy them all, their naive primitivism about the erection being
sacred.
    'Pay for it.'
    'I'd consider it.'
Will this clowning, disrooted scamping, keep Vince out? Black him
out. Travel, drink, almost similar landscapes.

First childhood of love is the permanent hell. Radiant contrived child, young at forty. Ever wistful, star aware, half cook-hungry. Autochthonous, yes, and free. It's too early, it's too late. The taking of star years, my dears.

(Dissolute always drunken Dedo Modigliani burst into a café: 'I've just been through Dante's hell — wonderful wonderful hell.' The sport of hell, soft breeze playing about you, chittering of birds you don't know.)

Bougainvillaea walls, lemon trees to squeeze into a bottle of gin, Belver Castle, Miró's studio, the sparkling bay. Not busy. Flights of steps, mad dog, palms, scented punishment. Almonds sweet and bitter, distrust of the annular, I will remain ringless. Balcony with chair and table for the vista parcial: Gaudí's baldachino across blue water, the Seventh Fleet.

Down in his hotel Batista, dark fat crow, plucking at his meat. Ex-skipper of the floating brothel, bah now everyone has to work. To the ciudad by bus strap-holding . . . Plaza de la Reina . . . heavy moulded houses arms over door . . . lament for the walls knocked down only in 1900 . . . shall I write a political poem?

Take a bus up steep mountain road. Stay with Ruthven in his cottage, door and window platform over a universe of shredded corn. Japanese print-view down a long way of stone to the sea. Taken with the huge potato omelette I wrapped with me.

Back to Palma, in the restaurant omelette trece pesetas, patatas guisades cuatro pesetas (very nice), mixture of patatas and coliflor. Very nice. 'Goo nigh. Wank you very much.' Weather warming and the long breezes coming from the sea up the paths. Paths of once-burning cinders. Ashes through the body. Singe.

God, flies on the street on the way to the American pub. Someone says what they like about it is the jukebox. What thou lovest well stays on the jukebox. Hell, the place is filling up. The boys are younger tonight, lots of girls too, not all faghags.

'Are you gay?'

'Eh . . . I don't quite understand that word.'

'Okay, are you a faggot?'

'Excuse me, are you from San Francisco?'

'Are you a faggot? Just because you have been rejected by some chick doesn't mean all chicks are like that. I've been rejected by a lot of dudes but there's no way I'm gonna be a lesbian, man.'

Others in the lemon light.

'Well, please fuck me now.'

'Not now, man.'

'I have been rejected by another girl, there's only men left.'

I remember the apples of his mouth.

I cannot speak any more of you. What I have to boast about is undelectable memory. I go out every night, much too sane to stay indoors with grief. I can enjoy. Sweet little electric line Calle Infanta Isabella to Soller. Peaches, oranges, roads, sweeping bends sudden olive orchards. Carob trees. At line's end a wide fall of steps, passing huge-ceilinged nineteenth-century fonda, to the street and the fisherman's bar at the harbour. Another day idled. I have conquered. Vince, you would like it here.

Shebeening to the immortal music of the shee.

Kilkee, New Oleans, Milwaukee,
1974-80

IVY LODGE
Tomas O Murchadha

TOMAS O MURCHADHA was born in Cork in 1945. After University College, Cork, he joined the Abbey Theatre and directed the first production of *The Tailor and Ansty* for the Dublin Theatre Festival in 1968. He has also worked as a director at the Taibhdhearch in Galway. Tomas O Murchadha has been living in south Kerry for some years, writing fiction and journalism. He is married to American painter Melissa Crawford Murphy.

'Wanna go toilet,' a woman screeched. She rocked backwards and forwards. 'Wanna go toilet . . . .' The January sunshine blinded from the wet bark of oak trees; she screeched at closed windows, black hairs on her face bristling with tears. Outside the staff club she rocked, appealing to the windows of the nurses, tortured by the empty sun, unsoothed by the red carpet of leaves, the black oak trees.

'Wanna go toilet.' Sun on the cold bricks, ice on the seat soaking her knickers. She would be there, rocking, forever, or until she burst, or did something.

In the staff coffee-shop some faces looked out; hazy they muttered into their cups, sheltering their eyes from the belting sun . . . a hand touching hair; a fall of sugar into coffee; a jukebox playing.

Someone led the woman away, and she quietened, pulling on the sleeve of the white coat to keep her balance.

About the grounds of Ivy Lodge hospital everything was moving: grass was thawing and lifting; from under trees and bushes starchy frost silvered stubbornly. At Ivy Lodge pond the ducks paddled calmly, though the lake itself was still a sluggish-brown. Up and down every passage and footpath people were walking: men in suits and waistcoats, workers in overalls, long lines of patients and each with a nurse at its head in white coat or navy blue cape; some of the patients glancing about like birds, others doubled over staring at the ground, some standing on corners calling out to other patients or to the staff: 'Hallo. Nice day. I've seen you before, remember?' There was an air of liveliness, as if the unexpected sun had warmed people's spirits. Along the hedges and among the trees an occasional squirrel had come out, to run along the branches and eye this new sun, testing its goodwill before going back to its lair among the oaks.

In the cafeteria lunch was in noisy progress: English faces mixed with Indian paleness and attentive Chinese; a group of heavy Spaniards ate quickly while a cluster of handsome Indian people merely picked at their food. At one table work was being discussed: 'These people are simply less intelligent than you or me. That's all. They need love. They're not *mad*.' At another the subject was music: '"Orpheus in the Underworld". You'll know the can-can. No? That's from it.' Steam hissed and gushed over all; pink girls danced up to the coffee-machine, plates and cutlery were swept onto a trolley by a light black Spaniard, while an Englishman like a side of beef ran everything, and remembered the old days. Nobody sipped diffidently or dawdled his spoon among the baked beans: everybody kept pace and everybody ate well.

In the staff coffee-shop it was quieter: a large woman sat alone with a little dog at her feet, a few people sat silently reading newspapers, while a tall good-looking man swept the floor — he wore a long grey overcoat and had very black Elvis Presley styled hair. The overcoat was tight and buttoned-up, and gave him a military appearance, but the hairstyle looked old-fashioned; on most of his fingers were coloured rings, such as children buy for pennies in toy-shops. He swept so hard that the timber of the brush banged the wooden floor. He was patient Andrew Pocock, aged thirty-seven, formerly of Reading.

At a table by the windows, overcoat hanging from his shoulders, sat a slight middle-aged man with a thin beard. He stared absently out of the window and plucked his beard with his thumb and index finger. He was the consultant psychiatrist, Doctor James.

Behind the staff club lay the driveway through the wood, the main gate of Ivy Lodge, and the road to London.

Wilson left the low green bus behind him. The day was bright and freezing and the exhaust hung above the road. The ground was dry and cold; he made his way across and faced up the drive to the hospital, pulling the collar of his coat about his neck. The yellow suitcase he was carrying looked larger that it was as it bumped against his leg.

He thought of cabbages, overgrown and putrid, swimming in green juice; buckets of brown slop and withered faces. Big heads: he saw children strapped into go-carts with heads as big as cauldrons. With short steps he avoided the pale patches of frost that radiated out from underneath the large hydrangeas.

'Excuse me. Where is the Night Office? . . . Thank you.' — that face cold but thankfully tight.

Inside the door he met one: in a white smock that revealed his genitals. Wilson smiled; his face trembled. The bright staring eyes followed him; he had to put down his case to knock at the door. 'C. Burke. Chief Night Officer'. He stumbled into the heated office and saw a man at a desk, speaking into a telephone; a large white man — like a Viking.

'Twenty-eight pillows,' the man was saying. 'Pillows. All feathers. Yes, twenty-eight feathers.'

Wilson saw his school classroom, everything a light yellow colour with a blue ceiling and the blackboard. Sunlight on the desks and a fat boy with a tweed suit. Bad teeth. Ollie Radford it was. Ollie Radford.

'Ah Wilson is it? Starting tonight eh? I'm Burke. A sixteen-hour job this you know. Well I hope you'll be happy with us.'

'Thank you. I'm sure. What exactly . . . where will I go to?' Why should it be Ollie Radford?

'St David's. You'll be with Kennedy. A sound fellow. Irish. So am I. Come on, I'll just take you over to your room. Male nurses' block, right over the cafeteria. Handy!' The man stormed out like a soldier, Wilson limping after him.

Alone in his new room he looked out of the window. He tried to think of Christmas, of holly and coal fires and the radio crooning softly. But out there it was all space, with figures moving everywhere.

He was afraid of the smell.

But all was quiet; there was no smell. Except a light sweet smell and a soft rumble of breathing. Each bed contained its white parcel. In the centre of the ward was a lamp shaded by a sheet, a table and two armchairs covered in sheets. It was eerie but warm. His bowels began to relax.

Kennedy had a clear boyish face with freckles and a neat grey suit.

The grinning face in the smock grinned in Wilson's mind again, but he smiled and shook the firm dry hand of Kennedy.

'You'll be on nights then? You'll get to know the ropes. Come on . . . I'll show you.'

He followed Kennedy into the dark end of the ward. A glittering eye or a frightened face; one amazingly asleep head. Kennedy wore a pair of furry slippers.

'Hallo professor,' Kennedy whispered to an old bald bird-head. 'Still awake? This is Mr Wilson, a new staff.'

The scraggy head perked up. 'You go to the movies?' he said, 'Monroe. She took a powder.'

'There's a thing!' Kennedy nodded seriously.

Wilson tried to smile. 'You like the movies?' he managed to say.

'Yeh,' said the professor, disappointed.

Kennedy walked on; he was a dapper figure, wide but low-sized. He looked at ease, carrying himself like a man who is content but not bored. Shining his torch on the beds he spoke quietly, as if showing a private collection of his own, something he prized. When they returned to the table he was beaming. 'You'll get to know them all,' he said, 'they're like children. If you hear a fart in the night you'll recognise the arse!'

They sat in the armchairs on either side of the table. The quiet was perfect; thirty grown men breathed in solid silence.

'Do you come from these parts?' Kennedy inquired.

'No. London.'

'Oh. Not too far. I'm from Ireland myself. Originally.'

'Oh?'

'Yes. I cum over 'ere twenty-five year ago. When I was seventeen.'

Wilson continued the patter as Kennedy drummed on the table with his fingers. Irishmen always told you where they came from first thing. There was warmth in this man's clear eyes and in his soft voice — a brogue with occasional English vowels thrown in rather affectedly. Wilson found himself imagining the man watching television and drinking Guinness: the way he would put down the glass by his side and smack his lips. He found himself smiling at Kennedy, as if they were old friends, relaxing together by a fire, recounting the old days when they worked together in Ivy Lodge: 'Remember the professor? Always at the movies. Monroe and Jayne Mansfield! Remember the time . . .' He wanted to keep the log fire . . . He looked at the man talking and drumming the table; the schoolboy-man.

Kennedy rose and stretched. 'Night medication,' he announced. 'Got to give them their bombs. It's all written out below in the office.

As he followed him around again Wilson felt as if his own body was too big: he was afraid to move his arms and legs. The man was a stranger to him; his grey suit was a light cold metal that rippled; his head was clockwork. Only the back of his neck would be warm to touch.

'Sweeties Johnny. One. Two. Two bombs for you Mr Elersley. One paraldehyde, two paraldehyde. That'll slow you down a bit. Swallow them y'fucker. Swallow them.'

They sat up and opened their mouths like chicks; some of them said 'Mr Kennedy' and dropped off to sleep again. One got out of bed and took a few shivering steps after them.

Time passed to the sound of breathing: as they sat in the half-light looking at the walls they listened; some of it was heavy and rasping, some loud and erratic, some soft and wet. A blue skeletal figure perched on the edge of his bed, his naked body thin and scarred; sleepy, he could not get back into bed — several times he tried but always failed. Now and then a hand fluttered towards the sheets and back again, to rest between his thighs. Wilson watched, almost in awe.

He looked at the bundles in the beds: most were completely hidden under the covers; one or two had legs poking out — but the faces he could see looked perfectly normal. A jaded sigh issued occasionally from the large hooked nose of the skinny creature trying to climb back into his bed.

'That's Lyons — a Jew. Pots of money.' Kennedy dropped words into the silence: been in the army; take them as you find them; married an English girl; three kids; no blacks here then; all Irish; not a bad job — a cushy number.

Time passed easily enough. Papers read. Supper at midnight. Occasional trot to the toilet — Wilson watched these trots with interest, noting that all were different: heavy and lumbering, light and anxious or old and shuffling. One stayed in the toilet too long and they had to go for him — he was staring at the wall, penis in hand. They led him gently back to his bed in silence.

Wrapped in a blanket Wilson struggled to keep unpleasant images out of his mind. He felt slightly sick in his stomach, but it was the sickness of fear. It was not fearful images of the patients that pushed into his mind now, but of Kennedy: he saw him in his grey suit leering at him, his face pink; in an army uniform without arms or legs; tied up entirely in a sack, kneeling by a white chair while crowds of people looked on. There were also images of his schooldays, sickly and rotten.

At six o'clock Kennedy brought coffee — thick and sweet. 'Weary?' 'Not too bad.' He did feel weary, and confused deep down where he could not reach. Supposing he couldn't talk to them, make comical banter with them as Kennedy could? Supposing they thought him strange? Or worse again, supposing he couldn't talk to Kennedy? He shivered deep in the darkness of his spirit; fear and self-pity crept out of the fog.

'Suppose you were screwing a bird,' Kennedy was chattering, revived by the coffee and the sense that dawn was about to begin. 'Suppose you were out to screw the world. You're in bed with this bird, right? Giving her a good seeing-to eh? Ha ha! — No love or anything mind. Just a screw. Well say a bit of respect too, affection like. You fuck her and fuck her and fuck her — you're there and you think you're great. You think your arse is eating chocolate. What a ride you're having eh? And she gets up in the middle of the night to have a piss — What do you make of it? How do you feel? This divine bird . . . ho ho ho! — that beautiful divine body gets out to have a piss? . . .'

For a brief moment Wison felt hate: that neat and healthy man — like a well-wrapped parcel. Then the coffee gradually restored him — he breathed and moved his legs and focused his eyes on the solid objects around him.

He smiled at Kennedy. 'You're a forty-two-year-old schoolboy, you know that? A great Irish schoolboy!'

Kennedy looked at him and grinned — yes, he was a schoolboy; he laughed, proud and flattered at being a schoolboy. They both laughed, smiling their laughter at each other — mischievously.

A head shot up from under a blanket — 'Aiee!' — it was a squashed yellow face, flabby, with huge puffed ears and a nose that had a crease down the centre. The hair was saturated in urine.

'Robbie! Good morning to you.'

'Aiee!'

Another head appeared, wrinkled and withered: 'Morning Mr Kennedy. Morning sir.'

'Morning Hopkins. What are you going to do today?'

'I'm going to pull off Aunt Rosa's drawers and shoot spunk up her cunt. What's the weather like?'

A Sunday in January; the frost remained on the grass all day, cold and black, a freezing dampness fouled the air. Here and there clouds of angry steam gushed in pillars from valves along the pathways. At Ivy Lodge pond the ice was dark brown and dirty; the ducks paddled their hopeless circle. Out in the low-lying fields along the railway, flat pools of water gave the grass a sickly look — like sweat on a pale forehead. Mud was everywhere — on footpaths and roadways, cattle-tracks and feeding-places, in the great valley dug out for the new motorway; huge cranes and diggers lay abandoned among frozen lakes, dwarfed by mountains of grey sand.

The hospital teemed with people: parents, brothers, sisters, aunts. As they walked on the blackening leaves, they passed each other, strolling up and down, across and back. With fur coats, walking sticks, bags of sweets and fruit; they might have been at the park, or by the seaside — they brought with them a hint of coal fires and television, swept carpets and cold meat with salad.

An old lady in a fur coat, an old man, tall, heavy. Between them their son, fawn dufflecoat hanging down in front, buttoned up to the neck against the cold. Arm-in-arm. Padded hat — an epileptic. They walked forward in silence, looking straight ahead. The son could be twenty, thirty, forty.

Two people came along the path, two women. Arm-in-arm. Neither looked at the other. Both could have been forty — they looked exactly alike: heavy cheeks, pale loose mouths, wide ungainly walks. Exactly alike, but the mother was bareheaded, the daughter wore the padded hat.

On a bench sat two parents and a son. Between them a biscuit-tin. She was feeding him cakes. With her hand. Bit by bit, because he would eat them too fast. He did not seem to know them.

Little old ladies, and large old gentlemen. Fords and Fiats and Morris Minors.

One grinning youth, well wrapped up. His parents cheerful and getting into an orange-coloured Ford Escort. Gaily saying goodbye. A fat corgi in the back seat. One foot in the car, one out, waving, hesitating. Sitting in, closing the door. He grinning at the window; they waving and leaning out — advice from mother. Take care. Keep warm. Or whatever. Car starting, pulling slowly away. Keep back. Goodbye. Car moving. Roll up the window. Drive away. Waving. He's running after us, drive away. Car accelerating. Into second. He's still running. Goodbye. Goodbye. Yes dear keep going. Third gear. Goodbye-ee. Goodbye-ee. Tearing down the road. Waving at them — the orange car and the fat corgi, frost on the road. Running. Faster. Blinder. Keep going. Waving. G'bye. G'bye.

'Books.'

'Yes Albert. Go to bed now.'

'Books.'

'They're gone Albert. Come on.' Wilson patted his shoulder.

'Books.' Big Albert Copeland knelt by the door. 'Books.' Looking through the glass. Six-foot-four with white nightgown. Looking for the day staff. To give them a *Daily Mirror*, torn evenly in two.

'They're gone Albert.'

'Books.'

'In the morning Albert. I'll give it to them in the morning. I promise. Come back to bed now.'

'Books. Books.' Resisting, eyes pleading, voice light and soft as a whisper. The huge back curved gently to the glass, scanning the empty stairs.

'Back to bed Albert. You can sleep with the book. Give it to them in the morning. OK?'

Led back by the elbow. 'Books.' Head turning, bewildered. Stately walk, shoulders and hips swinging, feet landing heavily. Into bed with all his other books, *Daily Express*, *Angling Times*, *Irish Post* — four inches thick of them under his back. Putting the *Daily Mirror*, torn neatly in two, on top of the pile, pulling up the mattress on both sides, tucking the over-sheet around his head and shoulders and under the top of the mattress to hold it in position like a tight white parcel.

'Cover up Albert. Bye-byes.'

'Books.'

'Day staff on in the morning Albert. Give the book to Aunt Rosa.'

'Books.'

'Yes Albert, Books.'

Extreme care to be taken with this patient. On no account should he be isolated from other pts. No medication to be administered without written approval of doctor. Extra staff to be on duty at all times. Tends to be violent and hypomanic.

P. James.

The patient was Andrew Popcock. In the staff-club they spoke of him.

'Andrew Pocock's back again. Tried to burn down St George's. Set fire to his bed. I don't know. I just don't know.'

'Should be in Broadmoor that boy. This is a corrective ward, not a bloody prison.'

'And who will take his boots from him? I'll not do it for one. Not me!'

'Got boots?'

'Yeh, big bloody boots.'

'He could lash out.'

'Ha! Lash out mate, lash out?'

A patient at Ivy Lodge for seventeen years, Andrew Pocock had been committed by the courts at the age of twenty, on malicious damage charges. Tall and handsome, the professor had christened him Gregory Peck.

He strode up the ward towards where Wilson was sitting at the white-robed table, his walk straight and steady, his boots ringing loudly on a parquet floor.

'Can I have a smoke sir?'

'Go to bed Pocock, you're not allowed matches.'

'Oh. Sorry sir.' He clattered away down the ward again, banging the door of his private room — set aside for him by Dr James.

Wilson breathed again in relief.

'Andrew's alright,' Kennedy said, when he came upstairs to give the night medication. 'They're all afraid of him, that's all. Those stupid women on the day duty. Don't know how to treat these boys. Sweeties Reggie. Nice sodium amitol.'

His voice was different for each one: to big Albert Copeland he spoke gently, as to a child — 'Have you some nice books Albert? Good. Have a nice read. 'To Robbie Hunt — the tiny creature with the squashed face — he spoke in a rough, jocular way: 'Are you wet y'fucker? Get up you sod. No bloody good you are. Care for a smoke?' He gave him a spent match, and the little crooked man, who was nearly fifty and couldn't speak a word, took it and smoked it, expertly and ostentatiously, flicking the ash with his little finger, and looking at his imaginary wristwatch importantly. The squashed old face grinned in huge pleasure, almost matched by Kennedy's boyish grin as he watched — 'Wouldn't you like to take him home?' Another he dragged and pulled out of bed, shoving back his head and forcing open his mouth.

The professor was waiting for him: 'I see Peck's back boss?'

'Aye,' said Kennedy, wordly wise, 'set fire to them again.'

The professor shook his ragged old skull, 'Captain Ahab,' he said, 'Captain Ahab all over again. Tst tst,' and he laid his head mournfully back on the pillow, chewing his tablets with a saintly expression.

He spoke to all in their own language: 'Wake up Hopkins. Was she nice then? Right, go back to sleep and give her a good seeing to then, all right? Tell her I was asking for her.'

'All right Mr Kennedy. I'll do that Mr Kennedy. I'll her her you was askin' for her and then I'll take her knickers off.' The leathery old face of Hopkins remained unmoved, but he gave a dirty little cackle.

Some he sent scurrying to the toilet, others he tucked in with a whispered goodnight, more he shouted at and threatened. When he came to Pocock's room he closed the door.

'Goodnight Andrew.'

'Goodnight Mr Kennedy.'

'I have your night tablets Andrew.'

'Thank you sir. Thank you.'

Kennedy sat on the bed while he took the tablets, and remained looking at Pocock for some time. 'Silly bugger,' he said impassively.

'I know sir, I made a mistake. I made a silly mistake.'

'You know you'll be watched night and day in here? Locked in. No visits to the town. No going out alone. St George's was freedom compared to this.'

'Yes sir.' Pocock didn't know what to do with his face — he half smiled and looked at Kennedy's mouth.

Kennedy stretched out a hand and touched Pocock's hair — the eyes fluttered upwards in confusion. Absently his fingers tidied the stray locks, over the temple and behind the ear; Pocock's expression flickered. Kennedy's hand came to rest softly on the crown of the broad head.

'I used to have hair like that Andrew,' Kennedy said, quietly, to himself.

'Did you sir? Did you?' Pocock brightened, relieved, 'It's an Elvis style sir. Elvis Presley wears it.'

'Elvis is dead Andrew. He used to wear it. Many years ago now.' He remained looking into the nervous eyes.

'Is he dead sir? Is Elvis dead?'

Strong hair. Black and strong.

'So is Buddy Holly. Plane crash.'

Combs out thick and heavy, I know.

'And Eddie Cochran. In a car.'

'Yes Andrew, they're all dead. Jim Reeves and Grace Moore and the Big Bloody Bopper. But it doesn't matter to you, does it? Because you never really believed in them, did you. Well I'll tell you a secret Andrew. Neither did I.'

All dead.

'I never believed. But all the time I carried around something . . . what was it? Like an empty bucket I couldn't shake off — it came everywhere with me, rattling and laughing . . . it was myself.'

Pocock's eyes were steady but Kennedy was not looking at them now — his head had fallen on his chest, his mouth open, the man in the iron mask choking on his own beard. Pocock jumped up suddenly as if a thought had just struck into his mind: 'Is Little Richard dead?'

'No. No Andrew. Little Richard is still going. He's quite a lively old gentleman I believe.' Kennedy smiled, regaining his usual composure.

Pocock snorted with laughter, his face wrinkled up almost in pain as his big loose mouth split his face; he roared and cackled with laughter, until Kennedy thought his big sturdy head would cleave in two. Then he suddenly stopped.

'Mister Kennedy?' he said anxiously.

'Yes?'

'They want me to hand in my boots. Can I keep my boots?'

Kennedy looked at the boots on the floor by the locker: they were scruff-marked, with the wedge toes turned up, creased and muddy; Pocock's face was eager and intent, his eyes strained and furtive.

'Stupid cunt,' said Kennedy, and with a burst of anger he fumed out of the room, 'keep your piddling little boots.'

'Good Golly Miss Molly,' came the joyful shout from the bed.

*   *   *

It was the M.V. *Innisfallen* that carried Malachy Kennedy, aged seventeen, to Fishguard in 1952.

He had heard the name Innisfallen before: it was an enchanting name, one thrown about in the days of summer when Joe or Bridget came. Joe brought a motorcar, and it came on the *Innisfallen* — a boat that could carry big motorcars, and all the people too!

And hadn't master Hegarty said that Innisfallen was an enchanted place where somebody met a beautiful woman on a white horse and went to the land of youth? And something about monks and saints and scholars? All that in Killarney, just across the mountains.

He imagined the boat to be as big as Mangerton — no, Carrantwohill, sharp and steep, and to be coloured white and gold, with the funnel up above the clouds.

He could feel Cork city when he and his father reached the Western Road in the hackney car, driven by Dan Jerry Sullivan the local butcher. Aunt Kate, his father's sister, lived on the Western Road, and so they had to 'call in on her — it wouldn't be right'. The hackney stopped and they went down some steps to her house — one of several all together — but Malachy's eyes looked down the road, where he could see the air thickening over the city, where cars became denser, and buildings grew taller and more strange-looking.

He kept quiet and still during the tea and scones: they sat — his father and Kate and Dan Jerry — the mens caps on the polished mahogany table, his aunt in a flowered apron she must have brought from the country, light from the window shadowing them. Outside: a tiny yard with drains, a flowerpot, and flowers growing on tops of walls.

In later years he could never remember what was said at that mahogany table, but the memory haunted him: the rhythms of the voices, the strange bared heads of his father and the butcher — unmanning them somehow — the fine cups and saucers, the yard; all the time knowing that the city was rumbling away just near at hand and that the *Innisfallen* towered up out of the heart of it, waiting for him. But he remained quiet and still, and refused a second scone, until Kate made him have it, and he blushing beetroot.

As they left the dark house Kate threw holy water at his face — half jocosely. 'Aren't you sad going away?' she called.

'Naw. I aren't sad at all,' he replied, blushing again, wondering if he should have said he was sad — but what was there to be sad about?

'The blessings of God on ye,' she said as she closed the gate.

'That's a quare thing to say,' his father remarked in the hackney.

'What so?' bluffed Dan Jerry, who knew.

' "The blessings of God on ye" like that.'

'Ah well people have to be saying something.'

But Malachy's father never forgave his sister Kate for that remark, and to her dying day he never spoke to her again, though he was seen weeping at her funeral.

The boat was indeed as big as Carrantwohill, and as glorious as he imagined it. Though it was a splotchy green colour, to him it shone and radiated with every possible delight. It seemed as if the boat was *his*, to do what he liked with, and that it would keep him enchanted for ever. Timber railings and lifebelts and little round windows — and men in uniforms with gold on their shoulders. And a bar! — a public house in the middle of a ship where his small round father and the tall thin Dan Jerry talked and drank and shouted, and stroked his head and shoulders and shook their heads at him sadly. They even began to make him feel sad, though there was so much to see: so many men walking around with big swanky cases, women with fur collars on their coats and accents like uncle Joe's — saying things like: 'Reaching Paddington five-and-twenty after eight. All roight love?'

As the two navy-blue backs, one round and wobbly, the other long and swaying, retreated down the gangplank, Malachy waved fiercely after them. They stumbled on the quayside, wavered, and just caught each other's sleeves. They grinned up at the little hatch, and they were gone.

On my own, Malachy thought, his entire body thrilling so that he had to run . He ran down every corridor in the steerage part of the ship, up every stairway and around the deck, looking down into the bottle-green water. 'On my own,' he chanted aloud. 'No Mammy no Mary no Pat no *him*. No griddle-cakes no rosary no cows no going to the hill. No Con Harrington to mock me no Cathleen Sullivan to laugh at me. No master Hegarty no Fr Dillon no Harrington's dog. No bog no rain no buttermilk no boots no stupid big raincoats. No washing my feet no chasing the bull no dirty eejits throwing lumps of turf at me on summer nights at the crossroads. Oh holy God and his blessed mother I'm glad of it. Nothing for me from this day only dear old London town!'

With a mighty roaring and churning the ship left the dock — they were on the water! Malachy kept going from one side of the deck to the other. He saw big houses and trees, and a stone castle down by the water, fine fields of grass and factory chimneys. And the great town of Cobh with its cathedral sitting on top like a hat. And the forts where the English soldiers used to be, when Cork was the most fortified harbour in the world. And Roche's Point, the lighthouse on the very edge of that world.

He watched Roche's Point disappear — become a tiny white dot. They were now passing Waterford or Wexford, and night was coming down. He could just make out the shapes of houses on some parts of the shore. He was standing in the back of the boat, above the flag, when the lighthouse finally disappeared. The ship was chugging steadily; the night was cold; the sound of singing came from below. It dawned on him that all the people on the shore — in the houses he could just make out, where the lights were beginning to flicker — would be staying where they were, and that all the people who were singing 'Kevin Barry' down in the ship were going away — somewhere else. He thought of the two men he had been with all day: drinking in pubs, sitting at the table with the light shadowing them, their backs retreating down the gangplank, getting smaller, their little stumble on the quay, holding the sleeves of each other's navy-blue suits . . . those were the moments he meant when he said, 'They should have told me.' As he watched the coast of Ireland — and the word 'Ireland' found its way into his throat and stuck there — disappear, he thought of that stumble on the quayside, and their glance at each other while gripping the sleeves, and he said, 'Why didn't they tell me.'

A stranger came up to him and pointed at his bundle: 'Ah lad. You'll never go back now.'

Malachy blushed again, quite beetroot he felt — like a tomato. 'What do I want back there for? Shur shur there's nothing back there shur only oul' bog an' oul' hill an' . . . an' oul' wather!' — and he ran away from the stranger, into the toilet, hugging his bundle and crying.

The ship was just beginning a gentle roll.

Aunt Bridget looked different at Paddington station — everything about her was different. She was smaller, her face was tighter, paler; there was coldness about her shoulders and her clothes seemed to make her walk clipped and hard. Her voice was the most different part of her: it was more English, less humorous, less relaxed; it was hardened and dwarfed by the black pillars and dingy Victorian ironwork above their heads; it was made smaller and certainly less significant by the taxis, the buses ('Buses inside the house') and the queues of bowler-hatted men, men stopping taxis with umbrellas, and red post-boxes — a whole city under one roof.

Malachy remained quiet and still, and greeted his aunt politely, saying the journey was 'very nice' and his family were 'all good, all fine thanks'. But there was also a stiffness: in the way he held his bundle now, more out from his body; and in his eyes a look of bruised determination to keep looking straight ahead — not to be gawking around him at everything.

As they emerged from the dirty oily station he saw the words 'Praed Street' marked up on a building, and he knew then and there that no matter what else he ever saw in his life in this country or in any other, he would always remember the name Praed Street, and never again would the name of a street hit him right under the ribs like that and make him gasp for breath.

He said nothing when he got on a bus for the first time in his life. He said nothing when he saw Piccadilly Circus, though he knew he had seen it before in a picture, and that it wasn't a circus at all! He said nothing when they went on a moving stairs down below the earth — away down farther than the biggest church spire would ever go up — and he said nothing when they got on the train that ran so close to the walls he thought it must surely hit something. But on that speeding train he had something to think about: a naked girl who had her picture up on the wall beside one of the moving stairs. She was sitting so that you couldn't see her pishkin, but you could see her arse, and she had blonde hair and she looked as if she might have big frightened eyes and a shy smile. Maybe she would like him to take off his clothes too.

'You're the quiet one Malachy,' said Bridget in her English voice — she had felt his shoulders shuddering next to her.

I'm quiet all right din,' he said, and he giggled into the window at the blackness flashing past.

'And what does "mentally retarded" mean din?' he asked Bridget that night, in the living-room of her flat in Willesden, where she lived alone. A friend of hers had secured a job for her nephew in Ivy Lodge hospital, to start the very next morning at 8 a.m. 'Is it mad? Like Mike Twomey's wife?'

'No, not mad. Less intelligent than others. They can't control themselves.'

'Oh like Mickey Gowl the fooleen that do be dribbling?'

'No. He can talk and feed himself and all.'

'Is it like the Harrington Battys so? All the Battys are dummies.'

'No, not like them either. It's just that they're like animals, they have no sense, no ordinary common sense like other people. Animals.'

'Mikey Gowl has no sense and he's like a monkey. He's always saying he's a great fella, and people do be rising him to say how good he is. The time they told him they'd bring him a wife he believed them. And he put on his suit and baked a cake for her and they came in, one of them dressed like a woman. And he thought she was a woman and when he made a go for her they broke the cake on him and gave it to the dog. And they left him crying and picking up the bread into a mug. Almighty God if he's not mentally retarded!'

Bridget smiled. 'Aye they had great times,' she said, and laughed into her teacup, laughed as Malachy hadn't seen her since they met at Paddington that morning. But then her face darkened again, and she assumed a stronger English accent: 'But it's not like that over here Malachy. Here we look after people who can't take care of themselves,' and she sipped her cold tea.

'Is it like the Shaggers? You know the Lynchs that lived above in Coom and they called them the Shaggers. They had nothing and the mother starved to death, you remember? And they only threw her out on the ditch. And then they were all put in the asylum because the young one was up the pole. They said 'twas her father done it. Is that mentally retarded? Like the Shaggers?'

This time Bridget loosed a great peal of laughter and leaned back on her sofa, showing the silver patch under her chin. A new colour came into her cheeks, a new blush of life, like the healthy blush she got from the mountain air at home. 'You're a tonic young Malachy I do declare,' she said, and she poured them another cup of tea.

Malachy, encouraged by the effect his chatter was having, ran on: 'Or like the one they called "Lady", do you remember Lady, that was having Mahony's bastard and went mad when she saw it blue and dead, and used to be dressing up dolls and singing to them and she stuck her head in the lavatory-bowl after and drownded above in the hospital remember? Or like Pa Quinn's father when Pa lost all the money on a horse in Tralee and he pulled out all his hair? I saw him myself out the back window and he pulling it out and throwing it in the glosha-stream and running after it to try and catch it again. Or Mountain Paddy with the turned feet, that can say nothing but numbers . . . .'

Malachy had to stop and look at Bridget. She was silent now, but she was holding herself and rocking, her eyes rolling in her head. In truth

Malachy couldn't say whether she was laughing or not, but she looked transfixed or mesmerised, as if nothing said just then could get through to her. Indeed he almost got afraid for the moment, as she was turning purple. For an instant he imagined her rising like a hot balloon and bursting through the ceiling, so much of a brown ball had she become; she might have brayed like a donkey or spat like a goose, or vanished into a little brass cog all the while turning inside a clock, she looked so unnatural to him just then. But he said nothing.

Gradually she came back: she coughed and gaped and wiped her eyes and moaned. But she didn't look at him: she kept her head turned completely away from him, in at the wall. As if she had just heard some terible news, and had to look away, anywhere else besides at another human being.

Puzzled by this he tried again: 'Or Cait Shea that left her three cows die, or Murty Dubh that was shadow-boxing balloons, or Julia Bull that went on her knees to oul' Jackie Thady at her own mother's wake . . . .'

But Bridget's face was still to the wall, and he could hear her breathe in gulps. The thin greasy hairs on the back of her neck revealed the blackened yellow skin where her shoulders rounded. Her bony frame seemed to be dusty and slack, like an old shattered donkey.

At that moment Bridget Kennedy was struggling with visions — images she had not allowed for many years, and had never in her life put into words. She was thinking of insects, teeming and crowding; of maggots under the sod — white and clean and squirming; and the warmth of the sod and its dampness, and its smell — the sweet black smell of the sod — and the taste of it on her tongue. The long screech of the fiddle in a jig or a slide. The straight backs of the men. The sparks after it was nearly dark; how the dancers would grow then into giants, and the shouts reach such a pitch they were almost still, like black metal statues, with sparks flying from under their feet.

The thin black woman who sold tobacco near Willesden Green station remembered the man who came to her one night under a wall of stones. So sudden she didn't know what it was; so powerful she thought it was a stick he had. And then it dawned on her: for a moment his flesh melted into hers — all the whiteness of him became a part of her — and then she hit him. She took a stone from the wall and hit him on the side of his head. With a curse he was gone.

She stayed where she was for some time, lying on the grass. She allowed the night air to cool her exposed flesh, and she felt it with her hands: it was smooth and firm. Then she rolled over and bit into a sod of grass — she tore it slowly with her teeth and sucked out the earth with her tongue.

They gave her the nickname of Crusher Kennedy, and every man wanted to try her after that, until she came to London a year later . . .

John-Joe Quinn had a way of telling a story.

Bridget turned her face to Malachy again; she looked to him now like a cat licking itself in a dark shed — gorged but still ravenous. 'Know your own Malachy,' she told him, 'cover your tracks. It'll cost you nothing to be polite. And above all, do everything normal. You'll never make a mistake if you do everything normal. You ask me what is mentally retarded? I'll tell you. Mentally retarded is your bread and butter.'

This, thought Malachy, is what London must be like — full of dark cold and sick holes from which men emerge now and then to clean themselves and to face other men again, with at least the appearance that life is warm and acceptable and substantial.

He was miserable and exhausted and confused, and he felt as a physical twisting pain the need to crawl into his bed under the rafters at home — his own bed, that knew every curve of his body and whose smell was also his smell, whose sounds were the ticking of his brain — where he was safe from all dark, from all consequences of sin, and from the fairies. Tomorrow he would think about it — about this London and what seemed to be 'unnatural' about it. Yes, tomorrow he would think — after all, he was at an age now when he should be getting clear views on things, wasn't he? But he resolved at the same time that in the bright English morning to come he would begin to be a man: to elbow his way into the world of buses and trains and moving stairs and electrical gadgets — and pictures of girls who might have blonde hair and big eyes, and a smile.

*   *   *

Pocock, up and dressed long before the others in the morning, walked around the dormitory. He sat on Robbie Hunt's bed, looking at the little squashed face, the hair saturated in urine; he was snoring fretfully, and calling out 'aiee' in his sleep.

'I like old Robbie,' said Pocock, with a broad smile at Kennedy. 'Hallo Robbie. Want a smoke Robbie? Nice little fella, poor old Robbie.' He spoke just low enough not to waken the little black creature.

'You're supposed to be in bed Andrew. But as you're here you might as well join us in a cup of coffee.'

'Yes sir. Thank you sir. Nice coffee. I like a cup of coffee. Can I do any little jobs for you Mr Kennedy?' He sat straight, looking ahead, and drank the coffee in one or two gulps. 'Nice coffee. Thanks.' He walked back down the ward to his room, quite an impressive figure, tall with loose, almost swaggering movements, holding his broad shoulders straight, walking from the hips and swinging his arms.

Wilson had to admit the resemblance to Gregory Peck. 'He looks all right to me,' he said to Kennedy, puzzled. 'You'd take him to be quite a normal bloke. The way he said he liked old Robbie there. That takes a bit of insight doesn't it, to like a creature like that? I mean you'd have to have some bit of confidence in yourself to think it even.'

Kennedy shook his head. 'No,' he said gravely, 'Andrew's not what he seems. That's his problem. That's his very big problem. You wait and see. He'll trip himself up sooner or later.' Then Kennedy smiled at Wilson, a strange smile, which unsettled the younger man — it was so weak, and foolish, and frightened. 'You and I, Wilson, are we what we seem? Even to ourselves? To our wives, our so-called loved ones? What do you know of Kennedy S.E.N.? He might be just a cream bun! Oh but that's just my Irish blarney. A wee bit of philosophy, ha ha! No, Andrew is a bad case all right. A bad case.'

Pocock came clattering up the ward again, 'Oh by the way Mr Kennedy, I'll be asking Dr James to send me back to St George's. Got all me friends an' all there see. I made a mistake Mr Kennedy, but I want to go back to St George's.'

There was something in the air around them that made Wilson feel a slimy breath on his cheek.

In the staff coffee-shop a jukebox gulped out reggae music incessantly to listless ears. Nobody seemed to be listening, just staring ahead or fiddling at a crossword and gaping around — yawning and rubbing their eyes. One man — Clive Smith — was talking animatedly to a Chinese student about Offenbach, humming the can-can and banging the table. The student was shaking his head glumly. A large woman was sitting alone with a dog at her feet, looking around as if she wanted to talk to someone.

'Play that funky music loud boy,' blared the jukebox, as if it was acting on its own initiative, apparently without the consent of anyone in the room.

The waitress sat at a table, going through the contents of her handbag, weakly, without any real interest — a handkerchief, nail polish, tweezers, a battery.

Smith jumped up and began to kick up his legs — still the Chinese shook his head. Some looked up in alarm and one or two smiled politely.

Wilson was sitting by the window gazing out. It was a dull grey day, threatening rain. In the grounds people were still walking incessantly in all directions. One male patient wearing a bright green knitted hat stood outside the window looking in. He had been there for an hour, staring impassively at the glass.

The waitress shouted: 'Coffee?' in a strident, off-key voice, and made an aggrieved bustle to get it, noisily ringing on the till.

Smith called: 'Hey Terry, you know "Orpheus in the Under-world?"'at a newcomer.

'Yes,' came the apathetic and cautious reply.

Smith's head — totally bald — was gleaming with the effort of his explanation.

'Ling here doesn't know the can-can. Never heard of it!'

Ling smiled stiffly, the newcomer sat by himself, Smith looked about him helplessly. The jukebox pumped on; only the waitress acknow-ledged it unknowingly with the palm of her hand.

Wilson blinked as he saw the line approaching across the grounds: swaying and nodding, waggling, tottering, see-sawing. At first he didn't recognise them, then he felt alarmed; he saw Pocock and tiny Robbie Hunt, and his stomach leapt as if in fright. They were dressed! In overcoats and caps and scarves. For some reason he couldn't believe his eyes. there was Hopkins, the old goat, with his quick little walk, holding hands with Motherway — a good looking fellow with a clear healthy face. There was big Albert Copeland of the books, leaning backwards so that he might fall over; Rodney Bell wearing a huge dirty gaberdine, his evil eyes glinting; limping Reggie Morris, further hampered by a massive herringbone; Colin Forbes in a dream; Ayres in a new car-coat, looking every inch a respectable semi-detached mortgagee. All of them were limping or doubled over in some way, except Pocock, who was proudly leading Robbie like an uncle. Aunt Rosa, the tiny wide Spanish woman, led them, beaming and gesticulat-ing. Somehow to Wilson for a moment it didn't seem right: that the tall military-looking figure had almost burned thirty people to death; that the little lurching figure next to him should smoke a matchstick so elegantly; that Ayres, the gentleman in the car-coat, would eat that coat, as he ate his blankets, if it wasn't made of gaberdine. He saw suddenly that they were real, and that he had come to like them — no, it was almost, he realised, as if he were one of them. In some ways. The straggling line was approaching. They would pass right by his window. In a panic he left his seat, bumping his knee, and ran into the toilet, where he stayed until they had passed, holding onto the pipes and swallowing.

When he returned to his seat, trembling and puzzled, he looked after the disappearing line, which was just bobbing and limping around a corner. It was the thought of how they would have shouted and waved at him — been pleased to see him, asked him questions — that he couldn't face; and the thought — which hadn't occurred him before — of them dragging their way through the day, every day, year after year, slackly putting down their tormented days and weeks, battered by torpor and pain.

Why couldn't I face that, he thought, Kennedy could face them. He'd have a bit of blarney for every one of them, and they'd love it. Why not me? But do I face even Kennedy? Anybody? Where is the link between the appearance I put up to Kennedy, and the directness and warmth of these half-wits? And what do I know of Kennedy? Cream bun? Maybe we're all cream buns!

The large woman with the dog was shaking and trembling in some private laughter of her own. Her hand covered her eyes and her flesh rippled while her shoulders heaved. The dog sniffed her ankle.

The evening light began to thicken into dusk, and a few drops of rain touched the window, streaked by a cold breeze. The man in the green knitted hat turned and walked away, shrugging his shoulders and looking about, trying to impress the night that he was going someplace in particular.

Bell was jumping with delight. 'Shall we kill the bastard?'

'Yeh.' Hopkins was not enthusiastic, lying withered in his bed.

'Stone dead?'

They were talking about Pocock, who was watching TV downstairs with Kennedy.

'Yeh. Stone dead.'

'Ooh!' Bell wriggled in ecstasy. 'Rip the fucker open!'

'Yeh.'

'Kill 'im stone dead.'

'Yeh. Kill the fucker stone dead.' The leather concertina face of Hopkins showed no interest, gazing from his pillow.

'I hate him.'

'Yeh.'

'We'll kill him.'

'Yeh.'

'When he comes up.'

'Yeh.'

'Stone dead?'

'Yeh.'

'Do you like him?'

'No. I hate him.'

'Kill the fucker.'

'Yeh. Kill the fuckin' bastard stone dead.'

Staff Wilson interrupted: 'Go to bed now Bell. You can kill him in the morning. Hang up your clothes.'

Bell got ready for bed in chortling good humour, and Hopkins went instantly to sleep.

Wilson sat with the *Daily Mirror*, leaning over towards the night-lamp. All was quiet. Bell brought his clothes to the closet and returned naked to bed — tense with glee, his eyes flashing, his buttocks bristling with dark hairy evil. Wilson smiled after him.

He made himself a cup of tea, smoked a cigar and finished the crossword puzzle. Ayres trotted out to the toilet like a man rushing through a crowded street, elbowing and dodging, a faraway look of determination in his eyes, his night-shirt grasped tightly above his waist.

Wilson's mind was blank, ready for the dreamy images to begin their erratic and twisted trek from one cubbyhole of his brain to another, filling the night with fitful unease, when he became aware of a sobbing. It was a deep, genuine wresting sob, which flowed free and loud, not a child's shrill demanding sob, nor a man's silent one; it was like the sob of an adolescent, dismal, wretched and relentless.

It was Rodney Bell!

Wilson wondered what to do: ignore it, and put it down to idiocy; tell him to shut up, and put an end to his own sympathy; or go and comfort him, which he wanted to do, but felt might be the wrong approach — encouraging pampered behaviour, or some such. He ignored it.

Then he became aware that Bell was coming slowly towards him, up the ward, a step at a time. The sobbing continued, miserable and unconsoling, the scraping out of the barrel of not-knowing. Wilson could see the rough pale body, its eyes looking at him. Bell came closer, until he was standing before the armchair, his shoulders jigging like a machine, his mouth and eyes stretched and puckered as a child's; tears had drenched and flattened the black mat of hair on his chest; his penis was gripped tightly in both hands.

For several moments — many minutes perhaps — Wilson looked at him. The nurse's mind was quite blank, his little finger resting in the corner of his mouth. Bell looked back at him helplessly, his eyes bright yet dull.

Then Wilson decided, quite deliberately, that he must act. He took a breath, stood up and put an arm on Bell's shoulder. 'Shush,' he said.

Quickly Bell's arms wrapped him around the waist and his head went low down on his chest. He held Wilson tightly, like a clamp.

'Now now! Shush shush. Back to bed.'

They staggered back down the ward, locked together like that, Bell almost toppling over at every step, Wilson almost choked by the stranglehold. Both of them tiptoeing to avoid stepping on the other's feet.

'Bye-byes now Rodney.'

'Yeh.'

'Or I'll kill you. Stone dead.'

'I've done a bird,' Pocock announced.

'Eh?' said Wilson.

'I done a bird. See.' He put a drawing on the table. It was a bird on a branch, with delicate confident lines, bright colours in crayon, and leaves and branches precisely traced.

'Oh its lovely Andrew,' cried Wilson, genuinely impressed.

'Aunt Rosa gave me fifty pence for one. You know, the Spanish lady.'

'You should do more of those. You should go to art classes.'

'Yes sir.'

The drawing was stylised and accurate. The bird was exotic, eastern, and had a sleekness that gave it a solid palpability or gravity; it had an expression about it of surprise, or innocent wonder. the branch and leaves looked so fine and brittle they seemed intangible or pointless. There was a fragility in this exquisitely plumed bird perched on such frail twigs, a vanity, or void — something almost approaching the nullity of a Japanese watercolour. Wilson was astonished.

'Doctor James says I can go to art classes.'

'Good. Very good.'

'Yes sir.'

'You must go, you know. Really you should.'

'Yes sir I will. Do you think I should sign it?'

'Of course.

Laboriously he wrote: 'Andrew Pocock, Ivy Lodge' under the twigs. His handwriting was awkward like a child's, and almost spoiled it. 'I might sell it,' he said and clattered away to his room.

'Did you see Andrew's drawing?' Wilson asked excitedly when Kennedy came upstairs with the night-tablets.

'Been drawing budgies again has he?' Kennedy laughed.

'It's very good,' Wilson protested. 'It has a certain quality.'

'And little Robbie here has a certain quality known as urine. He's pissed himself again. Come on Robbie.'

'Aiee!'

Wilson was stung. He wanted to shout. 'Really it's good. He should be encouraged.'

Kennedy turned. 'I just work here chum. I sell cars by day — that brings in fifteen quid a week tax-free. I've got a big wife and three big kids. *I* should be encouraged.'

Wilson was startled by the fierceness of the response, but he knew he should go further: 'Come on, you like these people.'

'Yes. Yes I like them. They're my bread and butter so I like them. But I've got my own budgies to draw. And I'll tell you something: I drew a few budgies in my time. A few quare budgies!'

Wilson laughed, but he wanted to say more — to know more of Kennedy, and he wanted Kennedy to know him. He felt there was something in Kennedy he wanted to touch, something that went beyond the mateyness he affected, and in which Wilson felt snared. But he couldn't speak; he felt barren and spineless.

'Where I come from,' Kennedy was continuing, 'the women scorn and laugh at the men — just because they are small farmers. The bachelors crowd around me and buy me drinks. I tell them the women jump on you over here. Six to every man!' He was laughing. 'It's true isn't it. You push them up against a tree and open your flap — that's it isn't it. You're working away, in and out, in and out, like a channel-swimmer: "Had a good day love? Aye. Christmas next week!" Then you see the next one. It's a great country you've got here Wilson, I'll be the first to admit it. A great country.'

He stopped speaking and they looked at each other. They both held their breath as long as they could, for they were frightened to breathe. They were afraid to look at each other, but they were more afraid of looking away — so they continued to stare into each other's frightened eyes. During that time Wilson's brain was racing like a film projector out of control: he saw himself as a child sitting on a rock; he saw a green field and a picnic and a small barking dog; he saw clean towels and freshly baked bread. He thought of his own age, the number of his age, and other numbers that dated his life — eight, seventeen, twelve. And he thought of his most recent numbers, twenty-five, twenty-six, twenty-seven, and of Kennedy's number, forty-two.

At last Kennedy's breath gushed out — not a hissing boisterous gush, but soft and shaking. Wilson allowed his breath to escape silently; for a moment he was afraid he would fart. In the silence they tried to pick up a workable arrangement to carry them forward into some kind of bodily composition that would allow movement and even speech.

'I buried my budgies,' Kennedy eventually articulated.

Wilson flinched, blushed and turned away. 'Where? he asked, to say something. Now he knew how badly Kennedy must feel at this moment — his voice was coming too dramatic, like an actor whose voice is pitched to an emotion he cannot hold.

'Where? — I don't know. In Ireland I think, but before I came here. Maybe somebody buried them for me.'

It struck Wilson absurdly that an actor's job was impossible: you cannot feel and speak at the same time. How far does it go, he thought, but he wanted to respond, he wanted to acknowledge a look or a feeling, but it was too mysterious. He felt impotent and effete.

'But why is Andrew drawing budgies?' Kennedy was getting onto a more normal plane, getting his wind back. 'Is it for art? For the fifty pence? No — he's doing it to survive, because this place is killing him. When Andrew starts drawing budgies it's bad news, believe me. You just wait and see.' He sat back, exhausted and released.

'Mm. Mm.' Wilson replied. He felt a sense of elation — as if he had just witnessed a miracle: they had come through! The storm was weathered and they had succeeded in pulling a rational order back like a cloak around time — he felt like planting a kiss or a flag on Kennedy's forehead. The word hope came into his mind, but he could not say it, or put it into a sentence.

Again Pocock came padding his way up to the night-table, in bare feet and white nightshirt. They both smiled up at him, as if he were a colleague, or an old school friend.

'I bought a ticket, look. Twenty quid? Cor, that'd come in handy.' He put a raffle-ticket on the table, first prize £20, second prize £10, third prize bottle of whiskey. 'Draw is three weeks next Sunday. Cor twenty quid eh? Twenty quid!' He smiled in weak enthusiasm.

Wilson's elation collapsed as abruptly as it had arrived. They had been too ambitious, their techniques of avoidance too strong. He saw the three of them — two nurses looking up at an imbecile with a raffle-ticket, in the circle of pale half-light from the shaded lamp — and he felt pity for them all, an ugly stale kind of pity for all man's triviality, inefficacy, and servility. And especially he felt pity for himself: a dud, a victim of mediocrity, a prey to ignominious isolation.

Now the word love tumbled into his mind, and rattled about in it, like a ping-pong ball in a furious pulsating fit.

Wilson was slumped in the night-nurse's armchair, half-asleep, half-dreaming, his head falling down and coming up again, a pain in his neck. Lyons whined and snorted occasionally; Ayres was silently unravelling and eating the threads from his blanket, his hands rising, descending, twisting and snapping the white cords, while he soundlessly rolled the wads in his mouth.

He felt himself white on the operating table, a light in his eyes. There was Doctor Ayres, in a fine grey suit, straight and elegant, a briefcase under his arm. There was Pocock in a white gown, passing the knife, the scalpel, rings flashing on his fingers.

He was in school, but fully grown, in a policeman's uniform, sitting at his desk. Mr Kennedy was the teacher, and he was flogging the class. Closer and closer he came. Should he allow himself to be flogged? He, a grown man and a policeman, symbol of authority? But would Mr Kennedy understand? He held out his hand for the cane, but Mr Kennedy struck him on the neck.

Now he was in the school yard, watching himself being attacked; all his friends were there: Malcolm, Humphrey, Peter and others. They bore down and covered him in a scrummage. He couldn't see himself any more, but he knew they were beating him mercilessly. He saw

Malcolm's face, covered with green moss, in the scrum: he was crying, but he was hitting down with an old black kettle. Banging. When the group parted and drifted away there was nothing left on the ground but an old shoe — three feet long, like a circus-clown's shoe, but it was slimy and covered in green moss.

He remembered seeing that shoe in a museum. It had belonged to a local giant a century ago.

Now Hopkins was walking about with his short little steps.

Malcolm was sitting on a sofa, drinking whiskey. 'Now you'll have to get married, George,' he was saying, and he lifted the telephone. 'Yes?' he said into the receiver, and then handed it to Wilson, who was terrified; he took the receiver and looked at Malcolm, whose eyes were cold and challenging. He put the receiver to his ear and it let out a tired whine.

Motherway was sitting up in his bed, Hopkins was standing by his own bed, looking at Motherway and wringing his hands.

'Kiss me Charlie Hopkins,' Motherway said in a low voice.

Hopkins looked at Wilson and again anxiously wrung his hands. Motherway repeated his demand.

'Can I sir?' Hopkins asked pleadingly. 'Can I kiss him?'

Wilson stayed silent.

'Please sir?'

Wilson sat dumbly.

Kiss, kiss, kiss. They smacked each other's lips. Hopkins went back to bed smirking.

'I love Johnny Motherway sir,' he said solemnly. 'He knows it. Motherway knows I love him. Don't you Johnny?'

'Low-grade Hopkins. Low-grade Hopkins,' Motherway began to chant.

'See sir?' Hopkins was upset. 'He's calling me low-grade.'

'Kiss me Charlie Hopkins.'

'No.'

Wilson's head fell down heavily. He drifted in a boat, while crowds of people lined the shore to watch him — hundreds of them. He had no oars and no engine, there was no wind and no current. An occasional wave rocked him sickeningly. All was silent. The people just stared at him and he stared back at them. All was still, except for an occasional move from the crowd — a hand brushing a face, a stray lock of hair, a shrug of shoulders. He knew none of them, but he knew he would recognise every one of them again, he could see them so clearly. But it was too late: he was drifting on the welling water and would have to remain in the boat until it was swallowed up in the grey horizon.

Kennedy brought them coffee. It was almost dawn.

'Reggie Morris had a fit during the night. Grand Mal,' Kennedy remarked.

'Oh I'm sorry, I must have been — '

'Not at all. I don't mind. I prefer working with someone like you. Easygoing, like myself.'

'Yes. Easygoing is right.' Wilson nodded and he gave a laugh he knew was artifical. 'I really love the coffee,' he said. 'In the morning. It's good.'

They looked at each other for a few seconds, and then both of them began rubbing their eyes and yawning.

'Oh-hum. I'd better make out the night report,' said Kennedy. 'Another night's work done.' And he went out.

Wilson finished his coffee and lit a cigar; smoke slowly filled his eyes, ears and brain; his aching body seemed to be melting. The sound of breathing on all sides was reassuring and soothing, calm and constant.

*   *   *

In his first two months at Ivy Lodge Malachy did nothing exciting. He sat in his tiny room or watched television, and went to his aunt Bridget's at weekends. She would give him rashers and sausages and fried eggs, and they would play draughts or ludo in the evenings. He would look at his aunt, thin and greasy, with lipstick and hair-do, and listen to the traffic outside the window. They were chilly and joyless occasions, and he often felt like flinging an egg at her, or running down the high-street shouting and waving. But he knew she looked forward to his visits, and put on her good clothes and make-up for his arrival. The train journey back to Ivy Lodge was always dreary.

The work still frightened him: he felt someone would leap on his back or cut his throat. He also felt that all the other staff were better equipped to deal with these lunatics than he was — the Irish staff seemed to have a garrulous comradeliness that he could not share in, and the English had a natural weight that gave them authority. He usually ate alone in the cafeteria, or with a bunch of the Irish, but he often longed to sit among the English student-nurses, who had an effusive way of chattering and an open, free way of gesturing, laughing, or tossing their heads, such as he had never seen in the girls at home. They called aloud to men to come and sit with them, and their demeanour did not change in men's company. You wouldn't think they were women at all, he thought, but he knew there was more to it: he knew that these women *were* women, in some way that the girls at home were not, and it fascinated him. He watched their faces as they spoke, their casual movements as they took off their coats, the way they ate — dainty but without inhibition. He noted their peculiarities — one would take several bowls of soup, another never had potatoes, another had several helpings of dessert, and so on and this too held him in rigid fascination. Most of all he noticed their laughter: there seemed to be a particular kind of enjoyment there that he was not in step with — he suspected that at times they were laughing at something away beyond nursing, or the hospital or even men, something so essentially female that only women could fathom . . . and he was enthralled. He watched their faces with delight and wonder.

Once he sat at a table with four of them, using as an excuse that an Irish male nurse was already at the same table. But he blushed at the very beginning, and, apart from a few words to the Irishman, remained silent throughout the meal.

During those two months he kept thinking of Helen Shea, the local 'fine heifer'. Once he had cornered her at the crossroads and put his hand under her blouse. He felt the soft flesh for an instant and the rough bra, and he tried to kiss her lips but they exploded into a gassy laugh in his face. A thousand times that pliable touch flashed through his mind as he watched the nurses in the cafeteria.

Then one night at a staff dance a woman's hand went inside his trousers — the first human hand to touch him. He went for her headlong and breathless and spurted out on the grass behind the dancehall. She quietened him — he was shivering, and gasping: 'Oh God! Oh God!' — and she soothed him and whispered his name in his ear.'Malachy,' she whispered, and laughed, and the name never sounded so sweet before. He calmed, and saw her there — the beautiful eyes and lips that wanted him to plunge into them, and the curve of her cheek and her temple that were a woman's. There was a harmony in her face and head, in her body beneath his, where her legs curved out, in the breasts he could feel against his — a harmony which he knew would bring him a new definition of himself, an illumination of the world and of the other people in it.

She calmed him, and she helped him to come to her again. Like a soft explosion her body received him, and then she laughed — and that laugh thrilled him even more, as he looked at her wet eyelids, and he too laughed. For the first time he responded with his own laugh to *that* laugh of a woman, and he said, 'I want to screw you and screw you and screw you.' And they laughed.

He could play a few reels on the mouth-organ, and when he had three or four whiskeys he found he could be as vocal and as witty as any of the Irishmen. His youthful, freckled face and his strong frame made him popular, along with an unspoiled exuberance, which increased as he found more confidence.

In a few months his reputation as a womaniser, drinker and 'a good sport' grew, until he was the acknowledged 'wild Irishman' of Ivy

Lodge. People called out to him wherever he was, and the girls — even the more timid ones — vied with each other to sit at his table and talk and laugh with him. The extent of his escapades became legendary, and the stories became even more exaggerated: one told of his visiting (or 'seeing to', his own expression) six or seven nurses at an open-air party one night, another of his having a young married English nurse in the ward with him early in the morning.

Soon all the patients at the hospital knew him and would laugh whenever they met him. 'Hallo Mr Kennedy,' they would call, and wait expectantly for the reply, which always came. His distaste and fear of them disappeared, and he became known as having excellent potential as a nurse.

He had never felt so happy before: for the first time he found something in himself which other people could respond to and like — something which was essentially his own. It was a new Malachy Kennedy he looked at in the mirror every morning, and an exciting one, to be tried out and tested during the day, always successfully.

As a student-nurse he was keen, with fresh ideas and a strong energetic interest. He sharpened a classroom with his quick questions and his relaxed and cheerful manner. His teachers and the staff hierarchy came to know and like him — some even looked forward to their classes with him, as he never failed to revive their own youthful enthusiasm, and to make them feel again their idealistic drive for the job.

Sometimes if he was sitting alone he would be overwhelmed by the idea of how full and free his life was, and he would begin scratching restlessly or hopping about in his seat. He would think of the faces of people, or their laughter and chatter and the movement of their bodies. His stomach and spine would begin tingling and thrilling until he had to jump up and leave the room. Then he would knock on someone's door and organise something — a bottle of whiskey, a game of cards, or a few tunes on the mouth-organ. Often he would end up in a woman's bed, the sharp smell of sex in his mouth, and a sense of disbelief in his mind: how could it be so good, so easy, so lucky! Sometimes in those moments the image of wet rocks, stony fields or muddy bogs would flit into his quiet mind, and make him feel happily nostalgic. His weekends became more full about this time, and his visits to his aunt Bridget less frequent.

One night — he had been at Ivy Lodge about six months — a knock came on his door as he was about to fall asleep. It was late and he had been drinking with some friends. He never locked his door at night as he often had visitors.

'Come in mate,' he called.

The door opened.

'Have you got a light my friend?' came a strong deep voice.

'Sure thing chum.' He didn't smoke, but always kept matches by his bed for such an event. He found the matches in the dark and struck one. 'Right-oh then mate,' he said, blinded by the light at first.

Then the face came down to the flame. It was a black face — the first black face that Malachy Kennedy had ever seen in his life. He froze along his whole body — even his toes seemed to go weak. The loft at home, the fairies, the Lissataggirt Field, Mary the Butter, the grey beard and horny face of Paddy Knowledge, all leapt and jangled in his clattering mind. He could not speak. In a panic he wondered if the man was naked — a sailor perhaps, or an Arab. The eyes were white like a mountain goat's, the lips were scarlet like a painted woman's, the face shone, not only black, but blue and green and orange; at the throat were black creases and on the chin were hairs like a horse's tail.

For many moments he was certain he would die. He had time to regret his lapses from religion, and to think of his mother's face and soft fluttering voice. He even thought for an instant of his father's bare head at his aunt Kate's table on that last day in Ireland.

The smoke came in blue and yellow gusts, livid and sparkling.

'Thank you my friend,' and the face was gone, the door closed.

In the morning the hospital was buzzing: two negroes had been hired as ward orderlies. That day Malachy and two others went to the office of the chief nursing officer. Within a week the two negroes had left the hospital.

'Welcome home Malachy.' He shook hands with everyone in the pub; it was a strange feeling to shake hands with all these people, old men and married women, all making a fuss and pleased to see him.

'Were you homesick?' This question was asked many times, always with a laugh, and Malachy always laughed when he replied: 'Just for a few months. After that it's like being at home. You walk down the street and you always meet someone you know.' In fact he had bought two calendars — one for his bedroom and one for his pocket.

'How was the crossing?'

'A good crossing. Like glass it was.' He had been sick for four hours until he fell asleep on the wet floor with his head under a seat.

'Plenty money I suppose?'

'A great country chum. A great country.' He had to borrow the fare to come home.

'What are you drinking chum, pint of bitter? Stout is it?

'We drink bitter over.'

'Did you see anyone from the parish?'

'I met John Jack Tom. He's driving a brand-new Morris.'

'He is so?'

'Doing well he is. Contracting. You know.'

'I know.'

'Mary O'Shea is in Kilburn. Married an engineer.'

'She did?'

'A protestant.'

'Well every man to his own.'

'Yes o' course I don't hold with all this religion.'

'I know yes.'

'Ireland is way behind the times chum. You know.'

'I know.'

'Over you take out a bit o' skirt and you give her a good seein' to that night. None o' your hidin' from the priest or that. Not a bit. Give 'em a seein' to and see 'em no more. That's my motto.'

'Right too.'

'Only nature in't it?'

'Nature is right.'

When his father asked about the job: 'What do you do with the fooleens?' he evaded it. He mentioned exercising them or holding down the disorderly ones, but he didn't tell of cleaning their mess or washing them.

When his mother asked about the local church he invented a parish priest from Donegal and an entire flock of Kerry parishioners. He didn't mention at all that there were female nurses in the hospital.

He was relieved to go back.

Years passed. He fell in love and suffered. Nothing serious. Just the milky-white body and the heart-churning. A longing to break from his own body and become her: fuse their grey brains. If possible. He went crying to Bridget one night — his legs would not hold him up, his face was gashed with tears, his teeth were stripped like a dog's. She said, 'She's only human, whoever she is. She's only human child.' His aunt Bridget was kind. The girl married a milkman. Of all things.

Then the army. Aldershot, North Africa. Whiskey and women and more whiskey. The smell of men and the barrack-room talk. Crinkled photographs in wallets, old letters, pin-ups, farting in the night and polished buttons in the morning. The baking heat and then the cool transparent evening, and the shouting, the drinking, the bitter cigarettes and the sweat. One night as he stepped into a roaring steaming cellar he saw a face he knew: it was Michael Connors, who came from his own valley. As if he had been struck in the chest with a hammer, Kennedy fell back against the door, stunned and pale. For several seconds he could not move, nor take his eyes off the figure of Connors, who was laughing and chatting with some Englishmen. His shoulders were broad: *carrying turf and hay*. He was slightly stooped: *walking slowly through bogs*. He had a high forehead and wide-spaced eyes: *the tweed cap*. His hands were enormous and rough: *digging and picking potatoes from the sandy ground.* His eyes were quick and his teeth flashed: *Michael Connors could dance a set* — the thoughts frightened Malachy Kennedy. Michael Connors could throw a salmon on the bank in the long grass or lift a cock of hay on a pike to the reek-top. That man with the tan of North Africa on his face could swing his body to the scythe or bend his back on the stone floor to say the rosary in a dry steady intonation. He knew the voices, the rhythm of places, the sound of falling water. The sound of sheep coughing in the night. Malachy nearly screamed, but instead he flung himself outside again. After he had walked a few steps the pungent spicy smells and the intoxicating sounds again enclosed him; but he realised that he had sweated as he never had before: his clothes were saturated in it, and clung uncomfortably to his knees, his groin, and his armpits.

He went back to his old job at Ivy Lodge after his National Service. The place was still the same, with the same intrigues and the same scandals. Who was interested in who or who was being made a fool of. Malachy was welcomed back, and resumed his part as the wild Irishman, but he felt different: it was not so exciting, so new and fresh; he did not feel so free, the exhilarating possibilities for conquering new worlds did not seem to be there in the same way. He felt heavier, not so restless and impatient for things to happen. Sometimes he found himself, instead of joining in some revelry, staring blankly at somebody's nose, or at a woman's wobbling chin, or a wrist-watch flashing up and down in the light. He often sat in his room for hours just smoking, or dozing on the bed.

On his twenty-second birthday he stayed in his room most of the day, telling nobody. 'Today was my twenty-second,' he told himself, as if taking stock. 'I got a card from my mother. Pink and silly. "Mr Malachy Kennedy. Male Nurses' Block, Ivy Lodge Hospital."' M.K., he thought, remember carving M.K. on a tree. I'd like to see what happened to it on the mountain with the rain and the wind. Not much I suppose. Not much happens at all. Well I loved a few women. At least I loved a few . . . . The thought cheered him briefly, but then he grew fitful again, and left the room. He went down to the door of the Male Nurses' Block, looked around him a few times, turned and went back up to his room again.

Before his twenty-third birthday Malachy was married. It was not until his eldest child was six years old that he returned to Killarney again.

*   *   *

Patient Robbie Hunt attacked by Andrew Pocock in the p.m. Pocock punched patient Hunt several times in the abdomen and face, and had to be restrained by staff Williams and nurse O'Brien. Pt Hunt received attention from Dr Abdullah at 4 p.m. Pt Pocock remains restless and disturbed, constantly walking about and referring to St George's. This pt is a danger to pts and staff. R. Fernandez

Robbie Hunt lay bunched like a fist under the blankets. Nobody knew why he was called Robbie. His casenotes gave his name as William Joseph Hunt, and his sister, who used to visit him before she died, had always called him Billy.

Pocock was pacing about. 'Twenty quid eh. Next Sunday. Bloody 'ell. Twenty quid. Could use that.' Dressed in his white nightgown he went from one window to another to look out. Having been deprived of his boots his toes now stuck out through the holes in his navy-blue socks. 'Twenty quid. I'd get me back to St George's wouldn't it, twenty quid. Second prize ten quid. Not bad that. Ten quid eh? Third prize bottle of whiskey. Six nine three six. That's the ticket. Six nine three six. Bottle of whiskey eh? Cor — could use that. Could have a drink. Ha ha! Have a drink! Twenty quid . . .' His hair was dry and tossed and he looked slightly stooped — not so tall and imposing as he had been. His expression kept changing: empty smiles flashed across his face, being replaced by a drooping vagueness. His hands were shaking badly all the time, and a spot of froth bulged in the corners of his mouth.

'Andrew will you go to bed. You'll wake everybody up.' Kennedy was firm but not severe. 'It's against the rules. Come on now. Bed.'

'I bought a ticket sir. Six nine three six. Draw's next Sunday. Five days. That'll be all right eh? Twenty quid. I'll go back to St George's then. I want to go back to St George's. I'll go next Sunday.' His face wore a false smile as he spoke to Kennedy, and his eyes darted about everywhere. 'I got a new watch look. Me sister gave it. From Reading.Look, ten-past-eleven see. What time is it? What time is it . . .? Ten-past-eleven. That cost twenty quid. I'll bet. Twenty quid eh?'

Wilson watched, fascinated by the jerky movements, the darting eyes, the hands which shook violently, as if he were doing it deliberately. Once, while pacing from one window to another, he caught his reflection in the glass — he smiled, the same false flashing smile, as if he were trying to flatter himself. Or as if he were afraid of himself.

'Andrew I have a pain in my head from you. Go to bed now, there's a good fellow.'

'Have you Mr Kennedy? Have you a pain in your head? Yeh. I bought a watch. What time is it?'

'Ten-past-eleven Andrew.'

'Yeh. Ten-past-eleven. Six nine three six.' He smiled, and then his mouth drooped again. His eyes were dull and yellow — there was fear glinting in them, when he wasn't trying to smile.

'You punched poor Robbie, Andrew,' Kennedy said.

'Yeh.'

'What did he do to you for Christ's sake?'

'Nothing.'

'Poor Robbie couldn't punch a butterfly. He's the most harmless poor sod in the place. Why not pick on somebody bigger than him.'

'He irritated me sir. He's always doin' it, irritating me like. I got rings look.' He held out his hands. each finger had a ring on it, some had two. They were cheap tin rings, costing a few pennies in the patients' shop. His fingers were red and swollen and scratched from them. At first the extended hands were steady, and then, as if he just remembered, they began to shake. They shook violently, and his arms shook, and his shoulders, and his cheeks shook.

'Andrew!' said Kennedy in alarm. 'Cut it out.'

'I'm shakin' sir,' he whimpered, 'I'm shakin'.'

Wilson and Kennedy helped him down to his room and into bed. Even his legs were shaking, and the blankets soon fell off onto the floor.

'What's the time sir?' he said, his eyes rolling, his mouth working in attempted smiles.'What's the time?'

They spoke soothingly and tried to reassure the stricken creature. Again Wilson felt detached: he saw the two staff in their grey suits, in the yellow electric light trying to mother a human being who was beyond them, and who probably didn't trust them anyway. Perhaps Pocock knew that as soon as they closed the door they would revert to a normal way of speaking and behaving — a normality he would never be able to join. And what's this normality anyway, Wilson thought, we'll be 'hard-men', we'll make jokes and get through the night. Then we'll go off selling cars or drinking beer or listening to the radio. When we want . . . something else. . . . Love? He noticed that his heart leapt as the word came into his mind. He noticed that he tapped the doorknob twice with two fingers. He noticed that as he walked with Kennedy he was examining the ceiling, and he wondered if Kennedy was perhaps examining the floor. Again he tap-tapped each bed as he passed it, and tap-tapped the table when they reached it. Just as Elersley the autistic patient would do it, tap-tap. He was aware of what he was doing but couldn't — or didn't — stop himself. If Elersley were prevented from his tapping he would fly into a rage and bite someone. Love — love, thought Wilson, and his stomach was shooting with fright.

'That toilet is a disgrace,' Kennedy was saying. 'They piss on the floor and the piss gets under the lino and there you have it. A stink. And in the summer — phew! It's unhealthy. Anything could be breeding in there. And this is a hospital!'

They were sitting in their chairs, which were covered with white sheets. Wilson was aware that he wanted coffee and a smoke, but he also wanted to talk.

'I mean to say,' Kennedy continued, 'when I make my report and I say the toilet is stinking, who reads it? Who does anything? Nobody chum. They don't have to sit up here all night do they? And in the summer, phew! It's unbelievable.'

Wilson wanted to talk, nothing else.

'It's stupid,' Wilson said. 'It's criminal. What would the *News of the World* make of that? They'd go to town on it, wouldn't they?'

'Now the *News of the World*. That scares 'em you know. It sure scares 'em. Mind you there are a lot of other things . . . .'

'I know. Don't I know.'

But Wilson was watching Kennedy and noticing how he flicked at his nose with his thumb and then touched his spectacles into position. He also had a way of crossing his legs and rubbing his hands on his knees. Wilson wondered what his own characteristics were. Did anybody ever notice him picking his nose . . . and taking out his handkerchief? He often did it.

'But it's not a bad little job.' Kennedy went on. 'As jobs go it's easygoing. Easygoing is right. Isn't it?' Kennedy looked across at him, his hand to his spectacles.

Wilson knew that the word 'easygoing' was a favourite word of his, and that it was important to him in some way. He also knew that Kennedy wanted him to say 'Yes it's a nice job' for two reasons: to reassure himself, and because he wanted Wilson to say 'Yes I like working with you and I'd like to stay working here with you for the years to come'. Kennedy was looking at him, holding up his spectacles on his nose. Wilson thought of two possible replies: 'No, it's a stupid piss-wiping job', and also 'How do you live with your wife? Do you love her? Do you love your children?'

Instead he said, 'Yes. A nice little number.'

Kennedy sat back in his chair and gave a little yawn. 'Chris Burke was asking me about you tonight.'

'Oh?' Wilson tensed. Chris Burke was the Chief Night Officer, the huge Irishman who looked like a Viking — straight as a reed with a sombre silence about him that made him unpopular.

'Yes, he was asking me about you,' Kennedy continued. 'If you were satisfactory and that. I said I never worked with anyone better than you.'

'Oh?'

'Yes. I said you were punctual, careful, that you had an interest in the job.'

'Oh-ho. Yes? That's . . . er . . .'

'And I said you were understanding.'

'Really?'

'"That's one thing about Mr Burke," I said. "He's got understanding that lad. He's got a lot of . . . well, understanding."'

Wilson swallowed and tried to breathe evenly. He found his knees jumping about and he slapped them with his hands. His eyes were going around the room, looking at all corners. The tune of a popular song came into his head and he almost hummed it out loud.

'And Mr Burke said he was pleased to hear that, and that he's heard good reports of you from everyone else too.'

'That's good.' Wilson was sweating — he felt cold. For a second he imagined himself smiling at the tall pale figure of Burke, and shaking his cold soft hand.

'"But your report is the most important," he said, "and if you say he's alright then he's alright with me too." Those were his very words. And I said you were alright with me.'

Wilson wanted to run, to bang the door between himself and this man with the weak expression on his face, who was touching both his index fingers together in front of his nose and looking at him, expecting him to reply. He felt a revulsion for the neat grey suit and the clear skin of his cheeks — for one second he wanted to kick him in the stomach and hear the wind bursting from him; then crack open the clear skin and smash the bobbing light in the glasses. See pain in his eyes. 'Thanks,' he said. 'That's good. I'm glad of that. Thanks. I'm grateful for that anyway.' And as soon as he was able he said, 'Would you like some coffee? Will you have a cup? Two spoons?' And he went down to the kitchen, to the cold air and the stainless steel.

Wilson walking over the dunes at Skegness. Under his arm a box. In the box a man's head. It was for dinner. He hoped his parents would like it — that his mother would boil it and that his father would not think it too fatty. The head was shaved but the teeth were still in it. It was not the face of anyone he knew, but yet Wilson did not feel right about eating it. Perhaps the brains would taste alright — blue and salted. The reeds rippled briskly in the breeze and some sand was blown about. The sea was a very light blue and the tiny waves were almost silent.

Mr Burke was phosphorescent. He illuminated the whole night. Two moons shone in the black sky behind him — drumming and dancing. Up and down thumped the two moons. Mr Burke was taller than the two oak trees. He was eating them. They would taste like mushrooms. He ate the two black oak trees and screamed. His white face went green with joy.

Wilson woke suddenly, his heart thumping. Wide awake he breathed heavily, thinking of the fried egg he'd had for supper. Lyons had just screamed — he was sitting up in bed. The long naked form of Chalmers was crouching by the radiator. He was shitting small hard balls and eating them. Lyons waved his hands about his head and screamed again. 'Shut up Lyons!' Wilson called, and Kennedy pushed him under the blankets. Wilson pulled the stringy form of Chalmers to the toilet, where he squatted like a monkey, his hands and face smeared with shit. Hopkins — wakened by Lyons — followed on his skinny little legs, with Chalmer's hard knobs of shit in his hands. 'I picked it up Mr Wilson. Chalmer's shit — I picked it up for you.' Elersley — the autistic — also wakened by Lyons — came to the toilet, his tongue burring like a bird, tapping the doors and windows. Hopkins dropped his burden and dodged the white-gowned figure. Wilson said, 'Alan!' but Elersley swept Chalmers off the lavatory with one quick blow. The naked shit-covered figure banged his head on the sink, sprawled on the wet floor, and went bawling back to bed, his hands to his ears. Elersley was six feet tall, white-faced, black-haired; sitting on the lavatory-bowl in his white nightgown he looked like a young Italian monk of the Renaissance.

It was quiet again, and the two nurses sat back in their armchairs. They were weary and clammy, their skin prickled with dried sweat, their minds were heavy with the hours gone by, and the hours to come. The slow breathing and snorting took on the rhythm of a clock, they felt their own heartbeats slow and dull. The air was thick and sluggish with the smell of faeces, a warm rich smell, to which their noses were almost numb. They spoke a little — some story of the past, or a plan for tomorrow — and then relapsed into a blank blindness, where the dim light on the pink walls became a milky warm blur, and wheels began to trundle — down into black caverns.

A house was burning. Wilson's house — his mother upstairs asleep in her bed. Burning slowly, without flames, but she would die in her bed. In the other room his brothers were sleeping — Chalmers, Elersley, Lyons, Robbie too, the bunched fist under the blankets. They would all die in the burning. He had to climb the stairs to get them out. But tons of books kept toppling down the stairs and as he scrambled he slipped on the books. Thousands and thousands of them, yellow hardbacks and blue old Penguins, dusty and scrappy they banged his knees as he slithered and the torrent carried him down the stairs. *The X Bar X Boys* in red covers, *The Guns of Navarone, David Copperfield*. They smelt dusty and damp. He could see his mother's hand, poor and troubled, and the head of Elersley, white-faced and astonished. The stairs collapsed.

A man with no face grabbed his wrist and danced. He wore black, and his non-face was rough and blue. He danced about.

Wilson was in a place where there were frozen bodies. Fully dressed, in rows like bunks. They were all old people, frozen, with their grey hair and stooped backs. A wren perched on a block, its tail erect and bobbing, ready to fly.

Now he was awake, painfully rubbing his eyes and banishing the unwelcome images. Why are they so unpleasant, he thought. Does Kennedy have this bog inside him? Does everyone carry around this filth with them during the day? Under their bowler hats or bishop's mitres or housewives scarves — if everything suddenly flipped over, by some sort of cosmic twitch, would we all drop to our knees in the high-street and roar for mercy? But he thought of the little wren perched on the icy block, and smiled. At least I gave life to something, he thought, and stretched himself, perhaps it was the fried egg. He stood up and took the flashlamp to check the beds.

Morris had both legs out on the floor; Ayres turned green eyes at the lamp as he delicately unwove his blanket; Elersley was sound asleep, looking like a large contented child; big Albert Copeland was wrapped in the blankets like a mummy; Motherway had wrapped himself into a half-sitting position so that the first thing he would see when he woke would be his penis; Bell was snoring and Hopkins looked like a scrap-heap of bones and hair.

Through the Judas window Wilson saw Pocock sitting on his bed, drawing. He was talking to himself: 'This is a bird Aunt Rosa. I drew it. I drew another bird for you. Nine o'clock I drew it. Bloody 'ell nine o'clock. I went up and I said I drew a bird . . . . Mr Burke is a nice man. Mr Kennedy is a nice man. Dr Abdul is a nice man. Dr James is nice . . . I done a bird Dr James. Nine o'clock.' Here he put aside the drawing and stared at nothing, one hand trembling, his lips working.

Wilson went in; immediately a change came over Pocock: he leapt up.

'Nine o'clock Mr Wilson. Bloody 'ell nine o'clock. Who's on? Aunt Rosa?'

'It's only five Andrew.'

'No. It's nine o'clock. Look.' He showed his wristwatch, which said five-past-nine.

'Your watch is wrong Andrew.'

'No it's five-past-nine. Where's Aunt Rosa? I want to go out. I want a smoke.' He was excited and shouting.

'Andrew it's five o'clock.'

'Oh what a life. Oh bloody 'ell.' He paced up and down the little room. 'Let me out sir. Please. Let me back to St George's.'

'Go back to bed Andrew. Get some sleep.'

'But it's five-past-nine.'

'Andrew!'

'I done a bird Mr Wilson. Look.' With a sudden change of mood he picked up the drawing and showed it. It was exactly the same as the previous one — just as delicate and elegant, but exactly the same in every detail, not a line or a curve was different.

Wilson stared at it, half-appalled and half-saddened, wondering what he should say. 'It's lovely Andrew,' was all he could think of.

Pocock was again trembling slightly, and catching his breath; his face looked dark and frightened. His voice was cracked and shaky. 'Blimey five-past-nine,' he said again, breathing quickly.

'Andrew, before I came in you put your watch forward four hours didn't you?'

Pocock looked at him, narrowing his eyes.

'Didn't you?'

The big fine head nodded, shamefaced.'Yes. Yes sir I did actually, yes.'

'Therefore it's really only five-past-five now. Right?'

'No. No it's five-past-nine. Look. Where's Aunt Rosa? Tell Dr James I'll be in St George's. I'm going at ten o'clock. Dr James told me. On my bike. I got to pack my bags. Mr Wilson, let me out . . . ' Here Pocock raised his two fists and his face contorted in despair, his teeth bared, tears running from his clenched eyes. 'Let me out!' The hoarse voice rose into a falsetto scream.

Kennedy appeared in the door, quickly grabbed Pocock's two wrists and spun him around, throwing him face down on the bed; Pocock let out one small cry and then relaxed.

'I done a bird Mr Kennedy,' he tried to say, but it was smothered in the blankets.

Before Wilson could protest Kennedy had shot a hypodermic into Pocock's buttock. 'Eight milligrams of paraldehyde,' Kennedy said as he stood up. 'That'll slow him down a bit.' He was panting.

Wilson looked at Kennedy. He could see that Kennedy was excited and sweating slightly after his exertions. He felt both angry and sad; he felt like shouting at Kennedy and comforting Pocock. Certainly he felt like doing something unusual, something drastic — like walking out and not coming back. But he knew that Kennedy had simply misunderstood: the two upraised fists, the screaming; and he knew that he could not comfort Pocock, no matter what he did.

'Injection. Ten-past-nine,' Pocock was murmuring, still face down on the bed, a thin streak of blood on the exposed buttock.

Wilson followed Kennedy back to their armchairs, feeling numb and shaken. He kept silent, sitting in the armchair, blind and deaf, as if he were in the middle of a great church organ — somebody playing vast resounding chords.

Kennedy was talking: 'Women just don't understand kids,' he was saying. 'They'll give them lollipops or stick them in front of the television. Anything to keep them quiet. They just don't care. And they're lazy you know. Dirty and lazy. Oh yes. They don't care you know. Once they're married and they have kids that's all they want, they can be smelly and fat so long as they have their kids. That suits them . . . .'

Wilson was biting his little finger and looking at the wall.

'They don't care. Their dirty knickers and their jam-rags. They don't care.' He was waving his hands and rubbing his nose.

After some minutes Pocock appeared, his hair hanging loose, his shoulders stooped, his feet unsure and tottering. He had tied his leather belt about the waist of his nightshirt, making Wilson almost giggle as he thought of some photographs he had seen of Geronimo, the Apache chief, in his old age. He came as far as the place where they were sitting and looked at them, his eyes swimming, his head sinking. He tried to smile a sheepish smile, but he only succeeded in looking angry, his face almost black, his fine teeth parted. He made some efforts to speak, but his eye caught the bunched-up figure of Robbie Hunt, and he sank down on the edge of Hunt's bed. 'I like old Robbie,' he croaked, again attempting a desperate smile. 'Good old Robbie. Good fella.'

Wilson saw the treachery in Pocock's weakness: his cowardice, his negative character, his self-deviousness. And he saw perhaps the same treachery in Kennedy, and in himself also.

*   *   *

Tony Scott and Andy Pocock leaned against the railings by the Guildhall. Tony was short and fat, Andy was tall and very thin. Tony wore a leather jacket with studs across the back, drainpipe trousers and winkle-picker shoes, his hair was fair, though he was already almost bald. Andy wore a short coat, narrow trousers and winkle-pickers, and an Elvis Presley hairstyle. It was 1959, they were cold, and there was a look about them of shabbiness, perhaps even hunger. They were smoking cigarettes and looking at the passing traffic. A dry, cold winter's day, coming on to dusk.

'Fuckin' bus,' said Tony, and they followed the bus with their eyes.

'Fuckin' London,' Tony said.

'Yeah,' said Andy, and they threw away their cigarette-ends, mouths bitter. Neither had ever been out of Reading; they just met every night and walked around.

'Come on,' Tony said.

They turned away, Tony walking slightly ahead, his shoulders stooped, hands in pockets. Andy walked with his hands in his pockets, but without Tony's swagger — he kept his elbows by his sides, while Tony's were stuck out. Tony's eyes were sharp — he glared at a car, then at a woman with a green coat, then at a brass plate on a doorway. Andy's eyes followed his, but only glanced at each item — mostly they focused on Tony's feet.

'Golly Golly Miss Molly,' Andy said to himself, and Tony chuckled.

They were walking briskly now, and smiling at all the things they saw.

'Forbury Gardens!' Tony said and Andy laughed; they bustled in the gate.

The tops of the trees were black; papers and brown leaves clung to the road; the grass was bristling. A few people walked swiftly through the park, the traffic-sounds were now a murmur. A slight breeze was blowing, the evergreen bushes rattled and swished.

'The Abbey,' Tony said.

'OK,' Andy replied and they quickened their steps.

Tony danced a bit to warm his feet.

At the ruined Abbey they sat on a bench and took cigarettes from Tony's packet, lighting up briskly and sitting back. They blew the steamy smoke up into the air. The ruined stone walls were darkening, nettles shook their heads beneath the windows. They smoked and stared at the broken walls. Soon they were cold, they felt the dew coming through from the wooden bench, their cheeks felt damp. Tony looked at Andy, who saw the yellow pimples on his white chin, and the black spots beside his wide nose. Tony looked away and they sat there, still smoking, Tony looking at the walls of the Abbey. They threw away the cigarette-ends together, but their silence continued until they became very cold and still. As they became colder Tony became restless, at first rubbing his hands together and then banging the back of the bench, but Andy became still, though a finger wandered around his nose. He just sat, his head slightly bent over his knees, his finger in his mouth; drops of water stood in the corners of his eyes, his nostrils, and his mouth.

When Tony stood up Andy didn't notice at first, as he had walked a few paces away and was doubled over, looking at the ground. Then Tony began to turn around on one foot, but Andy still didn't see him.

Tony put out his arms and spun himself, going faster and faster. 'Look at me,' he called, 'I'm Elvis. Look.'

Then Andy looked up and saw him spinning.

His leather jacket had gone up around his chest and shoulders so that he looked like a hunchback. 'I'm Elvis,' he shouted, and his lank hair fell over his face, 'I'm Elvis,' but he was breathless and slowing down already.

Andy looked at him but could not smile because he was too cold, instead he started coughing. He coughed into his fist until the water poured from his eyes and his throat was sore and his face felt colder from the water. He moved back to the seat. Still he coughed, although he didn't feel the need to any more. Tony reeled dizzily, looked around in alarm as his head swam, and then he fell back on the seat, on top of Andy, his head on Andy's shoulder, his mouth next to his ear.

Andy could hear his breathing, and feel his damp breath on his ear. 'You're not Elvis,' he said.

Tony's arm went around his shoulder and held him, pulled him over, grabbing his lapel with his other hand and forcing his head back. He put his forehead against Andy's, his nose against Andy's nose.

Andy could smell sick from his breath, feel the dampness of his forehead and the roughness of his nose. 'Push off,' he said.

Tony let him go and stood up. He looked at him uncertainly and said, 'I wasn't trying anything.'

'OK.'

Tony rubbed his hands together, standing in front of him, and after a moment he said, 'Honest I wasn't.'

Again Andy said, 'OK,' and looked up at him.

'OK?' said Tony, raising his eyebrows in question.

'OK.'

Tony smiled; Andy smiled too.

'Come on,' said Tony, 'we'll go down the Market and have a cuppa tea in the Gem.'

They walked back through the park with their arms around each other's shoulders, trying to keep in step, but Andy was always tripping and each time he tripped Tony let out a loud scream of laughter. Now the streetlights were on and the lights of the traffic and the shopwindows and the exhaust of the cars made it night, even though there was still a pinkish-green sky above the rooftops.

The Gem was almost empty, but Tony danced on his winkle-pickers up to the counter, where he did a little shuffle, and called, 'Two teas love,' to a rippling Italian woman. Then he suddenly called, 'Bill-ee!' to a tiny withered little man who was slurping tea. 'They all know me here,' he remarked, though the man had ignored him.

'A tanner love.'

'Ta love.' Tony paid the sixpence and waltzed over to the burly-looking jukebox.

Andy stood with the cup and saucer in his hand. 'What are you playing?' he said.

'Let's sit down, eh?' Tony threw himself on a chair and Andy followed him.

The jukebox clicked and hummed, while Andy looked at it with a big grin on his face.

'How're things in the Market then?' Tony called to the man with the tea, but again he didn't seem to hear.

You can shake an apple off an apple-tree, came the echoing bellow from the jukebox.

'Elvis,' said Andy, delighted.

Shake-a-shake-sugar but you'll never shake me.

Andy giggled and squirmed but Tony was busy stirring his tea.

As the song wound on its heavy way Andy began rocking from side to side, calling, 'No sirr-ee, yeah stick because I'm — stuck on you.'

Tony was watching him, and began tapping the scarred formica table, forgetting about his tea, drumming on the table with both hands for a while. But then he just looked at Andy, who had a loose smile on his big lips: his eyes were almost closed, and he was rocking backwards and forwards and clicking his fingers; a black curl of hair had come down into his eyes, and he was flicking it from side to side with his head. As Tony watched his own eyes half-closed, and his lips drooped sulkily.

When it was over there was silence. They looked around at the empty tables, the salt-cellars and sauce-bottles and grimy menu-cards.

Then Tony said, 'Hey imbecile, give me a cigarette.'

Andy produced the cigarettes and Tony grabbed them from his hand. He took one look out the window, smoking as if he had forgotten about Andy, who was sitting on the edge of his seat waiting for Tony to speak to him, his teeth chattering a little.

When he spoke again Tony used a loud strained voice, with a slight American accent: he told of carrying secondhand carpets on his bicycle, instead of using a van — how he had tied the carpets to the handlebars and to the saddle and gone from Lower Caversham to a house near the University. Andy didn't follow the story, but he laughed, and he saw that the laugh pleased Tony, so he laughed louder.

Then Tony told another story, about an auction, more carpets, and someone called Mr George. It was something to do with divorce, and a woman living with two different men; 'And Mr George sold him two green carpets and a wardrobe. Twelve ruddy quid!' Andy laughed fit to burst.

Tony's face was shining.

'Andy,' he said when he had finished laughing, 'do you know what Andy?' and he touched him on the arm. 'One of these days I'm going to buy you a bowl of soup.'

Andy looked at him but said nothing.

'OK?' said Tony almost casually.

'OK.'

Tony patted his arm gently and nodded his head. 'Come on then chum,' he said, and jumped up, heading for the door.

Andy followed him, almost having to run to keep up. Tony was rushing ahead, swinging his arms.

'Hang on. What's the hurry?' Andy called, but Tony went even faster.

They turned right and soon they were at the Abbey ruins again. Tony went straight in without looking behind him, hoisting himself through a window and disappearing inside.

'Come out Tony,' Andy called, feeling slightly panicky — things were going wrong, and he knew it would get worse. He climbed though the window. Inside it was pitch dark and he could see nothing. He called Tony's name and walked a bit, but hit his shins against iron. A bird or a bat fluttered so close to his head that he felt his hair rising. He was afraid. 'Tony,' he called, 'I have a pain.' Then he saw him, sitting on a stone doorstep. 'Tony.'

'Sit down,' Tony said in a voice that quivered strangely.

Andy sat next to him on the cold step. At first Tony wouldn't look at him, but kept his head turned away.

As his eyes grew accustomed to the dark Andy could see the back of his neck and the two ears sticking out. 'What's wrong? Turn around,' he said.

He turned, and Andy had to look away: his eyes were wide and swimming, and seemed to be deep and black, his lips were rounded and full of lipstick, and seemed to be purple in the dim light. His cheeks were burning red with rouge.

'You remember the bird?' Tony said in an urgent tone. 'The bird I showed you?'

Andy nooded his head.

'Have you drawn some?' His voice was high-pitched and unnatural.

'Yeh,' said Andy, 'I done a few.'

'Good,' Tony said. 'Good,' and he touched his arm. 'Because if you get good at it Andy, I'll show you how to do a fish. If you're good at the bird mind.' He flicked his shining lips and went on in a low whisper, 'Cos I want you to be good see. I want you to be an artist, so that your paintings will be in posh people's houses and people will say, "Andrew Pocock the artist, that's who painted that oil-painting. Andrew Pocock." But only if you're good at the bird. Then I'll show you how to do a fish.' He was breathless, and holding Andy's arm by the elbow, squeezing it; his face was puffy and Andy thought he might cry, as he had often done before at times like this.

'OK,' Andy said, and nodded his head.

'Promise,' Tony hissed, and squeezed his arm tightly.

'OK,' said Andy, wishing he'd stop, 'I promise.'

Tony relaxed, seemingly satisfied now, and he went on to say: 'But then you'll team up with someone else won't you? You'll forget Tony Scott and get some posh bit o'skirt eh? He had a weak smile and half a wink on his bloated face that made Andy squirm.

'No,' he said, 'I won't team up with anyone else.'

'Not half. When you're famous. You won't have time to come down the Market and see your old buddy. Old Tony Scott what showed you the bird. Tony what you knew so well, like nobody ever knew before. Nobody ever knew me like you Andy, and I never knew anybody like you.' He put his arm around him and drew him close, 'And nobody ever will either chum, not me. Nobody will ever know me now. Only you.'

'I promise chum,' Andy said, and flung his head on Tony's chest, 'I promise. And if my sister lets me I'll marry you. We'll live together and be a man and a woman.'

'Yes, yes, said Tony. They clung together, stroking and kissing each other under the walls of the ruined Abbey, pressing their bodies together until they shuddered into a sobbing breathless quiet. They stayed there, looking at the one or two stars and listening to the town's traffic, until the moon appeared above the broken walls.

PAIR ON ARSON CHARGES

Andrew Peter Pocock (19) and Anthony Henry Scott (29) came before Mr Justice Logg-Tenant at Reading Crown Court charged with the malicious damage of several cars, and with evading arrest.

Supt. D. G. Norton in evidence said that on the night of January 18th a number of parked cars were reported to be on fire in the neighbourhood of Forbury Road and the Guildhall. Two men, identified at the time as Pocock and Scott, were seen running into King's Meadow, but a subsequent search revealed nothing.

During the following week neither of the two men turned up at their homes. It appeared that they had absconded entirely, he said. Five nights later (23rd) two cars were burned in the Henley-on-Thames area, and the defendants were found sitting and watching the fire, apparently warming themselves at the blaze. They offered no resistance, and indeed, Supt. Norton said, they seemed either uninterested in the proceedings, or actually welcomed arrest.

Inspector Grimes of the Henley constabulary said that the pair were in an emaciated condition, having slept in barns and in ditches for the five nights. A quantity of lipstick, mascara and rouge were found in the possession of Scott. Inspector Grimes said that on interrogation they both admitted all charges, but that the answers of Pocock were obviously those of a mental defective.

The sister of defendant Pocock, a Mrs Rovatinsky of Lower Caversham, gave evidence that Pocock was an imbecile, and not responsible for his actions. She said he was fond of matches and that she was worried with him in the house, for the sake of her three infant sons and baby daughter.

Mr Justice M. K. Logg-Tenant said that Scott was obviously the villain in this case, being much older, and having some kind of power over the unfortunate Pocock. Scott appeared to be a layabout and troublemaker of the first water, he said, having three previous convictions on petty offences.

He sentenced Scott to six years penal servitude and confined Pocock to a centre for the mentally handicapped.

*   *   *

Philip Lyons roared: standing naked in the aisle and gesticulating, 'aa-oom!' his wiry body twisting as he swung his arms above his head.

'Go to bed!' Kennedy was alarmed.

'Aa-gh!' He rushed at Elersley's bed and pulled at the autistic's nightshirt.

Elersley screamed and kicked him in the face. Blood streamed from his nose. The white face of the autistic was frantic and gibbering, he sank his teeth into Lyon's thin blue flesh. Lyons squealed until Kennedy and Wilson prised them apart, Elersley burring and chattering in shock and indignation.

Lyons then grabbed Ayres by the throat and tried to drag him from the bed, blood from his nose spattering on the sheets and on Ayres' face. Wilson caught Lyons and pulled, but Ayres fell out on the floor, his tongue sticking out and his face quickly turning purple. Reggie Morris roared from his bed, then crashed his head through the glass of the door, while at the other end of the ward Bell had overturned his bed and was shouting. 'Come on. Just try it.' Kennedy kicked Lyons's wrists with his foot, but still they held, while Ayres was twitching into unconsciousness. Christ he'll die, Wilson thought, as Ayres vomited up clots of blanket wool and partly digested food.

The scabs and sores on Lyons's shoulders rasped against Wilson's shirt as he clung to the bony back. He could smell the sweat and faeces, as strong as an animal; around the neck he felt bristles and the warm slippery blood. Lyons's skin had a texture like concrete; the wiry hair prickled Wilson's lips. Kennedy gave Lyons a mighty kick to the groin and he curled up screeching, loosing Ayres, but immediately springing to attack Reggie Morris, whose face was already running blood from the glass.

As Lyons began tearing Morris's nightshirt Albert Copeland slowly swung his huge frame out of his bed; he dragged his nighshirt off over his head, walked calmly to where Kennedy and Wilson were trying to hold back Lyons, and presented the nightshirt at arm's length. Lyons took it, looked at it, put it on, took it off again and put it back on again as the two nurses looked on warily. Dressed in the nightshirt, he took a few fluttering steps backwards, then a few to the right and left as if unsure of something. He looked into the breast pocket of the shirt and drew out a small scrap of green — a piece of grass or a leaf. Instantly he relaxed, put the leaf in his mouth, and went back to his bed, chewing slowly, his hands behind his head on the pillow, blood still oozing from his nose. His eyes watched the two nurses nervously. Copeland lay wearily back on his pile of old newspapers, and wrapped the sheets intricately around him, remaking himself into his white parcel.

Wilson stood on the edge of Ivy Lodge pond, staring at the brown water. A fallen oak-tree stuck blackening branches out of the lapping waves. Like a silly monster, a spurious Loch Ness shadow, worthy only of sly winks and pitying smiles, it dropped its leaves and limp acorns into the water. Its roots still gripped the soil of the bank, exposed like a gaping mouth. Ducks pecked occasionally at the floating acorns.

He had just watched Andrew Pocock and the patients of St David's being led into the hall for a concert by a local theatre group. Pocock was wearing his long grey overcoat, but instead of being a tall impressive figure, he was doubled over and shabby; the coat looked like an ill-fitting cheap blanket. Instead of leading Robbie Hunt proudly by the hand, he was himself being led by two of the stronger patients, and Wilson recalled how he had seen them before and had run to hide from them. 'I saw him again today,' he said, to himself, still watching Pocock as if this scene was already in the past, frozen in his memory even while still happening. Going into the hall, where gay music was already playing loudly, the shambling figure of Pocock might have been going into a morgue.

On duty the previous night Wilson had been reading Pocock's casenotes. Over the seventeen years there were frequent accounts of absconding, of setting curtains on fire, of going to the hospital-block to have rings cut from his fingers, of attacks on patients and staff. There were two letters among the casenotes. The first was postmarked in Reading in 1963:

Dear Andy,
   I miss you. I hope you can get out of there. We will go for a walk around the Guildhall. I got a job in the market for £8. I haven't teamed up with anyone since I got out of that place. It was awful that place but Andy I didn't forget my Andy. I saw *Blue Hawaii* in the Odeon it was great. You know what you promised and try to get out.
   Sincerely,
   Tony.

The second was written on a piece of scrap paper in Pocock's own scrawl:

Dear doctor James,
   I kicked Robie today I'm sorry I tried to choke him he irritted me he's always is Pleas doctor let me back to sant Georges I want to go back pleas let me back to sant Georges.
   THIS IS ME Andrew

                    *   *   *

The most recent remark was: 'Has no insight and continues to be hypomanic.'
   Wilson walked away from the pond, across the playing field towards the main road. It was now nearly into March, and he had been at Ivy Lodge two months. It was another steamy frosty evening and there was no sign of spring. The grimy hedges, the weary pools of water, the black trees had never seemed so dead. He walked with hands in pockets and head back, trying to grab whatever little freshness was in the air.
   In ten years time Pocock would be a man of nearly fifty. He shuddered. He himself would be nearly forty . . . a substantial man. What would it be like? He had never known any substantial men he realised, never felt the grasp of a firm hand. All the men he had known had been mastered by some apparently irrevocable desperation, some missing link they seemed unable to bridge. Would he ever be able to wear a watchchain, reek of tobacco or grow a white moustache?
   He felt as if he had never lived, or that he had been lying asleep somewhere, like Rip Van Winkle, for all these years, waiting to be born; once he had expected to become a part of something, some movement known as life to which he could give all his love. But it hadn't happened, somehow. It was as if he had taken a side-road, a fly-over and the motorway was roaring away beneath him.

But as he saw himself on his fly-over the moment began to open up: he looked around him and he saw the green scum climbing the trees, tingling and seething with frost; it made his heart pound and brought a flush to his face. Was Kennedy here too? Was his fly-over in fact crowded with people?

What was he afraid of?

Rain crackled against the windows, March winds flung the trees about like dancers, rummaging the air with wild fingers and bent backs. They were warm in their armchairs and the patients were quiet, only an occasional trot to the toilet — or lope, or march, or waddle or shuffle or gallop — would interrupt the calm rhythm of breathing, of wind and rain.

Once the sound of heavy masturbating intruded. It was the professor, who laughed aloud as he masturbated, as loud and hearty a laugh as if he were watching a Laurel and Hardy film.

'He's on the short strokes now.' Kennedy cheered as the rhythm grew frantic before stopping suddenly. 'Sleep well professor,' he called out, but the professor was already fast asleep.

Wilson remarked how each one was different — by now he could recognise the slightest sound, a sneeze or a cough or a sigh, and identify the owner.

'Even a fart,' Kennedy agreed, and they tittered.

Suddenly there was a crash and a roar — Reggie Morris had fallen out of bed. 'Fukken bed,' he growled, as he dragged himself up. 'I won't go to bed. I'll kick you Kennedy.' He began to amble off down the ward, dragging his left leg and bellowing: 'I'll fukken kill Kennedy.'

'Poor Reggie,' Kennedy called after him, 'Come back and talk to us. Come on, do.'

Morris dragged himself back and stood before them, his massive head confused and anxious.

'Sit down Reggie,' Kennedy said kindly.

Morris immediately sat on the floor at their feet, scratching an ear and growling: 'No-o, I won't sit see.' He remained rubbing his ear and looking at their feet.

Kennedy regarded the sad-looking figure. 'He could have been quite handsome,' he remarked quietly. Morris had fine curly hair, a strong face with sensual nose and lips, and strikingly large even teeth. It was like a face in a wartime photograph of English soldiers drinking beer in a hayfield somewhere. 'You could have been a sportsman, or a pop-star. Or a barrister, yes a fine cut of a barrister you'd have made. Only for what happened to you.' He was quiet for a moment, staring at the curly head. 'You're a refugee Reggie,' he went on, louder, as if making a dramatic speech, 'like myself. A displaced person. No home to go to except Ivy Lodge. Son of Ivy Lodge, married to Ivy Lodge, died and was buried in Ivy Lodge. But once we had a chance, hadn't we? Somewhere among the teeming sperms you lost the game Reggie.' By now he was crouched over and whispering, almost into Morris's ear. 'Spunk roulette, Reggie, that's where you lost your marbles. Spunk roulette.' He looked up at Wilson and gave a mock bow, with a sheepish smile.

'You should have been on the stage,' Wilson retorted, but he was angry. 'Playing Nero or Pontius Pilate. Because it's your town got burned and yourself got crucified. You're sick.' Wilson was breathless and quailing.

Kennedy also was visibly shrinking; he had gone pale and his lips were twitching in fright. Their eyes were refusing to meet.

'You're scared Kennedy. You're afraid of your wife, your boss, your bank-manager. Even these boys here, you're frightened of them deep down, aren't you. You see them cutting your balls off, don't you. What are you afraid of?' And then he realised he was talking about himself, and stopped instantly. He had never spoken like that before, and he sweated as he looked at Kennedy's pale face, struggling to pull some reaction together.

'You're right.' He shook his head. 'You're right you're right you're right.'

'No I'm not,' Wilson answered, seeing that he had gone too far, and feeling slightly foolish.

'No you're right,' Kennedy was nodding his head and shoulders all the time, and biting his lips.

A man of his age! Wilson thought with some disgust.

'You see I discovered . . . at some point,' Kennedy was choosing his words very carefully and swallowing, 'that . . . that nothing is worth believing in. I discovered that when I was with a woman. I think. I fucked her and fucked her and fucked her. And she loved me for it. She wanted more and more. It could have been any woman, but one night, or morning or afternoon, I forget, it just crossed my mind. As simple as that, it crossed my mind that her skin, was only skin, her fanny was only a fanny and her mind . . . was just a mind. And I knew that that was worse than death. To know that . . . Or to believe it.' Kennedy's little gestures of fingers to his spectacles were so minute and timed as to be funny: it was indeed worse than death.

Morris threw back his head, opened his mouth wide and roared, 'No-oo-oo!' at the ceiling. His nostrils quivered like a horse's, his big lips came slowly together and his head dropped back once more. Sleepily he swung his head from side to side like a large heavy pendulum.

'So I married,' went on Kennedy, in a heavy voice,'I married a big Englishwoman from Suffolk. And when I brought her home . . . they made me feel foolish with her, she was so big. And she made me feel foolish too, thinking all the people spoke Irish in the pubs. Even my mother. Poor Marion, she hated Ireland.' He laughed, a dry dramatic laugh that hurt him. He was looking for a phrase: 'when I first loved a woman' stuck and seemed foolish; 'I left something behind' was vague, and not quite true anyway; 'old bones moving in the dark' sounded absurd.

Words failed, but Kennedy had the image in his mind of a rowan tree he had perhaps seen at some time. It was crammed in among some taller pines, and he had seen it suddenly — so small, so rich, in its dark green foliage and crimson berries. Had it reminded him, he wondered now, of a straight figure wearing a wraparound cloak, with burning cheeks and long curly hair, arms upraised holding . . . a sword or a glass of wine? He shrugged away the image as being painfully remote and illusory.

'So I came here anyway. For my bread and butter. To get away? Maybe that was it. Maybe I committed my first big mortal sin on the *Innisfallen* on the way over? Funny, isn't it.' He put his head down and thought again of the mahogany table, the flowers on the walls outside, the long figure of Dan Jerry the butcher, and of the receding gangplank.

Wilson looked at the bowed head, the crinkled collar; he swallowed and leaned closer; he put his hand across the white sheet that covered the table and held it within an inch of the neat black hair. 'It's still there,' he breathed, too quietly, so that he had to clear his throat and say it again. 'It's still there, buzzing around and waiting to jump out.' He knew that Kennedy could sense the hand over his head; he held it there and the head stiffened; he withdrew the hand quickly.

Kennedy looked up with a sheepish, boyish smile, stretched himself luxuriously in the chair and then rubbed his hands briskly together. 'Above all,' he said energetically, 'do everything normal. That's my motto. You'll never make a mistake if you do everything normal. Come on to bed Reggie. Time for bed. I'll bring you up a cuppa tea. OK?'

Morris raised his great sleepy eyes and growled: 'Cuppa tea Reggie yet?' and his gaze strayed to where the light from the shaded lamp was catching a drop of rain running down the window.

'Time time time. My watch watch watch. Draw draw draw. Six nine three six.'

It was dawn and Pocock was sitting in one of the armchairs. His trousers were the baggy ones kept for the high-dependancy patients, without pockets, belt or flies. He had become a persistent bed-wetter. Wilson sat on a stool and watched him; Kennedy was downstairs writing his report.

'Is today the day for the draw Andrew?' Wilson tried to appear normal, though he was full of pity and embarrassment for the shaking croaking figure.

'Draw draw draw.'

'Twenty quid eh Andrew? If you won! That'd be the day eh? Twenty quid.'

'Holly Holly Holly.'

'Buddy Holly? You like him?'

'Peggy Sue.'

Wilson was pleased to get some recognition from him. 'Peggy Sue, that's right, and "It Doesn't Matter Any More" eh?' Wilson began to sing.

Andrew's head moved in a kind of rythym, but his eyes were flying about. 'Watch watch. Time time?' he said.

'It's nearly six-thirty Andrew. Half an hour to go and Aunt Rosa will be on.'

'Watch watch.'

'Six-thirty Andrew.'

'My watch, my watch, my watch, my watch — '

'Alright Andrew, that's enough.'

Pocock was quiet for a while, his mouth working, his hand occasionally going to his temple as if he were trying to remember something.

Wilson began drawing back curtains, letting in the cold grey light, and opening windows for air, as they always did before leaving in the mornings.

When he returned Pocock suddenly looked straight at him and said, 'Oh sir. All the years.'

Wilson simply looked back at him and said, 'I know Andrew. I'm sorry,' and he held the shaking hand for a moment.

Then Robbie Hunt stirred and set up his 'aiee, aiee' call. He was once more saturated in urine. Wilson stripped the bed and heaved the unwilling lump out. He stood shivering and stamping his feet angrily.

'One of the mornings,' Wilson remarked cheerfully to Pocock, 'he'll be found drowned in his own piss.'

Andrew gritted his teeth and tried to smile, then he croaked out: 'My watch. My time. My watch,' and began to shake and moan again, whining: 'Bloody 'ell, bloody 'ell, oh bloody 'ell.'

Wilson had to shout: 'Quit it Pocock for Christ's sake,' but he continued shaking and shattering. 'Mr Kennedy will be up in a minute Andrew, and he'll bring you a cup of coffee. All right?'

Pocock nodded miserably, and said, 'Hallo Robbie,' to Hunt, who was hopping up and down and waving his fists, his enormous load of genitalia swinging purple between his legs.

Wilson went about checking for wet sheets. Ayres turned blank eyes on him. Reggie Morris growled 'Fuck off', Motherway was cuddling his penis and smiling in his sleep, the professor's shaggy eyes opened and he declared: 'Nice morning staff', Chalmer's face was covered in excrement. On the floor by Rodney Bell's bed there lay a gold watch, the strap folded, the face turned upwards. Bell opened one glittering evil eye and Wilson realised what had happened: Bell had stolen Pocock's watch. Just then there was a huge crash and a terrified scream, followed by the sound of a toilet being flushed, and breaking glass. With a feeling of horror and fear Wilson ran back to the toilet. He heard Kennedy shouting and running up the stairs.

Robbie Hunt was wedged upside down in the toilet bowl, his head under the water, his feet stuck up in the air, his huge genitals hanging downwards; the window-sash had been broken with a stool — Pocock was gone.

Kennedy arrived wildly in the doorway as Wilson was on his knees, Robbie's body lying on the floor.

'Pocock's gone,' Wilson said, 'he must have jumped. I think Robbie's dead. He's not breathing. Drowned. In the lavatory.' He gave one shrill laugh; the sound of it startled him.

For a moment Kennedy looked like a child suddenly bitten by a pet dog — his face flat with hurt surprise and guilt. 'Drowned?' he repeated stupidly. 'Drowned?'

'He must have gulped down the water.'

They both stared in silence, looking around the room at the walls, the urinals, and the broken window. The body on the floor was quite still — undeniably still; bloated and yellow on the wet linoleum. Wilson tried to stifle another ripple of laughter.

Then Wilson saw Kennedy's face changing: it became tighter, paler, a look of leaden determination came into his eyes; he looked straight ahead, seeing the words 'Praed Street' written on a wall. The shadow of a sly smile crept under the surface of his skin, and he pointed at Robbie. 'Give him the kiss of life.'

'What?'

'You heard me. I left you in charge here Wilson, and you allowed Pocock out of his room. I'll have to inform Mr Burke of that.' His voice was quite steady, he looked almost satisfied.

Wilson looked at the ugly deformed face, the gapped rotten teeth, the bared gums, the stubble of beard. A smell of sewage rose from the squat flattened head. Bits of faeces and paper clung to the face, in the hair, in the eyes, in the mouth. The smell made him gag, and he had to hold his mouth.

'Come on,' Kennedy said tauntingly, 'get kissing.'

Wilson put down his mouth and kissed the livid blue lips. They were warm. He pinched the nostrils together; they crinkled across the centre crease of the split nose. He breathed into him. The yellow flabby flesh around the eyebrows touched his own. The crooked chest-cage rose and fell.

Suddenly Kennedy was angry, and Wilson could hear that the anger was boosted by terror; in fact the man was almost crying: 'On my shift. Jesus Christ on my shift. Oh God all the years! Oh Jesus dead. Dead!' and he turned helplessly towards Wilson and kicked the foot of the dead body. 'You fool Wilson. You fucking English bastard.'

Wilson felt utterly calm, more calm and detached than he had ever felt in his life. In fact, kneeling over the unconscious body of the twisted cretin, with the cold damp morning air touching his forehead from the broken window, he felt curiously happy — as if time was standing still. 'You'd better get on the phone,' he said coolly.

He continued breathing into the grotesque body, quite oblivious now of the repulsive smell. In fact the air he was breathing tasted fresh and clean in his own lungs. He remembered a day he had once spent walking in the Lake District. He had not seen anyone for a whole day, the smell of water and stone and warm grass was in his head, his body felt warm and alive. Towards evening he had startled a deer from the undergrowth right at his feet; his body tingled again now, as he remembered the animal prancing away from him down the mountain, over the rocks and into the advancing dusk of the next valley.

He felt the lips move beneath his own; he felt the chest and throat contract. He sat back on his heels and watched the shitty little man gulp and choke and finally breathe.

He carried Hunt back to his bed and covered him up — he was still unconscious but breathing easily. He sat back in the armchair and waited, not even listening to Kennedy's voice on the phone. He had a curious feeling of relief: there was no use in chasing Pocock, he'd be somewhere out in the woods by now, heading for the main road. He'd be brought back before lunchtime, and Robbie was only stunned. But for Wilson something had changed completely; he wasn't sure what it was yet, but he had never felt so free in his life before — it was as if he and not Pocock had escaped.

Hopkins raised his old goat's face from the pillow and looked across at Motherway. 'There's Johnny,' he nodded approvingly, 'Motherway's a nice boy. More like a girl really, in some ways. Very smooth arse for a boy Motherway.'

'Morning Hopkins.' Wilson smiled at him.

'Morning Mr Wilson. Nice morning sir.'

'Do you still love Motherway then?'

'Yes sir I love 'im. I'll always love 'im sir. I give 'im buttons off me night-shirt, see.' And he pulled two buttons off, crossed over to Motherway's bed and shook him. 'Here Johnny. Buttons!'

Motherway took the buttons and snarled: 'F'off, low-grade.'

Wilson laughed. It was quite bright now and the day-staff were ringing the bell downstairs. There was sunshine and it would soon be warm.

* * *

Malachy Kennedy did not see his aunt Bridget for years, four or five, perhaps, or six. One night on duty in the ward he had a phonecall — from a hospital in north London. He had been married at this time about fifteen years. He went alone to see her, and when his wife questioned this unusual behaviour he said, 'I'm a nurse aren't I?'

The first thing he saw was a parrot of a woman jogging up and down in a chair. Silver-white hair and a yellow cardigan, elbows stuck out, frail blue legs useless beneath her; a high-pitched 'coo-coo' sound came with the movements. This is not her, Malachy thought, this is not Bridget. But it was — Bridget was this puppet-woman — trying to get up, determined to stifle the bright glossy walls of her private room.

'Malachy,' she said, 'get me up.'

He lifted her stiff chicken's body.

She shrieked: 'Oh Jesus Jesus.'

They limped unmercifully to the bed and breathless he planked her down.

'How's your father?' she rapped out right away.

'He's not too bad Bride,' Malachy answered.

'Aye,' she said, 'he've a fine back on him Pat have. How's Kate?'

'Kate is dead Auntie Bride. She's dead five years.'

'Oh she is. Kate. A terrible thing.'

'Would you like a cup of tea?'

'Tea. Yes.'

He pressed the bell, hearing it ring somewhere close by. He rubbed his hands together, relieved that they were dry and hard. He pressed the bell again to hear it ring. He was a nurse, wasn't he, and he would be prepared for them. She was perched on the tubular bed, holding the quilt by her side, as if she would fly off.

'Marion is well,' he stuttered, 'and the kids . . . . All very well.'

She ignored him. He went to the open window and closed it with a smack. In the new silence he heard her breathing — fast and desperate like that other breathing of women. The door opened.

'Could you manage some tea please? For my aunt Miss Kennedy? And a cuppa for me while you're at it. Thanks love. Well Bridie how are you keeping then? How are you?' He was getting control now, straightening his picture of himself in his blue suit.

'Get my bank book,' she said, and she pulled a key from between her breasts. 'Go to my flat. You know the chest of drawers in my bedroom. It's the top drawer. Bring it to me. You hear me?'

'Yes.'

She was breathing heavily all the time.

'You're the divil Auntie Bridie. I'll say you are. Are they treating you well? Do you need anything?'

'Piddling little bitches. I need nothing.'

He kept talking until the tea arrived. 'Thank you. I'll pour it myself. Is Miss Kennedy a model patient then? I'll bet she bosses you around?'

'She's a darling really. But stubborn with it.' And with a flick of hips the nurse was out the door.

'Her father was from Queenstown. A soldier if you don't mind.' Bridget grabbed the cup with both hands and slurped it like a baby.

There was silence for a full minute.

'Malachy,' she looked at him, her eyes quite steady, and big — her face having shrunk, 'I don't care at all about dying.' She said it in a businesslike quick way. 'But not out there.' She indicated the rest of the hospital, the general wards. 'Bring me two hundred pounds in cash. You hear me.'

He nodded.

'I'll piss myself here and I'll die here. You can bury me where you like. You hear me?'

He nodded again.

She relaxed with a big breath and something like a smile, and put down the cup. 'There's no kick in that tea,' she complained sullenly. Now she was quiet, staring contentedly at the clean walls, although she might have been following some thought in her head. Then she said to herself, 'It may not be perfect,' as if reckoning up something, 'but Bridget Rose Kennedy doesn't pine for the Milky Way. If I was cheated it was by my own hand, and at the wrong end of my life. Now Malachy, bring me the money.'

After that they sat for a long time listening to the quietness of the sheets, the hospital sunlight, and to the old woman's rooted breathing; he was a nurse no longer, his bedside manner had deserted him. He was Malachy Kennedy, just arrived at Paddington, the bog still on his boots; Bridget was the old hairpin stuck in the fireplace, sucking her pipe and smelling of soot. They both crouched, round-shouldered, about the curling smoke of the turf fire.

As he left the huge grey building the gravel under his feet seemed too bright and hurt his eyes. Some tulips in a black flowerbed stood straight and silent; a deep heat of summer surrounded him and lay heavily on his shoulders. In his pocket the worn brass key.

*   *   *

Pocock was returned by the Reading police within six hours. A bus driver had handed him over to a constable on duty at the terminus. He was given tea and biscuits, and later he caught a glimpse of the Guildhall from the policecar. That same night he had a fit — it resembled grand mal, but it may have been brought on by drugs. Next day Dr James signed an order committing him to a mental asylum. He left Ivy Lodge in Dr James's car — a red Alfa-Romeo — wearing his long grey overcoat. He did not wave goodbye.

Ayres lay on the bare sheet with his green eyes staring at the ceiling. He seemed preoccupied, and a little troubled. But there was no blanket! Only a few stray rags of thread scattered around the bed and on the floor. His fingers pulled vaguely at the air and he was still chewing.

'He's had his bleedin' breakfast!' said Kennedy, astonished. They both stared in disbelief. 'He's eaten a whole blanket!'

He submitted stoically to an enima — seemed to welcome it even — and it worked almost immediately. His face grew more clouded and abstracted; he smacked his lips and grunted, as if he had a problem on his mind which was very near inspiration point; his body wriggled and he clawed the air systematically, as if making signs that he meant to be understood. Then he gave a long drawnout wail which rose a pure octave into a full howl of pain and indignation. He raised his legs in the air, tensed, and the blanket shot out like a bullet, hitting the iron bedpost with a reverberant clang. It was a brownish cylinder, twelve inches long and four inches in diameter. It was as hard as a rock.

'Direct hit!' yelled Kennedy in delight.

'An artist!' Wilson cheered as Ayres relaxed again, a flicker of green in his eyes.

In high spirits they went about the business of the morning, changing sheets, sending the patients trotting to the toilet, making cheerful banter.

'Who did you have last night Hopkins?'

'Aunt Rosa sir.'

'Was she nice?'

'No sir. I got hairs in me teeth.'

Kennedy pulled the curtains and looked out — a soft foolish smile came into his face. 'Look,' he declared, 'it's snowing!' A carnival of flakes streamed and blew in the grew light of the dawn. 'Will it stay?' He turned eagerly to Wilson.

'Yes, yes. It'll stay. Look, it's sticking already.'

They almost imagined they could hear it, it came so thick and so silent. Like clots of wool. And tomorrow would be a bright white woolly day. They watched its white flags until they both became slightly ashamed.

'You don't have to drive in it,' Kennedy gloomed.

'It'll go through my suede shoes,' Wilson replied.

But they were both thinking of the crunch of it, the footprints, and the colours. The whole hospital complex looked like a model village, warm and black, with good old sturdy trees, and lighted windows. And as the dry grey dawn brightened, hatted figures came and went.

As Kennedy and Wilson left — after being relieved by Aunt Rosa, a round barrel of tar in the ice of England — they both felt like whooping, or starting in on a Big Day. But they said, 'Hope it doesn't freeze on top of this.'

Outside was like a swim in the ocean.

'Do you like it?' Wilson said loudly.

'No, I hate it,' Kennedy lied, his red gloves to his burning ears.

'It's exciting,' Wilson plunged.

'Damp,' Kennedy jeered, but his eyes had 'snowman' written in them, in big heroic letters.

They parted with shouts and flurries of powdery snow.

The cafeteria was noisy and crowded, with an air of gaiety, though nobody looked at the windows. Clive Smith was there, the great white globe of his head bobbing up and down above his poached eggs. 'Oh Hokey Hokey Kokey,' he was shouting at some students at the next table. 'Then you do it with your elbow, see.' They smiled vaguely at him, not understanding.

After breakfast Wilson lifted his mahogany frame up the stairs to his room. His flesh responded like an old donkey, pickled in its years of instinct. The maple floor and unearthly corridor carried him like a drifting spermatazoa to his chosen nest. The snow on the trees outside would sustain and suckle him, until he grew into a man.

Peters the attendant was mumbling outside: 'Not so bad now nice today yes nice now.' He was walking up and down, incessantly talking to himself, as he always did, about the weather: 'Snow today not so good no.' His voice was like the sleepy swish of waves on the shore of an undiscovered sea. His footsteps were fossils — the brachyopods of Lake Huron which Iroquois children tossed and played with. His words were the silver fish which dazzled the Aztecs in former millenia, the pots and pans and brass farthings of nether-Brittania. 'Nice today snow now not so bad cold though not so good nice today.'

Staff Wilson dreamed of a soaring snowball as he burst into sleep.